Managing Authentic Relationships

Facing New Challenges in a Changing Context

T0342264

Networking in the seventeenth century

Management is doing things right, leadership is doing the right things.
A quotation by a pioneer of management theory, Peter Drucker.
Already in the seventeenth century, this concept was apparently
well understood. This large militia painting by Nicolaes Pickenoy
from 1632 exhibits this clearly. Twenty-four militia men – sorry;
this is the seventeenth century, no ladies yet – pose thoughtfully
for a painting. They are aware they are being observed and they
commissioned this painting to illustrate their good deeds. They
are members of a civic guard, a sort of voluntary military group.
They have a good reason to order a group portrait as their captain,
Jacob Backer, has recently been elected mayor. He is shown with
his men for the last time before he has to leave the civic guard.
Soon he will occupy the most important office in the city. These
men know they will benefit from his promotion so they appear at
their very best. One active and alert, another contemplative and
wise – perhaps their attitudes depend on their ambitions? Each
man had his own preferences on how he was depicted. In the
seventeenth century, Amsterdam city politics was in the hands
of regents. These men of high status usually came from rich
merchant families or the aristocracy. Time after time they were
able to secure the highest political or managerial positions through
their extensive family relations or friendships. Powerful families
shamelessly favoured and appointed one another. However, the
civic guards still offered an avenue for someone from a humble
background to worm their way up. To get in, you had to pay for your
own uniform and arms, but you did not necessarily have to be a rich
merchant. It was one of the best stepping stones. Upon joining,
you knew you were being observed. You got the chance to perform,
which included presenting yourself well and being seen doing good
deeds. It really was a once in a lifetime opportunity.

Paul Mosterd, Deputy Director Hermitage Amsterdam

Managing Authentic Relationships
Facing New Challenges in a Changing Context

- Jean Paul Wijers (Editor and Chapter 12-13)
- Monica Bakker (Chapter 1 - 3)
- Robert Collignon (Chapter 4 - 9)
- Gerty Smit (Chapter 10 - 11)

Introduction by
Prof. René Foqué

Other contributors
- Marike Dragt, Head of Relationship Marketing, ING Wholesale Banking
- Boukje de Haan, Head of Communication and Fundraising,
  Foundation for Refugee Students UAF
- Paul Mosterd, Deputy Director, Hermitage Amsterdam
- Paul Spies, Chairman of the Board and Director, Stadtmuseum Berlin
- Tom Verbelen, Director, Municipality of Antwerp

Interviews with
- Janine Dijkmeijer, CEO, Nederlands Dans Theater
- Marielle Konings, Advisor Relationship Management, City of Eindhoven
- Alexandra Messervy, Founder and Chief Executive, The English Manner
- Rutger van Nouhuijs, CEO Corporate and Institutional Banking, ABN AMRO Bank

Content

Managing Relationships

Successful Encounters

Foreword

Managing authentic relationships has been important in every age. Barter trade was based on reciprocity; by exchanging goods or services, the needs of both parties could be met. Sensitivity to the interests of the other and a relevant exchange of needs are still the basis of professional relationship management.

This book will sharpen your sensitivity to stakeholder interests. You will be inspired to create added value to a network and optimize cooperation. This book offers a guide to strengthening trust. The guiding principle is a holistic view of relationship management – fulfilling stakeholder interests by being relevant, connected, and reliable.

As representatives of the public and private sectors, it is our pleasure to combine the leading practical and scientific views on Strategic Relationship Management in this book, thereby happily offering you an introduction to successful networking. We thank the authors and the members of the Advisory and Supervisory Board of the Institute of Strategic Relationship Management for sharing their knowledge and expertise to support the creation of this invaluable manuscript.

Managing authentic relationships is an art; an art you will learn to master by reading this unique book. Using this guidance, you can learn to make a measurable contribution to the strategic goals of an organization – the Return-on-Relationship.

Franck Erkens
Chair of the Advisory Board of the Institute of Strategic Relationship Management

Preface

I had many years of experience as an organizer of networking events when I decided to write this book. I was motivated to do so after seeing so many networking events fail. Putting hundreds of people in one room does not mean the right people will meet. That is not what makes a networking event successful.

At most networking events, the majority of the budget and attention goes to food or what happens on stage. Overcrowded rooms, loud music, or lengthy programs make it impossible for people to meet. Very little thought is given to whom to invite, how to make sure they will come, and how to guarantee the right encounters will take place.

This is where my experience in protocol comes in. While I was a student, I founded Protocolbureau, an organization specialized in providing operational support at high-level events. Protocol was originally developed by the European monarchies since a king or queen has very little time but has to talk to many people. Protocol is a way to stage personal attention based on specific predetermined goals.

By translating the royal protocol into a contemporary version, we were able to apply protocol at networking events, fashion shows, and even dance events. It gave us a way to guarantee the right encounters would take place.

Professionalizing networking events alone turned out not to be enough. Building and managing a strong network for the entire organization requires implementing professional relationship management on strategic, tactical, and operational levels.

I took the initiative to further develop our vision and did so with the help of a Supervisory Board and Advisory Board consisting of relationship management experts from the public and private sectors and academic experts.

The collaboration with Prof. René Foqué, Monica Bakker, Robert Collignon, and Gerty Smit started when we were given the opportunity to develop a minor in relationship management, first at The Hague University of Applied Science and later at the Hotelschool The Hague.

By this time, I founded my second company, the Institute of Strategic Relationship Management (ISRM), and we translated the minor into a program for professionals, the so-called postgraduate Strategic Relationship Management.

An organization needs to implement professional relationship management at all levels to be able to have a meaningful network and a reciprocal relationship with the right people. In an organization that implements professional relationship management, the strategy is translated into a Relationship Management Strategy, the relationships are managed properly, and the stakeholders are mapped correctly. The Return-on-Relationship is calculated. It is clear where the responsibility lies for the relationship management process. The meetings with stakeholders are measured, the networking events deliver the desired results, and the networkers are properly supported in their networking activities.

Furthermore, in an organization where real relationships are built, there is a shared understanding of what relationships are. It is impossible to develop successful relationship management without authentic relationships based on trust and reciprocity. From an organizational perspective, goals have to be set and processes have to be managed, but authentic relationships cannot be built on very precise or detailed expectations. This book offers a holistic view on the management of professional networks based on authentic relationships.

Professional relationship management delivers valuable and measurable contributions to the strategic goals of an organization and a network of authentic relationships:

- This book, *Managing Authentic Relationships*, starts (Chapter 1 and 2) by explaining what reciprocal relationships and meaningful networks are and why it is so important for organizations to know the right people.
- Chapter 3 is about developing a tailor-made Networking Vision, an organization's own view on why networks and relationships are important.
- In Chapter 4 the book continues with the Relationship Management Strategy, the translation of the why into the how.
- How to explore the broader set of participants in the value network is discussed in Chapter 5 about mapping the external stakeholders.
- The Relationship Management Plan in Chapter 6 describes the implementation of the Relationship Management Strategy.
- Chapter 7 describes the use of data in steering, monitoring, and improving relationships.
- Chapter 8 explores the economics of relationship management by calculating the Return-on-Relationship.
- In Chapter 9, performance is discussed in the context of Strategic Relationship Management.
- The internal responsibility for and implementation of the Relationship Management Strategy is addressed in Chapter 10, as is the organizing principle of networks with networkers, networking teams, and Managers of the Network.
- Chapter 11 is about change, as for most organizations the implementation of professional relationship management is new.
- The book concludes with a chapter about supporting the networkers (12) and organizing effective networking events with measurable results (13).

Prof. René Foqué wrote the introduction for this book and Monica Bakker the first three chapters about what relationships and networks are and why they are so important. Robert Collignon wrote Chapter 4 through 9 about managing relationships, and Gerty Smit Chapter 10 and 11 about the internal responsibility for and implementation of relationship management. I am the editor of this book and wrote the last two chapters about successful encounters.

For this book we interviewed the CEO of the Nederlands Dans Theater, Janine Dijkmeijer; Marielle Konings, Advisor Relationship Management, City of Eindhoven; the CEO Corporate and Institutional Banking of ABN AMRO Bank, Rutger van Nouhuijs; and the Founder and Chief Executive of The English Manner, Alexandra Messervy, formerly of the Royal Household of HM the Queen.

The history of relationship management is described by Paul Mosterd, Deputy Director of the Hermitage Amsterdam. He wrote about the four paintings in this book, the one on the cover and those at the beginning of each of the three main sections.

The contributions by Marike Dragt (ING), Boukje de Haan (Foundation for Refugee Students AUF), Paul Spies (Stadtmuseum Berlin), and Tom Verbelen (Municipality of Antwerp) provide practical examples of relationship management.

Jean Paul Wijers
Founder and Director of the Institute of Strategic Relationship Management

....

Managing Authentic Relationships

1. Authentic Relationships	2. Managing Relationships	3. Successful Encounters
Why are networks and relationships important? What are networks and relationships?	How to manage relationships? How to measure results? How to implement a relationship management?	How to stage effective networking events or meetings?
· Develop an inspiring Networking Vision	· Develop a Relationship Management Strategy · Map the stakeholders · Develop a Relationship Management Plan · Calculate the Return-on-Relationship · Shape the internal responsibility for and implementation of the relationship management	· Support the development of professsional networkers · Organize effective networking events or meetings with measurable results
CHAPTER 1, 2 & 3		CHAPTER 12 & 13
	CHAPTER 5, 6, 7, 8, 9, 10 & 11	

....

Introduction

by Prof. René Foqué

The subject that the authors of this book have made the topic of their reflections is extremely challenging and complex, but very pertinent.

Managing Authentic Relationships; A few preliminary considerations.

From an ethical perspective to relationships

To build a solid network of relations to support its activities, an organization or company must undertake a series of actions and interventions to achieve this and, in so doing realize from the start that ultimately every human action is determined by three conscious ambitions or motives.[1] Those motives cannot be reduced to each other and there is always a tension in the relationship among them.

The first is a manipulative, strategic-instrumental motive whereby relations are regarded exclusively as tools for gaining a dominant position in the world. This may be a full position of power, a dominant market position, or the elimination of as many competing networks as possible.

The second is the cognitive motive. If you wish to influence your surroundings through networking, you need to establish reliable knowledge of that social environment, of the implicit patterns that are in place, but also of the behavioral strategies and effects of interventions. The manipulative and cognitive dimension of our actions may not be reduced to each other, but they do complement each other.[2]

Finally, the third motive is the most complex one and therefore the hardest to define. It entails what we might call the meaningful dimension of our actions. Here the focus lies on the ethical dimension of networking, precisely that aspect that is essential when the authenticity of relations needs not only to be respected but also to be sustained and further enhanced. After all, involving people in a network of relations involves those same people in a shared normative set of values that gives their commonality an ethical contour despite their mutual contradictions or interests. It is not about bringing everybody into alignment with a simple and exclusive set of norms and values. It is about the values that, in a pluralistic society characterized by different and often even mutually conflicting views, have to be held high if that society or the established network is not to disintegrate.

In this context, the legal sociologist Kees Schuyt talks about "counter connections."

According to Schuyt, "a society needs counter-forces that hold society together in a different way than the well-known social factors." He sees an important distinction between social connections resulting from shared values (religious or ideological) on the one hand, and social factors that symbolically connect and match opposing parties, even though they do not share values of content, on the other.

Symbolic exchange [3]

The term *symbolic*, which not by chance is a key feature in the first guiding chapter of this book, is highly relevant to our society. After all, our society is increasingly characterized by vast discrepancies, fierce competitive relations, and conflicts of interest. In this context, society has great need of what can be called *symbolic exchange* so that plurality in society is not denied or oppressed but placed in the perspective of connection and partnership. In the original meaning in Greek, symbols indeed have a connecting force in a world of discrepancies and increasing disintegration. There the term *symbolic* is used in contrast to *diabolic*, the latter being indicative of the growing mutual irreducibility of discrepancies and subsequent separation of society, with war as the end result instead of peace, opposition instead of partnership.

Very often the qualification *symbolic* –in the context of a specific action– has a superficial meaning, suggesting that this action has little practical effect on our actions and, above all, that this action may not only have little practical societal impact but usually also lacks effective enforceability. In that case the meaning is *only symbolic*. That is not the meaning that should be used here.[4] As mentioned above, we should extract the etymological Greek meaning whereby the expression *symbolic* embodies a rich and highly layered meaning.

In Greek, *sumbolaion* initially meant human interaction in politics or trade based on fixed markers that everyone could recognize. *Sumbolon* also means that which links and connects people and which enables them to create a society with others. It also has a connotation of trust, both moral trust and confidence. Because the word trust has a dual meaning, the etymological background of the term also refers to the activity of consultation or deliberation. Finally, the term also refers to the process of mutual recognition among people whose diverse backgrounds make them strangers to each other or cause them to be in a state of conflict or fierce competition with each other.

Against this latter background, the symbolic exchange in society implies a focus on what the German philosopher Jurgen Habermas called "solidarity among strangers"[5] which refers to the inevitable divided and heterogeneous character of society, as addressed by Machiavelli already at the end of the 16th century. To him society is not an organic unity; Machiavelli saw society as inevitably divided and characterized by heterogeneity and conflict.[6] This division in society and cultural heterogeneity and conflict can not and should not be denied, but neither should they be left to arbitrariness or unpredictability. They should be channeled and steered to prevent the downfall of society by internal diversity and disintegration.

A symbolic exchange that still connects and pacifies in a context of division and conflict needs visibility and institutions that represent it in a recognizable way. Here the normative framework of a democracy is decisive. In the light of this, the symbolic statue of the Figure of Justice, especially, is a striking presence in our society. She is in search of balanced decision making in the conflicts she has to deal with. The symbolic image of the Figure of Justice with the representation of justice (the sword) in one hand and the balanced judgment of the respective opinions and interests (the balance) in the other hand, represents more than just an outdated legacy from the past. "These images of the Figure of Justice are a legacy that even now help us to believe in the need for representative images of shared values. To think about the visual traditions of the past is a way to deal with contemporary attempts to understand what justice means today."[7]

What applies for democracy and justice also applies for politics in which a strong and recognized symbolic force is vital to the balance, sustainability, and, ultimately, decency of a society. In a profound and subtle reflection on the political program of the new president of France, Emmanuel Macron, the political philosopher Philippe Raynaud claims that during the previous century French politics suffered a dramatic deficit in the capacity of symbolization, which was still recognizably active during the presidencies of De Gaulle, Pompidou, and even Mitterrand. Afterwards, according to Raynaud, French politics dramatically entered a period of short-term opportunism, strategy, and partiality. With Macron we enter a new period of grandeur, impartial authority. In other words, power is once again seen as an authority that is elevated above all the daily political controversies. The latter should be seen as a representation of a symbolic exchange that can guarantee connection and cohesion in the long run.

One could say that a republic is a political system that embodies a democracy in a symbolic image of the collective, indeed the public interest.[8] Here rituals and protocol formalities play an important role. The same applies to them as to the strength of symbolization in the Figure of Justice; "They are an important legacy that help us even now to believe in the need for representative images of shared values."[9] The fact that the Protocol Institute in The Hague initiated this project of "managing authentic relationships" is important and inspires further development. One could say the Protocol Institute in The Hague owes this to itself.

Thus, politics cannot be characterized by the irreducible contradiction between friend and enemy, between we and they, as claimed by the national socialist political theorist Carl Schmitt,[10] but by recognition, respect, and by the "desire to live in institutions that are correct and workable" with fundamentally different persons.[11] That is also the background that Kees Schuyt cautioned against; too much social cohesion, too much unilateral emphasis on shared norms and values. Instead, he talks about the importance of "counter connections," of nevertheless values that, like a symbolic exchange, can protect a divided society against fatal fragmentation and disintegration.[12]

Recognition and respect –of oneself and of the other– will only become possible when you live in a communal symbolic exchange. At the same time, this implies that the symbolic exchange of a society is the vulnerable Achilles' heel of that society; if attacked, the heart of the community and its viability are disregarded and ignored. In other words, the symbolic exchange entails not only the relations between the individual members of a society, but also and mainly the relationship of all towards shared common values in a community. Only then do intersubjective relations become meaningful.

Authenticity

The latter is especially relevant for authenticity when it is considered to be the basic ethical value that is at the heart of every decent relationship. After all, it refers to self-actualization, to the individual right, in its own actions, to hold true to its own sense of values without being dispossessed by external interests and strategies. Looking deeper into the meaning of authenticity, it soon becomes evident that self-actualization–authenticity–cannot be achieved single-handedly but only in a setting of intersubjective recognition that provides the requisite nourishment.[13] For this to develop, a recognizable symbolic exchange is needed. A society without any form of symbolization will never be able to contribute to the authenticity of its members.

Management

In view of all this, the difficult question is what type of management is necessary to contribute to the operation of the necessary symbolic exchange and thus create and sustain authentic relations.

Certainly, strategic insight, knowledge of the social area, and effectiveness are essential to any form of relation. However, managerialism, if complacent, may and will be fatal for authentic relations. To avoid managerialism is probably the biggest challenge of this book, as is the case for many organizations. A lot of preparation material for such an exercise is offered –which is already an innovation– but it does not yet offer an explicit and balanced positioning of the dimension of management. For this book to truly come to sustainable and innovative insights for the long term, a lot of reflexive work still needs to be done.

In recent developments, the large American management programs have clearly been proactive in liberating managerialism from its insular complacency. For example, in 1990, Prof. John Kotter of Harvard University made an important distinction between management and leadership.[14] Leadership is all about the development of a vision, of a normative framework of the future of an organization, motivating and convincing people to take part and to be clearly committed. Management activities are all about an organization, short-term planning, and efficiency and effectiveness; in short, the functioning of the system. The latter is important and even indispensable, but it is not sufficient. Such managerial tasks may not, in Kotter's analysis, be disconnected from leadership. In this respect, one of the important aspects of leadership is developing and protecting what we called symbolic exchange at the beginning of this introduction. Management thinking as such remains too limited to imperatives of the current system if not given the possibility to ask normative questions.

The philosopher of the University of Leuven, Herman De Dijn, refers to this as "a dramatic reduction of symbolic relations to systemic relations with far-reaching implications for justice and social ethics. Moreover, systemic relations are apt to be organized through the market, which itself is preeminently regulated by the system, namely the monetary system that allows connections and comparisons in a systematic and neutral way regardless of preferences."[15] Subsequently, one may fear that authenticity will be forgotten about and will fade completely from our consciousness.

This is cause for alarm and should be prevented at all times but not by denying the indispensable contribution of management. On the contrary. What should be avoided, however, is that management becomes complacent and withdraws itself from broader normative perspectives and detaches from the normative driving force of a symbolic exchange that connects and stimulates collaboration in a spirit of convincing leadership. This does not happen automatically but needs targeted investments in reflection and associated performances. But time is running out! After all, if this does not happen, companies or organizations and, in the end, society as such will be self-enclosed and fully absorbed by the mechanisms of merely operating. A word of warning, however, people cannot keep functioning in the meaninglessness of empty instrumentalism or of purely formalistic efficiency.[16]

Managing authentic relationships. It remains a complex challenge and above all, as this book shows, a work in progress.

Notes

1. A. Burms & H. De Dijn, *De rationaliteit en haar grenzen. Kritiek en deconstructie*, Van Gorcum, Assen, 1986, p.1-11
2. K. Schuyt, *Steunberen van de samenleving. Sociologische Essays*, Amsterdam University Press, Amsterdam, 2006, p.115
3. In this paragraph I continue my analyses as published in a previous publication: R. Foqué, "Op zoek naar een verloren toekomst", in: R. Frissen & S. Harchaoui (red.), *Integratie & de metropool. Perspectieven voor 2040*, Van Gennep, Amsterdam, 2011,p. 145-168
4. R. Foqué, "De onzichtbare grondwet", in: G. ter Horst et al., *De onzichtbare grondwet*, Ministerie van Binnenlandse Zaken en Koninkrijksrelaties, Den Haag, 2008, p. 39-41
5. J. Habermas, "Why Europe needs a Constitution", in New Left Review (2001) 11, p. 5-26
6. More information on his actual relevance: CL. Lefort, *Le travail de l'oeuvre de Machiavel*, Gallimard, Paris, 1972
7. V. Hayaert, "In de invloedssfeer van Vrouwe Justitia", in: S. Mareel, *Roep om rechtvaardigheid. Recht en onrecht in de kunst uit de Nederlanden 1450-1650*, Uitgeverij Hannibal i.s.m. Museum Hof van Busleyden, Mechelen en Koninklijk Museum voor Schone Kunsten Antwerpen, 2018, p.26
8. Ph. Raynaud, *Emmanuel Macron: Une revolution bien tempérée*, Desclé de Brouwer, Paris, 2018, p.148-156
9. V. Hayaert, op.cit., p.26
10. C. Schmitt, *Der Begriff des Politischen* (1932), Duncker und Humblot, Berlin, 1963
11. P. Ricoeur, *Soi-même comme un autre*, Éditions du Seuil, Paris, 1990, i.h.b. p. 199-236
12. K. Schuyt, *Steunberen van de samenleving. Sociologische essays*, Amsterdam University Press, Amsterdam, 2006, p.113-122
13. Ch. Taylor, *The Ethics of Authenticity*, Harvard University Press, Cambridge (Mass.)/ London, 1991, and the classic study by L. Trilling, *Sincerity and Authenticity*, Harvard University Press, Cambridge (Mass)/ London, 1973
14. J.P. Kotter, *A Force for Change. How Leadership Differs from Management*, The Free Press, New York, 1990
15. H. De Dijn, "Ethiek in de laat-moderne tijd", in: Idem, *Taboes, monsters en loterijen. Ethiek in de laat-moderne tijd*, Pelckmans/Klement, Kapellen/Kampen, 2003, p.15-30
16. J.-P. Le Goff, *Le mythe de l'entreprise. Critique de l'idéologie managériale*, La Découverte, Paris, 1995, p.278

Authentic
Relationships

Civic Guard Banquet with Colonel Jan van de Poll and Captain Gijsbert van de Poll, Johannes Spilberg, 1650-53, canvas, 297,5 × 589 cm, collection Amsterdam Museum

How do you want to be seen?
by Paul Mosterd, Deputy Director Hermitage Amsterdam

In the Netherlands, there are no larger militia paintings than the ones that are displayed in the Hermitage Amsterdam. They remind us of the Golden Age, a period in which trade and culture flourished in our country. Within just a few generations, an incredible economic boom occurred in the newly established Dutch Republic. The wealthy and powerful citizens who were then in charge had themselves immortalized in monumental paintings. Nowadays we see them as large, beautifully painted works of art. We can also decipher the codes and analyze the messages that are hidden in these artworks. The paintings served as a kind of LinkedIn-on-the-wall for citizens at the time. They hung in semi-public buildings and were intended for viewing and consideration. A beautiful example is this enormous painting by Johannes Spilberg (1619–1690). It is six meters wide, almost a meter and a half wider than the *Night Watch*.

The militiamen are arranged around a dining table, oozing success, wealth, and ambition. The city was doing very well so it had something to celebrate. Militia members who contributed financially received a place in the painting. Being portrayed towards the front of the painting was relatively expensive, and for a full-length depiction, you paid top price. It was certainly worth it though, because a work of such prestige could boost your career. It was an opportunity to demonstrate your good citizenship and to show that you acknowledged your responsibility to the city. You could also indicate where you came from as well as show how well connected you were. We can see this illustrated particularly well on the right. The commander of the militia group, Joan van de Poll, is the one with the napkin on his lap. He is elegantly dressed in black, indicating that he belongs to the urban elite of wealthy merchants. Meanwhile his archers boast splendid uniforms with brightly colored sashes and feathers. Perhaps Van de Poll feels he is above wearing a uniform? He sits separately, almost with his back to his men. Yet what is more important; he is seated with his younger brother, Jan van de Poll, an officer in his civic guard who is about to embark on a spectacular political career. After this painting was completed, Jan was elected mayor of Amsterdam seven times. His son can be seen behind his chair. The boy holds a baton of command. He seems to know more than the viewer does. The powerful Van de Poll family will continue to prevail.

1.   The Importance of Networks and Relationships

How important to reaching your goals is having a good network in our world today? When this question is asked to directors and other people in leading positions, most of them answer that high-quality relationships and the ability to maintain them are a key factor to their success. Relationships within your network can support you to reach your goals and be a sounding board for your innovative ideas. They can provide inside information, point out the blind spots in your policy, give recommendations, and support you in difficult times. The merits of your cause and strategy are important but access and a strong network are key, especially in these disruptive times of change in which you cannot rely on sole planning and control anymore. Who would have thought that many renowned banks would close most of their local branches? That the whole taxi world would be changed by Uber, that an enormous stream of refugees would have spread through Europe in 2016, and so on? In order to face these kinds of context-changing challenges, organizations need others and they need you.

Networks are a means of horizontal cooperation in order to create shared value while the different partners continue to have a high amount of independence. Via email, LinkedIn, Twitter we connect with each other, share information, and reach out for support. At networking events and face-to-face meetings we work on strengthening and broadening our connections. By investing in these relationships, we are building connectivity, friendship, trust, and loyalty, necessary ingredients to sustain our networks.

It may be some time before the benefits of authentic relationship management become apparent. This is why, despite its high potential for long-term advantage to an organization, it often has to be done in the slipstream of other core activities. But proper relationship management is an art of its own that needs attention and professionalization to bear fruit. This chapter will show how this has been the case in the past and also how important personal relationships are in our complex and digitalized era. Proper relationship management will be one of the key assets that makes the difference in a world that is changing faster than ever and in which relationships gradually have a tendency to become more flexible and distant. It is right now that a solid base of meaningful relationships is needed to make the organization more effective and resilient.

Friends and outsiders; networking in the seventeenth century.

Trust-based networks have existed forever. Ferdinand Bol, for example, is a famous Dutch seventeenth-century painter. He was the son of a surgeon in Dordrecht but

Ferdinand had his own dream. He wanted to become an acknowledged painter. In 1630, at the age of fourteen, he became an apprentice to the famous Rembrandt. A remarkable step forward in his career, but he lacked the support of his relatives and needed to find his own way to climb the social ladder. The Amsterdam admiralty, which was the economic and administrative power in the city, consisted of several closed networks, most of them based on strong family ties. People from within the network where called "friends," whereas people from outside the network were referred to as "outsiders." As an outsider, it was profoundly difficult to become part of these networks. The members enhanced their interdependence by gifts, invitations, and favors that at some point it was assumed would be returned. The network ties were based on reciprocity and trust and aimed to strengthen the group's own economic and social position within Amsterdam society.

After having risen quickly through the ranks in Rembrandt's studio while at the same time having invested in sustainable social connections with the Amsterdam elite, Ferdinand Bol established himself as an independent master around 1642. In order to be successful, it was not enough to be appreciated for his work; he also had to be respected for his personality in order to be awarded commissions. In the seventeenth century, reputation was everything, and Ferdinand Bol wisely understood that if he wanted to become part of these networks he had to adopt the style and moral behavior that resonated with the members of the Amsterdam admiralty. Only in this way could he establish a strong position as a painter and gain significant wealth and status. Still, it was through his marriage in 1652 to Elysabeth Dell, the daughter of Elbert Dirckz Dell, a very influential member of the Amsterdam admiralty, that he strengthened his position in the networks of the admiralty and magistrates which gained him continued commissions.[1]

He knew how to adapt his style and behavior, how to use the art of gifts and favors, to blend in in the higher circles as a middle-class gentleman from the small city of Dordrecht. Elysabeth Dell passed away in 1660. In 1669 he married for the second time with the wealthy Anne van Erckel. By this marriage he finally became a member of the Amsterdam admiralty's inner circle. From that moment on he stopped painting.

Without the talent to create useful and meaningful relationships within the circles he wished to join, it would never have been possible to increase his social ranking in such a profound way.

1.1   The transition to 4.0 organizations

As we can see in the example in the introduction of this chapter, gaining a certain market or social position and impact by networking is nothing new. Networks are the channels through which you sell your initiatives to people you depend on for cooperation and support. They give insight into the political dynamics and needs around you and help you to get your message across or to change your role within a certain field. Especially now, many organizations are in the middle of transforming themselves into network organizations, and the skill of creating long-term valuable connections is becoming even more crucial to be successful in the next decade.

This paragraph explains how society has changed in the last few decades and the impact this has had on professional relationship management.

1.0 decade

With the advent of steam power and the invention of the power loom in the late eighteenth century, the 1.0 decade took off. The Industrial Revolution radically changed the process of mechanization and the way goods were manufactured.

2.0 decade

In the late nineteenth century, electricity and assembly lines made mass production possible and society entered the 2.0 decade. From the late nineteenth century until the 1970s, the majority of power was in the hands of institutions and factories. These companies focused their business processes on managing physical assets and started to create budgeting models, organizational models, and planning systems in order to produce their goods in the cheapest and most effective ways. These systems were implemented to enhance the coordination of the organization in order to have a sense of control and reduce risk and uncertainty. During this decade we started to have the illusion that if we implemented the right systems and applied the right tools, we could control our environment and diminish risk to the maximum.

Another characteristic of this setup is the gap between the organization and the client/consumer. The latter had little influence on the product or service he or she wished to acquire. There was hardly any room for feedback or co-creation. The result of this attitude was strong competition for resources, information loss –because it was not shared properly– and a lack of a common overview. Efficiency and reliability were key. Being in true connection with the customer and building trust via transparent processes were not considered fundamental parts of the business process yet – they were seen more as a side activity.

3.0 decade

At the end of the twentieth century, with the advances of the Internet and globalization, the 3.0 decade set in. The gap between institutions and users shrank. We come from an era where institutions spread their messages and services through traditional media. In the 3.0 society, individuals have more opportunities to share their information with the world. As social animals freed from the traditional pillar society in the 1960s, individuals engage in community activities and share their personal knowledge and ideas across complex networked systems.

Communication becomes less of a one-way road and shows more characteristics of an equal dialogue.[2] This created a more complex environment for organizations to function in, since institutional and personal knowledge became more and more intertwined and sometimes even competed with each other. Knowledge that before was hierarchical and siloed is now diffused more horizontally. Diversity of insights is much more apparent. The challenge is to create the willingness, environment, and structure to nurture all these different knowledge paradigms at the same time, to balance them instead of choosing one over the other.

Wikipedia, YouTube, and personal blogs, for example, have challenged opinions of the medical establishment, statements of multinationals about their sustainability policies, and they have offered objective comparisons between insurance companies. Now, organizations are no longer like black boxes but start to look more like glass houses. The boundaries between inside and outside information is blurred, as are the boundaries between inside and outside Research & Development. Customers now engage in the development process, give feedback, share ideas, and sometimes even enhance products. This creates an environment in which companies are not separate entities anymore. They have less choice about whether to engage in interaction with customers, stakeholders, and criticasters. Procter & Gamble, for example, says on its website that through Connect + Develop as well as through the crowdsourcing platform Co-Create, P&G is collaborating with individuals and companies around the world to develop innovative ideas and products.

4.0 decade

In the 4.0 society, the combination of physical and digital technologies such as analytics, artificial intelligence, cognitive technologies, and the Internet of Things allows for the creation of digital enterprises that collect data from physical systems and use them to drive intelligent action back in the physical world. This revolution, which is most intense along America's west coast and in southeast China, is taking place at extraordinary speed, driven by technologies developing at an exponential rate.[3]

1.2   A new era

In our reality, societies 2.0, 3.0, and 4.0 are simultaneously present. The paradigm of the 2.0 organization is weakening, most organizations function in the 3.0 paradigm, and many organizations are motivated to step into the 4.0 age. In any case, the world will change in unpredictable ways. Artificial Intelligence will allow most repetitive tasks to be executed by computers. Due to the Internet and apps, knowledge will become available in increased amounts, and we can spread information towards enormous crowds faster and faster.

In addition, the location of power at a global level seems to be shifting. China's R&D departments are improving very quickly, its high-tech companies conquer the world's markets and most likely will exceed the innovation power of the USA sooner than we can imagine. More and more resources will become available for free. How long will it take before an alternative system for energy distribution comes into existence?

This technological revolution also implies a revolution in how we set up our businesses and how we relate to each other. In such a high-tech society, what is it that humans still have to offer? The technological revolution is unstoppable, but it will still be up to us to interpret what is happening, to give meaning to it together, to be creative, cultivate empathy, to co-create, to have ideals, and to make the world a better place.

This implies that the value of a sustainable network and meaningful relations will just increase in the upcoming decades. This network has to be as robust as it is flexible. Networks are like living organisms; their shapes and leading alliances are changing in real time.

> Ambiguity will be one of the main characteristics of the future.
> One we have to deal with.

In his book Leaders Make the Future, Robert Johansen calls our contemporary world the VUCA world. It is an acronym developed by the U.S. military after the collapse of the Soviet Union to describe a multipolar world that is Volatile, Uncertain, Complex, and Ambiguous:

- **Volatility** reflects the speed and turbulence of change.
- **Uncertainty** means that outcomes, even from familiar actions, are less predictable.
- **Complexity** indicates the vastness of interdependencies in globally connected economies and societies.
- **Ambiguity** conveys the multitude of options and potential outcomes resulting from them. Where once we could count on the seeming certainty and predictability of binary choices, choices and consequences are now far less clear.[4]

In this context it is important to realize the difference between complicated and complex. Freek Peters explains in his inaugural speech that *complicated* means the functioning of organizations as complicated, though predictable, machines like the internal workings of a great clock or a chemical factory. *Complex* means that organizations now have to function like flexible systems and respond in an adaptive manner to the ever-changing and unpredictable world[5] like the constantly changing movement of birds swarming towards their destination. None of them is in the lead. They need to be alert and aware of the movement of the others and respond adaptively. At the same time, there are no clear boundaries between the swarm and the environment. In a clockwork system, however, the organization can function more like an autonomous entity, but a complex swarm system is in constant interaction with its surroundings and can be entered by outward influences.[6] This increases its vulnerability and at the same time, when the system is doing well, endows it with great strengths. In order to succeed and flourish, organizations will need **V**ision, **U**nderstanding, **C**larity, and **A**gility as complementing forces to navigate in the vuca world.

Vision refers to the ability to see through the chaos and to have a clear vision for the organization. It relates to the leaders' ability to create **clarity** around this *true north* and to avoid external events trying to pull them off course.

Leaders need deep **understanding** of their organization's capabilities and strategies to take advantage of rapidly changing circumstances by playing to their strengths while minimizing their weaknesses. Listening only to information sources and opinions that reinforce their own views carries great risk of missing other angles. Instead, leaders need to engage directly with their stakeholders to ensure they are attuned to the changes in their markets and to cover the full spectrum of viewpoints.

Agility in this context means that adaptive tactics are required for rapid adaptation to changing external circumstances without altering the strategic course. Leaders need multiple strategy plans while remaining diligent to cope with unexpected events.[7]

Of course, life will not change extensively for every business. Neighborhood stores, heavy industry craftsmen – they will all continue to exist. But it is undeniable that the competitive environment is changing. Because of the possibilities of digital technology, the boundaries between industry sectors are blurring. Many organizations will face competition from companies and industries that traditionally belong to other sectors. Soon, and for some this period has already started, an organization's success will depend on its effectiveness in competing within rapidly emerging ecosystems, a variety of businesses from dimensionally different sectors.[8]

The car industry, for example, is now forced to compete outside its traditional sector of automobiles. Now its main competitors are companies like Tesla and Google who approached and disrupted the car industry from a digital perspective. The car is not so much a mechanical machine anymore as a computer on wheels. They changed the whole concept of driving and are now aiming at battery-powered self-driving cars.

Also, banks that currently experience some threat from new but powerful initiatives like crowdfunding and blockchain are forced to think about services of a new kind in order to stay relevant to the market. Idea Bank in Poland, for example, offers *idea-hubs*, e-invoicing, and online bookkeeping. Lloyds Bank includes legal assistance and email hosting, thereby expanding the scope and utility of their platforms by including services that used to be delivered by competitors from other sectors.

In this era of complex and constantly developing ecosystems, partnerships will be key. They will help you to fine-tune and clarify the vision, stay up to date on developments within other sectors to gain a thorough understanding of what is going on in the organization's environment, and also provide you the resources to respond to this environment with agility. So, striving for a diverse multisectoral network with people who are willing to share information with you, or companies that are even willing to share their data for mutual benefit, is highly beneficial. Solid partnerships have the potential to make the whole greater than the sum of its parts.[9]

1.3 The relationship-centered organization

Today's society is as much about cooperating as about competing. Connected through social networks, both online and offline, people and organizations are sharing information and resources. These networks do not only consist of organizations that are based on a typical kind of knowledge, they also include individuals with their personal knowledge and insights. Together they tap into collective knowledge and problem-solving abilities. What organizations need to do is find a way to access these networks and tap into this collective knowledge by developing meaningful relationships with their stakeholders.

The relationship-centered organization is a networked, agile, and adaptive entity that transcends traditional boundaries as it develops deep and collaborative relationships in a creative and consistent way by extracting full value from its various partners in order to reach its goals. As keeping pace with change and innovation becomes increasingly challenging and the complexity within and around organizations is growing fast, having a solid relational network with relevant power and expertise helps to decrease complexity and move through challenges in more agile and effective ways.[10]

With regard to companies and organizations, Gulati and Kletter define relationship capital as the "value of a firm's network of relationships with its customers, suppliers, alliance partners, and internal subunits." *The development of sustainable relationships helps organizations to provide better service to their customers or clients as well as to increase their influence for its greater cause that is shared and carried out by its strategic partners.*[11] A government entity involved in energy provision, for example, does not have direct ways to influence the perception and behavior of citizens concerning green energy but instead aims to influence political organizations and partners that do have direct impact on society to get its message across and influence the public to make greener choices.

An example of a 4.0 business model is the so-called platform organization like Airbnb and Uber. First, platform organizations are based on a business model in which both producers and consumers are connected to and interact via the Internet platform to create and exchange value. Second, they set the rules of governance for the interactions that ensue based on the needs of the customer. On these platforms, co-creation and sharing are the driving values of the community. Additionally, the content and contact are more personalized. Participants of these platforms are often both producer and consumer at the same time.

One of the risks of these kinds of platform organizations seems to be the issue of ethical behavior. Platform organizations have the ability to grow exponentially and are mainly self-generating and self-steering. Co-creation and sharing works splendidly within the network, but how does it relate to the stakeholders outside of its network? Hotels and citizens in Amsterdam are suffering from the explosion of Airbnb rentals, and Uber has been accused of a malicious privacy policy because of a feature that tracks the location of customers. In an organization that is hard to control and is growing at the speed of light, who is taking care of the ethical behavior of all its participants and making sure that its original good intentions do not clash with the interests of the societies in which it operates?

Perhaps partly because of this, we see a tendency toward alternative networks that are, like the seventeenth century admiralty in Amsterdam, more closed. When you think about publishing job vacancies, for example, do you publish them in the newspaper, on job websites like Monsterboard, or on LinkedIn? Most people probably already have experience posting or reacting to vacancies on LinkedIn. And why? Most HR managers find LinkedIn helpful in increasing the chances of identifying job applicants who share the same values as their organization. Also, the fact that this person is linked to someone else in their network raises the expectation that the person will act in a responsible manner, so as not to harm the other person who is connected to both the organization and the applicant. Still, LinkedIn groups are very accessible to outsiders. For an HR professional, LinkedIn is an endless pool of possible talent. And that is precisely the reason that, counterproductively, too many people in these groups keep sticking around passively which weakens the self-generating power as well as the relevance of the network.[12]

Future network; high-trust value networks.

The expectation of networks of the future is that they will be more closed and centered around a certain shared purpose in so-called *high-trust value networks* creating both social and financial capital to support their cause.

So even while technological developments allow us to be in touch with an ever-wider range of people, the tendency is to use these new technological possibilities to create networks that are:

· More personal.
· More closed to outsiders.
· Relatively small (to safeguard the self-generating power of the platforms).[13]
· Based on trust and reciprocity.

The seventeenth-century network of friends and outsiders probably looks very dated at first but it is actually coming back, just in a much more complex state, not bound to a shared geographical location and with less face-to-face interaction. Quite like in the decade of the Amsterdam admiralty, personal and organizational success will depend on networking power.

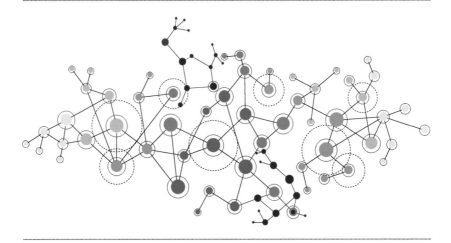

Figure 1.3.1 Interconnected networks

Networking power today is not just about entering meaningful networks but even more about connecting these networks to each other. It is the density of the network, the amount of interrelatedness of the network, that determines the power of it. For this reason it is valuable for every organization to first succeed in entering different networks and then mutually connecting them. In this way the information that is shared will spread even faster within the network, including requests for advice, leads, or support.[14]

1.4   Strategic Relationship Management; a purpose or a tool?

"We need to have a better Relationship Management Strategy" is something CEOs and managers often say. If asked, "why?", the answer often is "Because we need stronger ties with our stakeholders and we want to increase our network scope." If again asked "why?", the reply often is "because we want to sell more of our products." Ask a third time "why?" and there is confusion all around.

The mechanical approach that was so useful in building factories is now being applied to intangible processes and human interactions. In the meantime, these systems have become more and more fixed and are seen as a goal in their own right. The prescribed processes and protocols are now often more important than looking at the specific current situation and what is needed to actually improve it. This is often much more than systems and tools.

In the health care sector, for example, the instrumental approach has led to very painful situations. Protocols and procedures have become so extensive and detailed that health care professionals are spending more time administrating than doing their actual job – taking care of patients. They are more focused on the protocol to see what to do or to fulfill their administrative obligations than on the faces of their clients. The protocol weighs more heavily than the acute need to be treated as an individual. All this is the result of a fear-based society that wants to reduce risk to the maximum and aims to put responsibility on the protocols instead of carrying it on its own shoulders.

In some organizations, the Customer Relationship Management (CRM) system also tends to become a goal in itself. A lot of effort is put into making the CRM system more refined and effective as a way to enhance the organization's impact. Employees are supposed to dedicate themselves to registering their contacts and the interactions with these contacts in the system. In principle this can be useful but, in what context? What is the meaning of running such a system when the organization is not clear about what bigger vision and strategy the CRM system is supposed to serve? Or when even the internal stakeholders are not aligned properly in order to create the motivation and trust to share this information with each other? Relationships can only be managed appropriately when this management strategy is aligned with the right purpose and intentions.

> "The character of relationships between people is fundamentally vulnerable." – *Hannah Arendt*

We cannot totally "plan" our relationships.[15] People, especially in horizontal relationships, cannot be controlled. As philosopher Hannah Arendt wrote, "The character of relationships between people is fundamentally vulnerable." People can be spontaneous, creative, impulsive. You cannot make people do things without damaging trust and causing resistance. The belief in the concept of controlling relationships is an expression of *machine thinking*. Communication becomes strategic and outcome-driven. In order to do justice and show respect to the nature of human relationships, there is no other way than to allow some insecurity and initiate dialogue to increase understanding and the willingness to cooperate.[16]

> This does not need to be hard. I just recalled a memory from the early 2000s when the streets in Beijing still featured a lot of bikes. At that time, I was living there to study Chinese and I, like many other students, often went out on my bike to cycle to a nearby shopping mall or to just enjoy the experience of the city. Unlike in the Netherlands, people in China proved to be very flexible on the bike and behaved quite like the birds in the swarm. When a bike approached riding against the traffic, this did not lead to angry faces or power struggles about who has the right to drive on that part of the road. Instead, both bikers flexibly navigated their bikes around each other while understanding each other's intentions by keeping eye contact. When all went well they continued on their ways in a relaxed manner, already keeping their eye out for the next possible unexpected encounter. This way of dealing with each other – expecting the unexpected, staying in contact, counting on each other's good intentions, and navigating with sensitive flexibility to allow both to continue on their intended ways – can serve as an example on how to deal with relationships in an adaptive instead of controlling manner. Monica Bakker

Relationship management tools and strategies are necessary but do not add value to relationships on their own. The instrument should be used in the right way, at the right moment, by the right person with the right intentions. Especially intentions are a very important factor in the value-based economy that will rely so much on the quality of relationships. A purely instrumental mind-set blocks sustainable trust in relationships and needs to be balanced by intrinsic human bonds. As counterintuitive as it may seem, the absence of very specific expectations about what the other should "give" is key to the process of building meaningful relationships. It is by how we relate to each other and how we communicate together that we can change the environment of our organizations and communities. This exactly is what makes strategic networking such an important skill, now and in the future.

The twentieth-century market thinking in which competition, growth, value for money, and evidence-based action are its players' main drivers also influences our relationships. People can become a tool to achieve something, such as more profit for example. Clients become objects that must be improved, and stakeholders become our competitors. The wish to squeeze as much as possible out of the relationship harms the relationship and increases distance and distrust. This does not create successful companies in the future, since in this future it will be so much more about creating common value [17] and interactive service relations.

> The wish to squeeze as much as possible out of the relationship harms the relationship and increases distance and distrust.

The quality of an organization's network depends on alignment of the Relationship Management Strategy and tools with the overall strategy and vision and the intention with which they are performed. A Relationship Management Strategy carried out with personal integrity and focused on personal connection brings an exponential bigger return of trust, loyalty, goodwill, and benefit to the organization's network and ability to reach its short-term and long-term goals.

1.5   Developing strategic relations

The concept of conscious networking makes some people uncomfortable. They believe relationships should develop in a natural way. Steering a Relationship Management Strategy feels insincere or when the relations are not immediately relevant for the challenge at hand, like wasting time. Sometimes it even feels unnecessary if the organization has a very strong internal network and a significant level of self-reliance. But, relating to stakeholders, lining up allies, and mapping the political landscape are all part of leadership.

> Lining up allies and mapping the political landscape are all part of leadership.

The challenge is to grow and foster your network in advance, before you actually need it. We all depend on other people, and only by cooperating can we increase our impact and reach our goals. Charles Darwin became famous for his paradigm-shifting book On The Origin of Species, but the book was not the accomplishment of Darwin alone. He wrote 1,500 letters per year to a collection of biologists, anthropologists, doctors, and so forth. People from all walks of life contributed to his theory. Most of them had been part of his network for quite some time. Although Darwin got the credit, his theory was the result of a vast collective network effort. He could never have done it alone.[19]

> A common mistake is that organizations do not start expanding their network until they find themselves in a crisis. That is too late! People will be suspicious about your intentions. By that time, the network should already be in place and have a solid basis of reciprocity and trust.

Strategic Relationship Management requires attention and consistency in parallel with day-to-day tasks and ad hoc emergencies. Charles Darwin exchanged letters with his friends and academics from a range of different scientific fields for a very long time, maintaining a personal connection with them and sharing insights on shared interests – without actually knowing what the final outcome would be. The way he connected was authentic. Of course he needed their knowledge to develop his own theory on the origin of species, but the connection was based on sympathy and shared interests. If the network had been fostered just to serve his self-interest, these people most likely would not have been so keen on openly sharing their knowledge. It is by connecting from an authentic place that support and involvement are generated for the long term.

Having a solid network with strategic relations gives connective advantage; the ability to marshal information, support, or other resources from one of the networks.[20] It is smart to actively connect to people and networks that are outside of the immediate group of people who are like you. Having a broader network of people who are seeing from different perspectives significantly increases the quality of ideas. Like Darwin, you see more and know more. Organizations with more diverse networks have more power because they are the gateway for other people to connect to these networks and can connect ideas and resources that normally would not have been combined. Often you do not know these organizations and people from outside your own tribe very well. But exactly for that reason, they deserve extra attention. Connecting to them intentionally and bridging the gap between the two networks makes the organization more future-proof and more flexible to respond to unanticipated chances or turmoil. On the other hand, it is important to make sure that the network density is not too sparse. If the connections are too thin, there will be a lack of visibility, inside information, and real connectedness which implies that the size of the network lacks quality and therefore power.[21]

A diverse value network is a vital part of every organization if it is to thrive in the next VUCA decade. They are of great value for accessing new capabilities, sharing risk-taking, or expanding fields of influence.[22] A great example of an ecosystem that facilitates this is Shenzhen in China. Until thirty-five years ago, this city was not much more than a collection of fishing villages. Since Shenzhen was designated as a special economic zone in the 1980s, it has risen to become the predominant center of high-tech design and manufacturing in the world. Big Chinese tech companies like Huawei and Tencent are located there. Shenzhen was well-known in the past for being a huge copy center of western and Japanese products, by which it acquired the reputation of *shanzhai* – a word that describes counterfeit consumer goods. Interestingly enough though, it is exactly this background that makes Shenzhen so suitable now for high-tech innovation. Its value chains are highly flexible; it takes only two or three days in Shenzhen to make a product prototype, four times faster and three times cheaper than developing prototypes in-house. This is due to the collaborative nature of Shenzhen's producers and the close proximity of materials and service suppliers within the city. Shenzhen houses a complete manufacturing value chain and has incubated thousands of hardware startups over the past decade. Because *shanzhai* roots go deep in the genes of Shenzhen, rather than protecting intellectual property, most entrepreneurs focus on product improvement and innovation which is a great environment for R&D. Today Shenzhen registers more patents than Beijing and Shanghai combined. Shenzhen enterprises are fast, collaborative, adaptable, open, and relatively cheap. They hold a strong and diverse range of value networks making them ready to capture the next big wave of innovation power and making them an example of new ways of collaboration to the world.[23]

Applied to organizational structures, building both agile and powerful strategic relations implies letting go of the traditional concept of the organization as a hierarchical system while at the same time acknowledging that this hierarchy might still be a reality we have to deal with for a certain period of time. Organizations can be hierarchical and heterarchical simultaneously, heterarchical meaning the presence of several different overlapping hierarchies without the network being directed by someone from the top. This demands more internalization and the proactive engagement of all employees and stakeholders who wish to work for both their own self-enhancement and the greater cause instead of being dependent on clear top-down instructions and protocols out of fear of overstepping their boundaries.

It is important that the network is taken care of by the organization as a whole. A solid network is secured in an organization's CRM system and in its fundamental processes and attitudes. The consequence of this diminishing hierarchical and fixed structure is an increased weight on the quality of relationships – to communicate and have dialogues within and outside the organization to move forward in a manner that is carried by the majority and steers the organization in both a flexible and effective way through the complex landscape we are currently in.

1.6   Shared value networks

Why would people or organizational stakeholders want to collaborate? When they feel they have something to gain or feel an intrinsic passion for the cause. The common denominator is creating shared added value. For a strategic relationship to evolve from a transactional to a mutually reinforcing collaboration, the organization and its stakeholders all need to have a vested interest in the relationship. In order to create successful and effective collaborations, partners need to agree on a shared common cause that motivates the different stakeholders to cooperate; the driver of the cooperation. This can be around a situation that must be solved as well as about a desired situation for the future that is worth striving for.

According to Ronald van den Hoff in his book *Society 3.0*, the concept of shared value can be defined as "policies and operating practices that enhance competitiveness of an organization while at the same time advancing the economic and social conditions in the communities in which it operates." Shared value is not defined as just economic gain but includes social gain as more than a peripheral matter. Currently, the Internet is cutting transaction costs and facilitating fast knowledge sharing, mobility, and connectivity. This makes people more autonomous to engage collectively in new ways of value creation thereby increasing the complexity of the environment in which organizations need to operate. The only way to respond to that is by increasingly involving stakeholders in the realization of services and products. This does not always lead to a clearly identifiable goal, team, or project plan as we know it[25] but behaves more like a swarm; regularly changing direction, shape, and membership of the team. A value network is characterized by a shared starting point and a path of creation in a context of shared responsibility more than it consists of a fixed route, structure, and team. Value networks have the ability to connect to each other in changing and overlapping formations. There is an open structure for new knowledge and new contacts; acquired knowledge is free to share beyond the original team, which might lead to further cooperation.

> A value network is not so much an outlined path as a directed starting point with an unknown pace.

Still, the main values that guide an organization might not be exactly the same as the values of the networks the organization is connected with. The values in the organization's vision are often focused mainly on supporting the purpose of the organization itself, while the values for the organization as a part of several networks might differ slightly according to the shared drive and purpose of the network.

To level out these kinds of dynamics, it is important to take time and space to formulate a shared vision that is indeed shared by all network partners. Partnerships are not merely led by the exchange of interests but by the exchange between the added value to the shared vision and the accomplishment of individual goals. In that regard, collaboration is as much about shared vision and values as it is about negotiation.

In shared value networks, it is not all gain; some sacrifices will need to be made, especially when one or more of the cooperating organizations has a very strong culture and strong convictions about "the right way" of serving a certain cause. It might be hard to let go of its own judgments and to be open to the ways of others. These kinds of organizations are often made up of very value-driven professionals who can get entangled in competition with cooperation partners about which solution is supposed to be the ultimate. Although this is caused by a very authentic dedication to the cause, it will not serve the best outcome, which is likely to be a compromise between the different solutions, especially when all stakeholders need to stay motivated and involved. Effective and sustainable network cooperation also leaves space for the partners to elaborate how they choose to contribute to the shared goals.[26]

Collaborative partnerships or networks are very different from the organizational forms we are used to in which the objectives, strategy, core values, and tasks are usually clearly defined. The network itself is not fixed and the network is not always visible as a set group. It often has an inner circle of core partners, with a middle circle of co-creators and a peripheral outer circle. The more to the outer boundaries the stakeholders function in the network, the looser the ties between the several groups and towards the shared values of the core group.

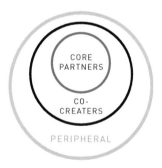

Figure 1.6.1 Collaborative partnerships or networks

In a context where the boundaries between organizations are fading, defining the "rules of engagement" becomes a crucial issue. In more open organizations, leadership needs to be clearly defined and accountable to keep the cooperation effective. The dynamics between different external parties can no longer be based on a hierarchical approach. The process of cooperation develops within the cooperation itself. This is a core characteristic of complex and emergent dynamics that cannot be fully controlled. For this reason, more than half of alliances fail. Stakeholders (groups or individuals) in principle think from their own individual interests, and as a result, there could easily develop a situation of competition that overshadows the desire for effective cooperation.

To reduce the risk of failure, Gulati and Kletter formulate four important criteria needed before you even start to secure significant advantage for all parties involved:

1. Careful selection (also see Chapter 5).
2. Jointly articulated expectations (also see Chapter 4).
3. Management flexibility (also see Chapter 6 and 10).
4. Performance incentives (also see Chapter 9 and 10).[27]

Still, allies will most likely be loyal to more networks and commitments than to just one. The challenge is not to be anxious about that but to use it to your benefit. If their connection with your issue is strong enough, they might be willing to work within their other networks for the causes you care about, or even to introduce you to their network and hence add a new partner to your circle. And sometimes, yes, their commitments will conflict with yours. But this does not need to be the end of the cooperation; the stabilizing forces then are *openness* and *trust*. This requires a history of open face-to-face conversations and respect for each other's dilemmas and different interests to work things out and find a solution that fits both parties. When this happens, it is important to accept that even the closest network partners cannot always be on the same page. The question is how harmful the differing interests are with regard to the common goal.

Tom Verbelen, Managing Director of Governance Affairs for the Municipality of Antwerp, recalls several situations in which political agendas and the aspirations of a long-term partner were not always compatible. Damaging or even losing this relationship would have been very harmful to the long-term goal of the city council, which is to increase the wealth and welfare of Antwerp. This long-term goal transcends disagreements on issues of more short-term and secondary relevance and forces the parties to continue working on trust, common understanding, and common ground. Polarizing the dispute has to be avoided – the challenge is to offer each other the greatest tolerance possible. The partners within the network do not need to agree on every dispute, rather the challenge is to focus on the bigger picture and mutual ground with each individual partner. The success of this depends to a great extent on the personal relationships between the representatives of the parties. In cases where the political representatives are tangled up in a conflict that might even be part of the public discourse, civil servants oriented towards the long term can still nurture the relationship on a smoldering fire.

Stakeholders feel initially attracted by the service and benefits the organization offers as well as by the greater goal it is striving for, but to achieve a connection based on trust, the relationship needs to be nurtured. It is not only about "what is in it for us," but even more about what to give, share, and strive for together. This also translates into individual professional relationships.

> "A befriended colleague once told me 'Whenever I am introduced to another person, I am not thinking *what use could this person be to me,* I am thinking, *what could meeting me mean to him or her?'* This attitude brings the way you and your organization relate to other people into a whole new realm." – *Monica Bakker*

1.7 Technical and adaptive challenges in relationship management

In whatever organization, whatever industry, relationships are a key element of the organizational capital. Historically, companies focused their expertise and business processes on physical assets (machinery, products, locations) and intellectual assets. Currently, organizations are increasingly developing Strategic Relationship Management, treating their relationships as valuable assets. They are moving from a transactional mind-set (interaction because of transaction) towards trust-based, long-term relationships that are beneficial for all parties involved. As a result of increased outsourcing, they increase their relationship on the vertical dimension that includes ties up and down the value chain. At the same time, they are shrinking their core and improving their customer solutions, many of which are a result of partnerships between several firms and organizations that add extra dimensions to their own product or service or increase their influence. This leads to an increase in horizontal relationships with equal parties.[28]

When we aim to switch from an instrumental to a relational mind-set, from a competing to a cooperating mind-set, from a financial profit to a value mind-set, we are talking about a change of behaviors and attitudes. Gulati and Kletter have designed a visual that shows the development of network partnerships from a transactional level towards a level of trust-based cooperation.

1. The ladder of Gulati and Kletter begins with transactional agreements that are based on a specific need or opportunity but never evolve into anything more.
2. At the next level organizations evolve into a more contractual relationship in which organizations agree to coordinate select activities that are non-critical with each other and stay close to specified contracts for those select activities.
3. At the third step, the relationship evolves into active cooperation on more critical tasks.
4. At the top of the ladder, the relationship has developed into a true sustainable partnership based on trust and reciprocity to achieve a goal that neither organization could have achieved without the other. The ties are more strategic and deeper.

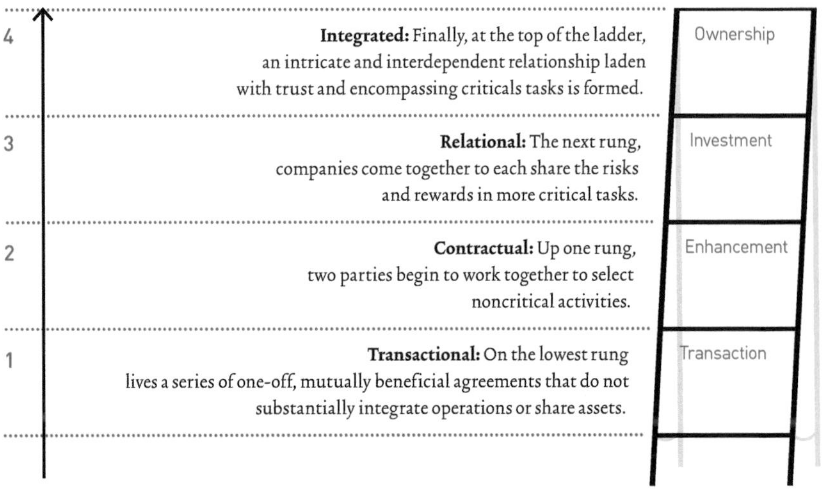

<table>
<tr><td>4</td><td>**Integrated:** Finally, at the top of the ladder, an intricate and interdependent relationship laden with trust and encompassing criticals tasks is formed.</td><td>Ownership</td></tr>
<tr><td>3</td><td>**Relational:** The next rung, companies come together to each share the risks and rewards in more critical tasks.</td><td>Investment</td></tr>
<tr><td>2</td><td>**Contractual:** Up one rung, two parties begin to work together to select noncritical activities.</td><td>Enhancement</td></tr>
<tr><td>1</td><td>**Transactional:** On the lowest rung lives a series of one-off, mutually beneficial agreements that do not substantially integrate operations or share assets.</td><td>Transaction</td></tr>
</table>

Figure 1.7.1 The ladder of Gulati and Kletter[10]

In the contemporary world, organizations are facing such complex environments that transactional or contractual relationships often are no longer sufficient to meet the challenges at hand. Every day, people have problems for which they do have the suitable know-how and procedures. These are **technical problems**; problems that can be solved with current expertise based on past experience, often by an expert. In other words, the cause of the problem is clear and, even though it might be complicated, it is clear how it can be solved. Just imagine you have an acute problem with a failing radiator and you call a repairman to solve the problem. When the problem is fixed, you thank him and pay for his services and most likely the relationship will not evolve into anything more sustainable. As you see, a technical problem relates to the transactional agreement as described above.

An **adaptive problem** is a problem without easy solutions. In modern language it is sometimes called a *wicked problem*. These problems cannot be solved by someone who provides top-down answers – on the contrary, the problem asks for new ways of thinking, experiments and adjustments from numerous places in the organization from the people who are actually experiencing the problem. Without learning new ways–changing attitudes, patterns, and values – people cannot make the necessary leap to be successful. When people look to authorities for easy answers to adaptive challenges, they end up with dysfunctional situations. They expect the person in charge to know and provide the solution, thereby pushing the person in the lead to come up with a technical solution for an adaptive problem, taking his or her refuge in routine solutions instead of leadership and co-creation. The problems related to globalization, innovation, sustainability, and co-creation are all of an adaptive nature. Organizational problems can also have an adaptive character.[30]

When there is evidence of a major challenge...	... do you focus on a technical fix?	or	... do you now need an adaptive response?
Subscriptions are down and people are booking individual tickets closer to the event.	*We need to offer them better incentives to commit to the season in advance.*	**or**	*We need a completely different pricing system and to build loyalty through direct participation.*
Our campus is old, confusing and used inefficiently.	*We need to invest in upgrading facilities and signage.*	**or**	*We need to leverage our off-campus successes into a new kind of home.*
Our expenses continue to grow faster than our income, and we are experiencing persistent annual losses.	*Our organization must generate more income and implement stronger cost controls.*	**or**	*Our organization must overcome its increasing aversion to risk by investing in new approaches.*

Figure 1.7.2 Richard Evans, President Emcarts Inc., examples of common adaptive challenges, showing 'business-as-usual' technical solutions vs. forward-thinking adaptive responses [31]

Since her appointment as CEO of the Nederlands Dans Theater (NDT), Janine Dijkmeijer and her team have worked on professionalizing the relationship management of the dance company. The dance company had already focused on strengthening its network for a long time, but somehow it had not reached its full potential. The focus was perhaps too short-term oriented, whereas most funding is granted by relationships that are fostered over the long term.

The first steps towards increasing the efficiency of their relationship management were to create clearer job responsibilities and organize alignment meetings, and they also set up an effective CRM system. But more had to be done to achieve an effectively coordinated network that provides consistent and sufficient funding–technical solutions alone were not enough.

> "The new relationship management approach required a more outward-looking tendency; the willingness to interact more actively and consistently with the outside world." – *Janine Dijkmeijer*

Relationship management at NDT focused mainly on its purpose; creating and performing high-quality dance art. The new relationship management required a more outward-looking approach. Now that times are changing and stronger ties are needed with governmental organizations, the private sector, other art schools, and the creative sector in general, technical solutions and even strong networking skills alone were not enough. What was needed was a change of awareness and the willingness to interact more actively and consistently with the world outside. It required a new habit of sharing information about relationships and stakeholders with the right colleagues and to be aware of what the temperature and needs are of the stakeholders outside the immediate organization.

Janine and the team had to find a way to open the organization's windows to the outside world. New principles of organizing were needed. NDT had to become a flexible network organization where the staff has the freedom to interact with the outside world, while remaining consistent with the strategic goals of NDT.

The other challenge was marketing versus development. Unlike the development team, marketing was mainly based on marketing strategies and visual attractiveness and less on content, intimacy, and long-term results. Here the team had to change its mind-set towards more sustainable relationship management in combination with a strong strategy to engage new audiences. The revenue, funding, and benefits of long-term partners are in general higher than of those who do not feel deeply connected to the organization.

Janine explains it this way; "You need a long breath to learn the technique of ballet. You need to trust that practice will bring you there. Once the technique is conquered, you need to trust it is there. From here your soul will start opening and the art form of dance will be transmitted. It is the same with relationships. You need to be willing to spend long-term effort without knowing what the result will be, in the meantime trusting the process."

This is the culture change that she is encouraging in her team and organization; to change into a network organization that is connected more to the outer world and can execute a sustainable, long-term Relationship Management Strategy while increasing the focus on content and intimacy. This requires leadership by perseverance and resilience.

When dealing with adaptive challenges, there is always resistance. People need to let go of old habits and beliefs, and they will challenge your approach. It asks them to tolerate uncertainty and redefine aspects of their identity. Still, in order to profoundly improve the situation for the organization as a whole, unpopular measures are often unavoidable. This will all be needed in order to make sure the new structures, systems, and procedures really fall into place, flourish, and generate the desired results.

1.8   The value of authentic relationships in a swift society

Starting from a relationship mind-set, formulating a shared vision and stating clear rules of engagement are crucial for successful relationship and network management. In the contemporary age of swift communication, we need to go a step further and give it roots by acting based on a mind-set that allows the relationships to gain meaning and staying power. We can develop the most brilliant strategy, the most effective internal processes, and the most magnificent event, but as soon as people feel the mind-set of the representatives of the organization is lacking genuine authenticity, credibility will be lost. Intentions, strategy, structure, and culture all need to be aligned. Values need to be embedded in structures and procedures that in their turn support the manifestation of the organization's values by its representatives.

Facebook, LinkedIn, Twitter, WhatsApp – information travels faster and faster. The hope of fulfilling desires and demands for individual self-assertion and community building is now invested in highly advanced technology known for the facilitation of inter-human contact and communication. Human messages rush and dash along the digital highways. Never did we have so much opportunity to connect to others and to express ourselves to such an extensive public. But how does this make us feel? How connected do you feel to a "friend" you have never met in person but only know online? How valued do you feel when someone informs you about a sensitive matter via WhatsApp? Although the electronic highway can be very useful and even fun, it can also make personal attention frail and shallow, ready to rush to the next person or channel before the situation is explored thoroughly. Electronic messages tend to be shortened and simplified so as to be noticed before the attention span shifts, a habit that prevents us from conveying profound ideas needing reflection or sharing messages that are profoundly connecting and feed feelings of trust and belonging.

> The price we all pay for having more and faster information is the shrinking meaning of its content.

In our fast-moving digital world, online communities are easy to access and easy to abandon on an ad hoc basis. Internet communities grow and shrink because of individual decisions to stay in or step out. This has its benefits; it gives a sense of freedom and the ability to maneuver without smothering social control or demands from other members to "stay in." But, they also lack certain values that the "old school" communities provided, values like true belonging, loyalty, and safety. [32]

Long-term commitments have their disadvantages, but the lack of them creates networks that are unreliable and lack traits like intimacy and deep-rooted trust.

Zygmunt Bauman states that "we are changing into a fluid society in which the old communities based on religion or political preference, institutions, and certainties have evaporated. It is no longer about a 'united we', but about a 'divided we.'" [33]

Governmental organizations like education and health care meant to advance social justice are increasingly organized according to market principles focused on results and regulations, resulting in a constant need for investments to realize growth and innovation. In the meantime, relationships between people and business units become results-oriented (often expressed in profit and efficiency) and instrumental in order to deliver the expected results. Of course, this also impacts the way people cooperate. And this in an environment in which global developments and international capital streams influence organizations and individual lives in ways that are impossible to control or predict. This tends to drive organizations towards risk-avoiding behavior expressing itself in increasing regulations and more short-term labor contracts, for example.

For individuals, it becomes increasingly difficult to rely on a solid societal order or to have a sense of control over their lives. The individual is supposed to continuously adapt to ever-changing circumstances. In modern society change and progress are prone to become goals in their own right – it is the era of rolling impermanence where bonds are frayed and intimacy disappears in the shifting nature of all social relationships. What is common today is to be on the move – to hop from one job to another, move from one social circle to another, to befriend and defriend, to be on a never-ending quest for novelty and improvement. [35]

This also has good qualities. To be flexible in forming and reshaping bonds can be of great strategic advantage. But it can also be slippery and fugitive, especially when there are no deep underlying values, other than progress and profit, to support this dynamic. When openness, progress, and flexibility are highly sought after, what about the value of responsibility that gives us the notion that we can depend on each other? Freedom and security are values that contradict each other here. Social cohesion is changing. Human beings as wage earners often with temporary contracts focus on survival and progress, and that might add to individuals' wealth, but it does not create a stable sense of belonging. [36]

How can we give our innovation and shifting networks a solid foundation in these times of haste and continuous change?

46

In the context of globalization, individuals and organizations need to adapt continuously to changing circumstances. Relationships become useful but swift, too often lacking profound intimacy and meaning. In order to build strong and sustainable bonds that can be of strategic advantage, sustainable, grounding values need to take shape within the relationship management approach in order to gain the resilience to withstand storms and the goodwill to get support in the long run.

1.9 Grounding elements in relationship management; attention, friendship, and loyalty

Organizations that strive for excellent relationship and network management acknowledge the importance of meaningful relationships. "Meaningful" relates to both personal communications and the strong underlying motivation that is intrinsic to the employees of the company who carry them out. Do they just aim to use their relationships for the profit of the company or do they wish to cooperate with their partners in a way that increases intimacy and trust within these relationships so that the relationship adds true value for both parties? In this paragraph we will discuss three basic virtues for meaningful relationships to develop. They can make a substantial difference to the way your Relationship Management Strategy will be received by your partners and should increase their personal connection and loyalty toward you and your organization.

Attention
You may have heard the expression "What you give attention to will grow." As cheesy as it may sound, there is a grain of truth in it. One of the core elements to growing meaningful relationships is *attention*. Meaningful relationships can only exist by the grace of the attention they are given. In our hectic times true attention is becoming scarce. Colleagues who you plan to ask about their difficult situation at home later (because right now you need to focus on finishing your project) might not be willing anymore to share this information with you later. Business partners who you plan to meet face to face later because you have other priorities right now might not be interested in developing a bond with you by then.

The time is now. We all know how difficult it is to pay attention to the right things, the right people, at this moment. Instead, we too often lose ourselves in paying attention to meaningless details and superficial communication, meanwhile feeling scattered and disconnected. Paying attention to what is important now is a way of being present in the moment. That is not the same thing as trying to stop time – it is a way of standing still during the ongoing passage of time. To be there, at the right time, in the right way, for the people who matter to your cause helps to create sustainable relationships. [37]

By giving true attention to your relationships and partners and putting them first, you will discover who they are, what their true needs are, and what is at stake for them.[38] In an interview with Rutger van Nouhuijs, member of the executive committee of ABN AMRO Bank, who is well known for being the one who has guided the launch of several big and successful companies on the stock market, stated that he among others succeeded in beating the competition by offering long-term personal attention. By getting to know his clients and finding out about their interests, desires and worries. By sending them information about developments that might interest them at crucial moments. By sitting down with them and travelling together. "To practice high-quality relationship management demands discipline," he said. "During all my years at the bank I have seen two professional partners or contacts every day, face-to-face. Creating meaningful relations is about hunting and farming. The hunting can be pretty easy, but farming takes time, effort, and, above all, attention in both good and bad circumstances."

Virtues are of great value in developing sustainable relationships. They bring stability to our existence and express themselves in balanced and gracious behavior that provides the safety and reliability that we are so much in need of. By paying attention to the present moment and developing true personal relationships with our business partners, we will find the space to stay with what is happening now and to set the right priorities. Attention helps to keep balance between an obsessive urge to control and swift chaos. It invites the allowing of things to happen at their own natural pace and to respond appropriately.

To support the development of high-trust relationships, the department of governance affairs of the Municipality of Antwerp has formulated several core values for its relationship management:
- Trust.
- Stability.
- Personal attention.
- Cultural Sensitivity.
- Transparency.

Personal attention is the most important factor in creating relationships that are meaningful, trusting, and resilient, says Tom Verbelen. He states; *"The other important factor is the underestimated factor of time. Time is one of the most precious things in our current society of disruption, fast-paced change, and swift relationships."*

Friendship
Another important element that gives meaning to relationships is friendship. In the past friendships were defined by real life social connections, people you know from family, school, sport clubs, or the Friday night bar. Nowadays everyone on your

social media is called a friend even though you have never met. These are actually connections. But these connections can grow faster than ever before. Many social networks help people acquire contacts and to connect with friends of friends of friends with one mouse click, thereby sharing and getting information with a range of people larger than their own network which helps to increase impact and resources. The new generation of young workers considers virtual communication normal and finds common ground to create networks based on shared values.[39]

This, however, does not take away the value of real-time relevant interactions – it is about both. Meeting each other, spending real time together, looking each other in the eye increases the sense of trust and belonging. It brings solidity to a relationship. Additionally, real-time tone of voice, nonverbal expressions, and small gestures provide additional information and allow for more sensitive responses than do online interactions. People relate to people, not to online profiles or positions. In order to grow, relationships ask to be more personal. They ask for a certain level of friendship.

The Greek philosopher Aristotle has described three kinds of friendship:

1. The first kind is the **friendship of the good**. Aristotle observes, "The perfect form of friendship is that between the good and those who resemble each other in virtue. It is those who wish the good of their friends for their friends' sake who are friends in the fullest sense, since they love each other for themselves and not accidentally."

2. The second kind is **friendship of pleasure**. This does not need to be cheap. It just does not involve a deep intimate bond and is mainly focused on having a good time together and enjoying each other's company. Like we do on Facebook, or with friends with whom we have dinner once in a while but do not share our private issues of the heart with. Friendships of pleasure are tenuous as they can change or end as quickly as the pleasure received changes or ends.

3. The third kind of friendship is the **friendship of utility**. These are friendships in which personal benefit is the dominant driver. The friend is not loved for his or her own sake but for the sake of some benefit received by the other. Aristotle notes that these friendships are not permanent, because if the benefit of the utility ends so too will the friendship. For some people, this kind of friendship may sound dishonest, but it is a normal kind of friendship in professional relationships and it does not need to be deprived of any virtue. Also friendships of utility can have elements of good and pleasure, thus adding meaning to them.

Most important for a relationship to be called a friendship is the need for reciprocal goodwill. Aristotle states that "A man cannot be friends with an object, for it would be ridiculous to wish well to a bottle of wine." It is not reciprocal.[40] Reciprocity is key in relationship management. It is not just about what you are trying to attain but even more about what you are wishing to give. That is where shared value is created. The delicate line between exploitation and mutual utility is something to stay aware of while creating the vision, strategy, and structure for the organization's relationship management as well as in the day-to-day contact with partners and stakeholders. What values would your organization like to express toward its relations? What would you like to give? How could you befriend them?

The ABN AMRO banker explained that he intends to develop friendships with his business contacts and customers. Of course, he starts by growing a friendship of utility, a relationship focused on creating mutual gain. But since he dedicated himself to not only hunt but also to farm his relationships by spending true time together, helping them by sharing information, and showing genuine interest, it has happened several times that the friendship evolved into a 'friendship of the good'. By then they had been through a lot together and developed trust and intimacy. As with good friends, he had been reliable and always kept their interests at heart. After spending lots of business hours together, they now see each other socially, at home, and with their families.

Loyalty

The third important element is loyalty. As a working definition, loyalty can be characterized as a choice to persist in an intrinsically valued relationship that involves a commitment to secure the interests of the relationship out of the wish to stay true and faithful to a cause, even in times when you do not get any pleasure in such a conscientious commitment.

Loyalty tends to secure the integrity of particular partnerships. It helps to act beyond narrow self-interest to sustain relationships and the causes they serve. The higher the quality of the relationship, both as fellow humans and in the various networks, the more inclined people are to treat each other fairly.

Loyalty to an organization or alliance is given up when it no longer shows itself to be capable of being a source of mutual satisfaction. When the loyalty is no longer considered reciprocal, people tend to withdraw from these relationships. Since we personify organizations, we can attribute loyalty to them or, more often, criticize their lack of loyalty to those who have been loyal to them.[41] For this reason it is very important for organizations and their representatives to be aware of the importance of providing meaning, reciprocity, and integrity. When we look at contemporary politics there seems to be a crisis on this level. People do not experience enough loyalty, reciprocity, and integrity from politicians anymore, resulting in abstaining from voting or, even worse, losing interest and taking distance from the political parties resulting in a damaged relationship between the politicians and the people. Loyalty can go a long way, and it is not something to take for granted. Like friendship, loyalty must be practiced with perseverance. It must be repeated in ever-changing situations, even when the going gets tough.[42] To come back to our banker, Rutger van Nouhuijs, member of the executive committee of ABN AMRO Bank, he stayed loyal to the business contacts he believed in, even in difficult times when the companies of his relations were not doing well. Contrary to his colleagues from other banks, he kept meeting his relations in person, inquiring about their situation, and waiting for better times. When these better times finally arrived, he had gained so much trust and appreciation for his loyal attitude that he was rewarded with extra business. And when he needed them for information or help of some other kind, he could often count on them. He did not respond impulsively to changing situations but maintained long-term relationships and alliances in good times and bad.

On the other hand, even when choosing to stay loyal, it is important to acknowledge the thoughts and feelings of the people who are actually having their doubts. Dolf Jansen, a Dutch comedian, in an interview on Dutch television in February 2018, expressed his loyalty to the NGO Oxfam Novib that was being criticized because some of its employees had organized sex parties in Haiti during its mission there in 2010 and 2011. He said that, although he strongly disapproves of this behavior, he still believes in the purpose of the organization and the good work it does in this world and does not wish to withdraw his support at this point.[43]

A lot of courage was needed to make this statement, and although some people appreciated his comments, there were also some who felt that he did not take the accusations seriously enough. This shows that staying loyal in hard times is not without risk of alienating others from your cause. What do you protect, the human dignity of the people who serve the system or the dignity of the people who are served? Loyalty appeals to your sense of justice, to not just abandon your beliefs when it becomes uncomfortable and, on the other hand, to hear and acknowledge the comments criticizing the system that you strongly support. It is a fine line to walk with great sensitivity and care with your own integrity as the most important guideline in making the right choice for you.

Showing long-term loyalty stands in contrast to the hasty dynamics of the fluid society as described by Bauman which is highly characterized by the preference for novelty, speed and relationships that can be abandoned on an ad hoc basis. Attention, friendship and loyalty allow us to create a proper foundation for our relationships. And to not just be a rudderless boat on the powerful waves of change, but to develop networks and relationships with a firm foundation that will withstand the test of time. In the contemporary world, organizations that aim for professional and authentic relationship management are very much aware of this and spend considerable time and effort in both evaluating their policy toward relationships and spending real time with people – as loyal friends.

1.10 Rules and dialogue as a way to sustain a community

As said in paragraph 1.5, cooperation among different parties with different interests requires clear rules of engagement in order to secure a sense of safety, accountability, and trust. In this paragraph, we will discuss the importance of rules and dialogue for effective and trusting relationship management.

What does it mean to follow a rule? It is not possible to obey a rule "privately." To follow a rule in the context of horizontal cooperation (as opposed to a vertical hierarchy of commands) means "to enter a social practice which is shared by others and which refers to a common understanding of the world." Rules refer to the narrative of customs or usages that give meaning and identity to a community. In this light, rules are not a restriction of freedom or a way to push obligations. The commitment to a rule is the commitment to the community that applies them. And they are serving the shared higher cause by supporting meaningful relationships among its members.[44]

Rules are crucial to make cooperation work. They provide a sense of safety, clarity, and direction. Just as in a protocolled event, they shape the framework for coherent procedures and interaction. At the same time, they are as alive as the community itself. Rules are guidelines for cooperative behavior directed toward the common cause. But times change, situations change, and the general rule is not always the best solution for a specific situation. Nor is the rule supposed to be followed blindly. Who does not recognize the situation in which a store clerk or government official says, "I am sorry, those are the rules..." while at the same time laying your documents aside and casting down his or her eyes, leaving you with the powerless feeling of injustice? Or the grating feeling you experience when you read in the newspaper that young children will be separated from their parents because of an extradition policy, and nothing can be done because "that is the law"?

In horizontal communities of deliberation like value networks and alliances, rules are dialogical and relational in nature. In dealing with rules, individuals are not absolved of their own responsibility to match the rules against their own conscience. Rules provide a direction for action, but reality is always more complex than foreseen. The individual stays an autonomous, acting, thinking person in a community that can provide sense and meaning to his or her actions. The open deliberation within a community, relying on the shared habitus, supports the continuing integrity of its rules and practices.[45]

To create cohesion and synergy among the different actors within a community implies that actors do have a restricted freedom for action within their own domain. The restriction is determined by the identity of the whole. To cooperate in this space, three elements are necessary:

1. Agreements on the level of the whole; about goals, resources, and governance.
2. Reflection on the effectiveness of the synergy between the parts; how do they function together, are there ways to optimize this.
3. Identity; "this is what we stand for, this is what we will go for."

The identity is dynamic. It develops itself in the dialogue about the choices between future opportunities and existing competences. At the same time, it gives direction and connection to its parts. In order to create a cohesive community, the goal is an infrastructure that includes the satisfactory cooperation of its parts, effective meeting platforms, and agreements that connect the parts while allowing for professional autonomy within the own domains.

In modern society, members of value networks and alliances increasingly wish their voices to be heard, to contribute value to the whole, and to feel taken seriously in the decision making process about the rules of engagement. This can only be done in co-creation. Differences are valuable and deserve to be honored in the process. To rely solely on cooperative trust creates the risk of being disappointed when one of the partners puts his or her own interests at the forefront, or to allow resentment to develop when one of the voices continues to be unheard. Acknowledgement of the differences and realistic negotiation can reduce the risk of sudden breaks in trust by providing clear rules and agreements for further cooperation.

The challenge is to act in a coordinated manner while maintaining the differences. To achieve this, André Wierdsma suggests basing a mutual agreement on three basic principles:

1. The agreement is meant to be temporary and the rules by which partners can withdraw the decision are clear. This increases the likelihood that partners feel safe enough to commit and move forward. Existing differences are made manageable to the benefit of the higher common goal.
2. The agreement allows space for autonomy in executing the agreed action. This increases the effectiveness of the agreement in different contexts.
3. The mutual agreement between partners within the alliance is considered a "negotiation result." It does not have to be everybody's ideal, it just has to be considered optimal considering the underlying differences in needs and interests.

But cooperation inevitably leads to situations where existing agreements turn out to be insufficient; the reality is always more complex than foreseen and cannot be totally covered by rules and agreements. This is something the Chinese have always understood. In China rules between business partners are more like guidelines. They are more focused on initial intention and trust than on fixing the final result. Circumstances and interests can change along the way – that is the nature of life.

What then happens is that the different parties sit down together to reconsider the rules in line with the new specific situation and come to new suitable agreements. Until new circumstances arise. In Western countries this concept of ongoing dialogue and possibly adjustment of rules often brings a sense of unease and uncertainty. Still, in these dynamic times of change, dialogue offers a way to respond to circumstances in an adaptive manner, thereby optimizing the creation of shared value together.

Wierdsma explains that there are two kinds of dialogue on rules and agreements regarding the "whole." One is about the interpretation of the rules and the second is about the legitimacy of the existing rules as such. In the first case, the partners practice a dialogue in which they develop an interpretation of the rules based on their shared values. Questions asked are for example; "Do we interpret the rules in the correct way?" "Do we attain our results in the right way?" and "Do we still focus on the right goals?" To create an environment in which partners feel safe enough to explore these questions and speak their truth demands sincere openness to different perspectives. But when practiced appropriately, it helps to make the right decisions and to determine the right cooperation partners.[46]

A dialogue about the legitimacy of the rules themselves is more complex. It means challenging the obvious. It is a process in which rules and values that are so interwoven with the common identity that they are barely conscious suddenly become food for discussion. Fundamental beliefs are to be discussed openly. Take this example; What if someone working at a bank is in a meeting about the topic "future opportunities for banking" and suddenly raises the question whether banking has any future at all? What if a person working at an NGO for development aid suddenly raises the question whether "helping" developing countries might not be helpful at all? This often generates a sense of unease and danger. People are afraid to judge or be judged and want to sustain the feeling of solidarity and community. Still, a community in which certain things cannot be discussed, and the voice of the people who dare to speak out is suppressed, is not whole. The voice is there and needs to be heard. The values of the organization are alive and should be deliberated, both internally and together with partners and stakeholders, as soon as they might impact the cooperation between them.

This is a slow process and requires the willingness to take the time and to deal with inconvenience and discomfort. In this time of fast occurring events that ask for immediate response, it is hard to create time to reflect or to question our own actions and principles. But we will need these gaps in time in which we slow down and reflect on the rules we agreed on to avoid functional pragmatism and to stay true to the values that drive our initiatives. In prioritizing between joint reflection on common values that precede rules and clear results, it might be tempting to aim for the clear results which seem objective and are less complex and vulnerable. But the solution of today might be the problem of tomorrow. Today's society expects organizations and alliances to act on their values and to add value to the world. Results are important, but *how* have those results been achieved? And *why* was the focus on *those results*? What are the values that guide us? To reflect on these values and translate them into rules and agreements that are shared and carried out by each of the partners contributes to shaping a meaningful and cohesive community.

1.11   Symbols and gestures to create meaningful relations

Symbols

Meaningful relationships are not just pleasant or useful but merely symbolic. The word *symbolic* is often understood as a measure or norm with few concrete indications for action and without much societal impact or effective enforceability. Therefore, in our modern times of results-driven organizations and swift relationships, symbolic relations often become reduced to systemic relations. Systemic relationships are mainly governed by market thinking in which pragmatic transactions are paramount and ethical choices not highly relevant. The guiding question in systemic relationships is; What does it yield?

Symbolic relationships on the other hand create community and belonging. They bring extra depth to value networks. To understand the true meaning of a word it can be useful to have a look at its etymology. The word symbol stems from the Greek word *sumbolon; that which connects people and allows them to create and maintain a community with others*. It also has the implication of trust. *Sumbolon* points to the process of mutual recognition between people with very different roots or backgrounds.[47]

It is by functioning in a symbolic order that mutual recognition and respect are honored. A symbolic order is not just the connection between the individual members of a community but even more the relationship between each member and the community's common values. Differences between people and parties are not to be denied, nor are they to be left to their own unpredictability. They have to be channeled and steered by creating a symbolic order that represents collectivity by cultivating common language, dialogue, procedures, and manners that are always open to a better argument. In a symbolic order, the different and innovative arguments of the other are accepted and encouraged to support the progress of the community. This is where value development and innovation can happen.

Another Greek root word for symbol is *symbolon* which originally means token; something you do or give that expresses your intentions. Symbols add meaning to the community's values, rules, and practices. They have the power to connect and unite, add credibility and strength and often beauty to communities. Think of the exchange of rings during a wedding ceremony, the transmission of the key when property is sold, or the crowning of a new king. But symbols do not always have to have historical value – new symbols and symbolic acts can be invented any time. Jack Ma, the CEO of Alibaba, is well known for his statement that people should always look at things from a different angle in order to be creative and initiate change. For this reason, as the writers of this book were told by a senior employee at Alibaba's headquarters in Hanghzou, every person working at Alibaba is challenged to do the handstand on breaks, which also contributes to keeping up high energy levels.

Symbols are marking points that invite the public into a shared narrative. This invitation can be accepted and create connection or it can be rejected and create division, in the process deciding who is in, and who is out. Symbols can be used to increase the awareness of tradition (as is the case of wedding ceremonies) or, conversely, break with tradition (as in the case of President Trump acknowledging Jerusalem as the capital of Israel, thereby denying it formally to the Palestian people).

> A symbol represents certain values. When values change or are supposed to change, the introduction of new symbols can add extra weight to endorse that.

Jeroen de Haas, the former CEO of the renowned Dutch producer and supplier of energy Eneco, decided the company's core strategy would be sustainability. When Eneco in 2012 introduced Toon (the smart thermostat that informs households about their energy consumption of their home), Toon became symbolic of Eneco's policy change and a clear statement that De Haas was absolutely serious about his intentions for green energy. This raised the credibility and likability of the company for a great number of customers. Symbols can thus understate the connection to the past, making the past productive for the future, or on the contrary, take distance from the past and show new intentions towards the future.

Gestures
Other symbols are not so much imbedded in tradition but are of a more personal nature. Let us consider gestures. Think of the German Social Democrat Chancellor Willy Brandt who in 1970 fell to his knees as a gesture of atonement for the suffering of the Polish people by the Nazi occupation in Word War II. Or more recently, Pope Francis washing the feet of refugees. A gesture is a means without a goal. But it still has an effect – by his action, the pope gave dignity to the refugees and at the same time increased trust in him as a person and, via him, the Vatican. It added to the legitimacy and credibility of this institution that aims to serve God and humanity. What are the values that your organization stands for? And when does it need a

gesture to also confirm these values to the people outside and inside the organization?

Philosopher René ten Bos states that a gesture – a promise, apology, or a request for forgiveness– is never purely functional. It is a personal offer in embodied action that reveals something about the drives and intentions of the person who makes the gesture. This person proves the meaning of his or her words by added physical action. The personal aspect, performed spontaneously and honestly, can heighten trust and credibility. However, the person offering the gesture has no control on the outcome. He can have a desired result in mind, but he cannot control whether an apology, for example, will be accepted or not. That is up to the people on the receiving end. The chance that they will accept the gesture will depend greatly on both the timing and the sincerity of the act, which are sensed intuitively, as well as on the context in which the gesture is offered. One of the hardest gestures to make successfully is the apology. Willy Brandt chose both the right timing and was authentic enough for the Polish people to believe his gesture. This improved the relationship between Poland and Germany. Tony Hayward, CEO of BP at the time, apologized in 2010 for the explosion and fire aboard the Deepwater Horizon and the resulting oil spill in the Gulf of Mexico. "The first thing to say is I am sorry," Tony Hayward said when asked what he would tell people in Louisiana where heavy oil had already reached parts of the state's southeastern marshes. "We are sorry for the massive disruption it has caused in their lives. There is no one who wants this to be over more than I do. I would like my life back." The self-centered streak in this apology led to great international criticism at the time, and the relationship with the public became even worse than before the apology. A gesture can make or break a relationship, it is not without risk and you should do it appropriately and sincerely, knowing when the moment is right, then it can indeed strengthen the identity of your organization.

Symbols can create distance from old narratives and initiate new meaning. They can narrow the ties between the organization and its public with just one powerful act, making Strategic Relationship Management more authentic and effective, and, above all, more personal. Because at the end of the day people relate to people. No matter how brilliant the strategy, it is the people who make it real.

1.12   The power of trust

We started with an example of the trust-based networks in the seventeenth century municipality of Amsterdam. These networks were closed and difficult to enter but provided opportunity, resilience, and security in turbulent times. By gaining a certain position and adapting to the style and values of these networks, individuals who were first considered strangers could become friends. Based on a shared attitude of reciprocity and trust, members of these networks helped each other to reach personal goals and simultaneously contributed to the networks' shared interests.

Nowadays we are entangled in contracts and fixed procedures used in order to create a feeling of safety. As we said before, these instruments have limited results. More often than desired, they complicate relationships and decrease the human dimension in creating suitable solutions. In the process, these instruments turn organizations into complex mechanisms, costing a lot of money.

Lack of trust is a major barrier to change and transformation whether in an individual, a system, or an organization. Low or no trust develops strong defenses against the new, different, challenging, or factual. It feeds a clinging to the status quo. A lack of awareness or insight thwarts substantial progress on adaptive problems because the main energy is focused on keeping things as they are or returning to the way things were. Retaining an illusion of being able to prevent or fight is symptomatic of low or no trust.

Trust provides stability and a sense of security in individuals, groups, and systems. It conveys a sense of accountability so that work can get done. It keeps chaos at a manageable level so that people feel safe enough to be creative and respond effectively to challenges and problems. Trust aids individuals and groups to deal with anxiety without resorting to dysfunctional behaviors that derail progress. It reduces the complexity between people. When we trust, we do the things that before seemed undoable. We can realize our shared vision. We can excel and contribute to the well-being of others.

"Trust is the glue that holds everything together." – leadership pioneer Warren Bennis [49]

In his lectures, René Foqué explains the two sides of the coin when it comes to trust. The first is called functional confidence, the second moral trust:

Functional confidence refers to reliability. It is about the belief that the other person's actions and words are congruent. This means a belief that the person will consistently adhere to a set of explicit principles. Are the rules clear and fair? Is the person or organization consistent? And can we rely on the person or organization to do what it promises and stick to its agreement? Do we rely on the National Railways that the trains will run on time and in case something goes wrong, we are accordingly informed, and the problem will be solved as soon and efficiently as possible? This is what is meant by functional confidence.

Moral trust refers to the integrity of a person or an organization. It is about trusting that the person or organization acts in accordance with the common good and not merely for its own benefit. It is associated with strong ties, shared vision, shared language, and a belief that the person will be discrete and receptive. It takes leadership in doing what is best for its employees, customers, and stakeholders, taking everyone into account. Do you trust that the board of directors puts the common good at the forefront, or do we suspect them of acting mainly out of self-interest?

This double meaning of trust refers to the etymological background of the word that also points to the activities of deliberation and dialogue as well as to the process of mutual recognition between people who because of different roots or backgrounds experience estrangement from each other. Both functional confidence and moral trust are necessary to reach full trust – when one or both are missing, the trust relationship is incomplete. As soon as you ask whether someone is reliable or actually has good intentions, his or her trustworthiness has already been impugned upon a little bit. It is all about the willingness to share, to be involved with your stakeholders, and show responsibility for your contribution to the greater good. It is about not only asking, but also giving; to show reciprocity. And not in the sense of "If you scratch my back, I'll scratch yours." That only undermines it.

And how attached to control we may feel; trust starts with *giving* it. This asks courage, curiosity, and commitment. Leadership often begins where boundaries start. Leadership means stretching boundaries between networks to create connections between them. This is called *boundary spanning*. Working toward shared goals and answering complex challenges asks a collective approach that includes the surpassing of boundaries and the willingness to leave one's own comfort zone and move into new, unknown territory.[50] How is your organization on both categories of trust? Is it stronger on one than on the other? How could you bring them both at the same level? What would it take to bring your organization into unknown territory?

> "Trust is the lubricating oil for relationships. It reduces the complexity of relationships." – *René Foqué*

The aspects of functional confidence and moral trust also come back in the Trust Equation of Charles H. Green. Credibility in this equation stands for the moral trust as described above with the extra factor of internalized knowledge and understanding of the message or service provided. Reliability stands for functional confidence – the added factor amount of safety and confidentiality that is experienced in contact with the person or organization. It is about the extent to which personal intimacy is experienced in the relationship.[51]

$$T = \frac{C_{redibility} + R_{eliability} + I_{ntimacy}}{S_{elf-Orientation}}$$

Trust-
worthiness

Figure 1.12.1 The Trust Equation[52]

Striking in this equation is the damaging factor of excessive self-orientation, self-orientation that expresses itself by sole focus on the own goals, own interests, own feelings. The inability to listen, to be open, empathic, to give or share. As we saw in the example of Tony Hayward's apology, nothing is more damaging for relationships than that. It is from giving that you will get, from sharing that you will grow, from common creating that your cause will flourish.

And despite how soft this may sound, when coming from a place of love, all this will fall into place more or less by itself. Love for the purpose of your organization, love for your work, for the people you cooperate with and serve. Then it will just be natural to act from the right intention and to want to be reliable. Excessive self-interest will just feel "off." The mayor of Amsterdam, Eberhard van der Laan, got a warm farewell from the citizens of his city when lying on his deathbed at home suffering from cancer, knowing there would not be many days left until he would pass away. As a mayor he achieved a lot for Amsterdam, but it was not only because of these achievements that the people gathered in front of his home. It was his love for his city, his attention to people, his honesty, his service, and his presence that made them feel connected to him. He created a connection with them not by just managing them, but, additionally, by being with them. It is from this attitude that trust comes naturally and with barely any effort. That is how strong it is.

1.13   Conclusion

In contemporary society when hierarchy and control are fading, relationship capital is a crucial factor for success. A sustainable and meaningful network helps to adapt to constantly changing contexts in an agile way. It provides information and support that help organizations to accomplish their goals.

These networks are developing into increasingly more personal, small-scale, and trust-based networks that demand high-quality relationships and the ability to transcend traditional boundaries and connect to these networks as well as to connect them to each other in order to enhance network density. Organizations with more diverse relations and networks have more power because they are the gateway for other people to connect to these networks and can combine ideas and resources that normally would not have been brought together. The development of sustainable relationships helps organizations provide better service as well as increase the influence of its greater cause that is shared and carried out by its strategic partners.

Meaningful relationships are not just instrumental in nature but are aimed at a bigger purpose and based on intrinsic motivation. Today's society expects organizations and alliances to act based on values and to add value to the world. High-performing organizations move beyond a transactional mind-set and build long-term relationships based on trust and reciprocity.

In order to create successful and effective partnerships, partners need to agree on a shared driver of the cooperation that motivates the different stakeholders to cooperate. The values in the organization's vision are mainly focused on supporting the purpose of the organization itself, while the values for the organization as a part of several networks might differ slightly according to the shared driver and purpose of the network. To level out these dynamics, a shared vision should be formulated. A value network is characterized by a shared starting point, the vision, and a path of creation in a context of shared responsibility more than it consists of a fixed route, structure, and team. The cooperation is about the exchange between the added value to the shared vision and the accomplishment of the individual goals.

In this contemporary context of globalization and ever-changing circumstances, individuals and organizations have to continuously adapt. Relationships become swift, lacking intimacy and solidity. In order to build strong and sustainable bonds that can be of strategic advantage, grounding values need to be strengthened in relationships. Examples of these values are personal attention, friendship, loyalty and trust–both functional confidence and moral trust. They increase the integrity and durability of our relationships, thereby adding to the resilience of our organizations.

In order for cooperation between different parties with different interests to work, clear rules of engagement are needed. In modern society, members of networks and alliances increasingly wish their voices to be heard, to contribute value to the whole and to feel taken seriously in the decision making process regarding these rules. Rules are dialogical and relational in nature. This era of rapidly occurring events requires immediate responses, but time to reflect on the guiding rules is necessary to avoid functional pragmatism and to stay true to the organization's integrity.

It is by functioning in a symbolic order that mutual recognition and respect are honored. A symbolic order is not the mere connection between the individual members of a community but even more the relationship between each member and the community's shared values. Differences between people and parties are a reality, but they can be channeled by creating a symbolic order that represents collectivity by cultivating common language, dialogue, procedures, and manners. Symbols and gestures are valuable ways to express identity and values by organizations and their representatives, as well as to create a shared narrative with the public.

We live in a complex world with little certainty and control. And even though we can manage our relationships, we can not control them. But we can connect them in a sustainable and meaningful way and create communities that offer products or services based on both economic and social value. The willingness to execute a Relationship Management Strategy – not as a goal in and of itself but as a guideline to connect to others and align partners in order to reach both individual and shared goals – enhances the loyalty and resilience of the network and the organization initiating and nurturing them.

Notes

1. Erna Kok, '*Zonder vrienden geen carrière. De succesvolle loopbanen van de zeventiende-eeuwse kunstenaars Govert Flinck en Ferdinand Bol*', De Zeventiende Eeuw, Volume 27, www.de-zeventiende-eeuw.nl/articles/10.18352/dze.1553/, 2012

2. Ronald van den Hoff, *Mastering the Global Transition on our Way to Society 3.0*, Society 3.0 Foundation, 2013

3. '*The Fourth Industrial Revolution is here – are you ready?*', Deloitte Insights, 2017

4. Robert Johansen, *Leaders Make The Future*, Berret-Koehler Publishers, e-book, 2014

5. Freek Peters, '*Next Generation 2025*', Galan Group, 25 September 2015

6. Freek Peters, '*Next Generation 2025*', Galan Group, 25 September 2015

7. www.managementpro.nl/leiderschap/leiderschap-in-een-vuca-wereld

8. Venkat Atluri, Miklos Dietz, and Nicolaus Henke, '*Competing in a World of Sector without Borders*', Mc Kinsey Quarterly, July 2017

9. Venkat Atluri, Miklos Dietz, and Nicolaus Henke, '*Competing in a World of Sector without Borders*', McKinsey Quarterly, July 2017

10. Ranjay Gulati & David Kletter, '*Shrinking Core, Expanding Periphery: The Relational Architecture of High-Performing Organizations*', April 1 2015, California Management Review, volume 47 no 3

11. Ranjay Gulati & David Kletter, '*Shrinking Core, Expanding Periphery: The Relational Architecture of High-Performing Organizations*', April 1 2015, California Management Review, volume 47 no 3

12. Ronald van den Hoff, *Mastering the Global Transition on our Way to Society 3.0*, Society 3.0 Foundation, 2013

13. '*Op Weg naar de Netwerksamenleving, op Weg naar de Zwerm*', Doxis Magazine, summer 2017

14. http://bigthink.com/experts-corner/the-potential-of-connectivity-in-the-21st-century

15. René ten Bos, '*Stilte, Geste, Stem*', Boom Uitgevers Amsterdam, 2011

16. André Wierdsma, '*Vrijmoedig positie kiezen: moreel leiderschap in vitale netwerken*', afscheidsrede als hoogleraar, 26 juni 2014

17. Ronald van den Hoff, '*Mastering the global transition on our way to Society 3.0*', Society 3.0 Foundation, 2013

18. Herminia Ibarra, *Act like a Leader, Think Like a Leader*, Harvard Business Review Press, Boston Massachusets

19. Dacher Keltner, *The Power Paradox*, Penguin Press, 2016

20. Herminia Ibarra, *Act like a Leader, Think like a Leader*, Harvard Business Review Press, Boston Massachusets, 2015

21. Herminia Ibarra, *Act like a Leader, Think like a Leader*, Harvard Business Review Press, Boston Massachusets, 2015

22. Ranjay Gulati & David Kletter, '*Shrinking Core, Expanding Periphery: The Relational Architecture of High-Performing Organizations*', April 1 2015, California Management Review, volume 47 no 3

23. '*Deep Dive: Shenzen an International Hub of Hardware Innovation*', 2018, Coresight Research, www.fungglobalretailtech.com/research/deep-dive-shenzhen-international-hub-hardware-innovation/

24. Ronald van den Hoff, *Mastering the global transition on our way to Society 3.0*, Society 3.0 Foundation, 2013

25. Ronald van den Hoff, *Mastering the global transition on our way to Society 3.0*, Society 3.0 Foundation, 2013

26. Hans Licht, *Netwerkregie: Samenwerken in en tussen Organisaties*, Scriptum, 2016

27. Ranjay Gulati & David Kletter, '*Shrinking Core, Expanding Periphery: The Relational Architecture of High-Performing Organizations*', April 1 2015, California Management Review, volume 47 no 3

28. Ranjay Gulati & David Kletter, '*Shrinking Core, Expanding Periphery: The Relational Architecture of High-Performing Organizations*', April 1 2015, California Management Review, volume 47 no 3

29. Ranjay Gulati & David Kletter, '*Shrinking Core, Expanding Periphery: The Relational Architecture of High-Performing Organizations*', April 1 2015, California Management Review, volume 47 no 3

30. Ronald Heifetz, *Leadership on the Line*, Harvard Business Review Press, 2002

31. www.artsfwd.org/are-all-organization al-challenges-the-same/

32. Zygmunt Bauman, '*Privacy, Secrecy, Intimacy, Human Bonds – and Other Collateral Casualties of Liquid Modernity*', www.iasc-culture.org, pp 26-27, published online spring 2011

33. Freek Peters, '*Next Generation 2025*', Galan Group, 25 September 2015

34. André Wierdsma, 'Vrij-moedig positie kiezen: moreel leiderschap in vitale netwerken', afscheidsrede als hoogleraar Organiseren en Co-creëren aan Nyenrode Business Universiteit op 26 juni 2014

35. Zygmunt Bauman, *Liquid Modernity*, Polity Press Cambridge, 2000,2012, pp165-166

36. Zygmunt Bauman, '*Pivacy, Secrecy, Intimacy, Human Bonds – and Other Collateral Casualties of Liquid Modernity*', 28-29, published online spring 2011, pp. 66-74

37. Paul van Tongeren, '*Leven is een Kunst*', Klement en Pelckmans, 2012

38. Kaj Morel, '*Bouwen op Betekenis*', inaugural speech Saxion, December 2010, Saxion

39. Ronald van den Hoff, '*Mastering the global transition on our way to Society 3.0*', Society 3.0 Foundation, 2013

40. https://stpeterslist.com/the-3-types-of-friendship-according-to-aristotle

41. John Kleinig, '*Loyalty*', https://plato.stanford.edu/entries/loyalty/, Harvard Encyclopedia, 2017

42. Paul van Tongeren, '*Leven is een Kunst: Over Morele Ervaring, Deugdethiek en Levenskunst*', Klement en Pelckmans, 2012

43. www.youtube.com/watch?v=pskjQ_3eo4Z8

44. René Foqué, Introduction in: *On Rules by Gherardo Colombo*, Amsterdam University Press, 2008

45. René Foqué, Introduction in: *On Rules by Gherardo Colombo*, Amsterdam University Press, 2008

46. André Wierdsma, '*Vrij-moedig positie kiezen: moreel leiderschap in vitale netwerken*', farewell speech as professor at Nyenrode University, 26 June 2014

47. René Foque, in: '*Integratie & de Metropool. Perspectieven voor 2040*', by R. Frissen en S. Harchaoui (Red.), Van Gennep, Amsterdam, 2011, pp. 151-156

48. René ten Bos in his lecture '*An Aesthetic View on Leadership*' for Comenius Courses at June 28, 2016 in Vught, The Netherlands

49. www.kithoughtbridge.com/search/global?s=trust

50. Erwin Damhuis, '*Van Verandering naar Dynamiek: Een reis in 24 etappes voor organisaties die in beweging willen blijven*'

51. http://trustedadvisor.com/why-trust-matters/understanding-trust/ understanding-the-trust-equation

52. Trust Equation of Charles H. Green

2. The Importance of Protocol in Networks

This chapter will explain the value of protocol in building networks and relationships. This has to do with the symbolic value of protocol and its value in managing time.

The original word for protocol is *protokollan* which means glue, the glue that kept the sheets of paper in medieval books together. So *protokollan* was connecting all the different parts into a whole, the same as trust does between people as described in paragraph 1.12. Protocol is in other words a major vehicle to increase trust in relationships.

Nowadays, protocol is the term for the rules of diplomatic and social discourse between heads of state, heads of government, and authorities as laid out in the Treaties of Vienna (1814–15 and 1961–63). Protocol focuses on respect and the creation of a good and comfortable diplomatic climate as well as the minimization of conflict and disagreement. Respect and an acknowledgement of status and hierarchy play an important role.

Protocol is often confused with etiquette. Etiquette can be defined as the rules of politeness between people – social manners. Etiquette is different in every culture or subculture and changes as society changes. Examples of etiquette are opening doors for people, proper ways of greeting, pulling a chair out for a woman and so on, while protocol tends to focus much more on the status of a person or an organization rather than societal status.

This specific focus on status has to do with precedence. Precedence can generally be described as "the rules concerning priority, arrangement, or the creation of a concrete hierarchy of functionaries in public positions according to public interest." The right of priority is based on the position that the functionaries occupy, whether in the judiciary, the military, or the civil service. The hierarchy of all public positions and official titles in a country is codified in an official order of precedence. Orders of precedence are installed and maintained by national governments and international organizations. Generally, the higher one's political mandate or the greater one's managerial responsibility, the higher one's position in the order of precedence.

Example of a national list of precedence (United States of America):

1. President
2. Vice-president
3. Governor (in own state)
4. Speaker of the House of Representatives
5. Chief Justice
6. Former presidents and former vice president
7. Ambassadors
8. Secretary of State
9. Justices of the Supreme Court
10. Retired Chief Justices
11. Retired Justices of the Supreme Court
12. Members of the Cabinet

Determining precedence is often the starting point in protocol. Precedence is used to make seating arrangements, whether for a conference, a concert, or a dinner. The rank of the guests and the rank of the chairs determine who sits where. But there are other examples of the use of precedence such as the order of flags and the order of welcoming the guests of honor at the beginning of a speech.

Modern protocol management

This book uses a modern application of protocol to stage effective networking meetings and events with measurable results. In Chapter 13, the principles of protocol management are translated into a method to organize effective networking meetings or events where there is time and space for people to meet and where the right people meet in a respectful and pleasant environment.

The art of protocol has never been more relevant in building networks

Royal Households are much better at building strong networks than many organizations in the corporate world. Royal Households understand the fundamentals of professional relationship management, but in the corporate world there seems to be a lack of this understanding. As founder and chief executive of The English Manner, a leading etiquette, protocol, and household management consultant based in the United Kingdom, Alexandra Messervy admits they struggle to get corporates to recognize the importance of protocol. "It is extraordinary that people do not correlate the importance of personal contact and the value of protocol in building relationships," she said in an interview with the writers of this book.

Alexandra thinks that is because we are caught up in endless tweets, WhatsApp messages, and Facebook notifications. We have lost the personal interface and there is a total disconnect. "I find it bizarre that people are conducting intimate bits of their life on an open platform like Facebook without offering substance or context. Everyone is so used to this way of superficial communication and most of us do not know how to get back to having real contact. Who actually picks up the phone anymore to have a real conversation?"

Networking is a good point of view for protocol and it can be a real tool for effectively organizing networking events. The rules of protocol offer predictability so everyone knows what to do and how to do it. Predictability takes the pressure off so everyone can concentrate on doing business and talking to the clients. People thrive on routine; it is a way to put everyone at ease.

Our profession has never been more relevant; building networks and relationships brings people together. It can even prevent wars. Protocol is about communality, recognition, and respect. You may be different, but in our profession we look at the common ground. Surely this can be translated to the business world?

2.1 The symbolic value of protocol

Often, people say they consider protocol to be old-fashioned, like the sound of trumpets at the start of a ceremony. Yet we still use some forms of protocol that have insufficient connection with today's values and perceptions. This results in increasing disconnection. But when we look at the protocol in courtrooms, how does this make us feel? It could make us feel safe as well as included in a bigger narrative that we share with our fellow citizens, one we all recognize and understand.

Protocol can still have an important function. Its rules provide clarity and safety when it comes to "how things are done." As paradoxical as it may seem, the framework of protocol actually does not limit space, it creates it. Protocol allows space for us to focus on the content of the meeting as well as on our interaction with others instead of constantly anticipating the unexpected. When a ceremony, meeting, or celebration is always executed in roughly the same way, following the same rules and symbols, this creates a sense of consistency. If meetings are always opened with a specific check-in ceremony, in which everybody briefly shares where they are at and what they expect out of the meeting, it creates an experience of consistency and trust.

At the same time, the specific set of rules and symbols create a shared narrative to the people who participate in it and fulfil the function as described in paragraph 1.10 and 1.11, that of a binding force between participants of different backgrounds who at that moment step into a shared narrative whether they were all present at the same time or not. The graduation ceremony at a university is something we have seen many times in movies. When we later participate in our own ceremony, it already feels kind of familiar. Comparatively, when someone else tells you later about his or her graduation ceremony, you can easily relate and understand. This would be even more so if you both graduated from the same university with its own specific protocol.

> Leiden University in the Netherlands already for many years has the symbolic tradition of inviting students to write their signatures in the same small room where the first Royal of the Netherlands, William of Orange, and also the current head of state, King Willem-Alexander, wrote theirs after they graduated. Being part of these unique traditions creates a feeling of belonging that lowers the threshold to real connection.

The same power that comes from following protocol can be derived from breaking the protocol. Imagine a CEO who dances with his secretary at the yearly New Year's reception. Or remember the little girl in the white gown in Rembrandt's *Night Watch* (Nachtwacht). In the seventeenth century, it was revolutionary to include a girl in

Figure 2.1.1 *The Night Watch*, by Rembrandt, Rijksmuseum Amsterdam

such a painting. By these acts, the CEO and Rembrandt broke the established rules. In the case of the CEO, this is part of the protocol – like with Carnival in some regions of Europe – it is quite acceptable to break certain social conventions at such events. It helps people from different statuses or back-grounds to connect, knowing that order will be restored as soon as the event is over. In the case of Rembrandt, however, the breaking of the rules was not orchestrated, leading to a discussion about which rules and symbols are desired and accepted within the community or network and which are not. This often generates much resistance but can actually serve the common good. As we discussed in paragraph 1.10, rules are not supposed to be fixed but open to a better argument. This helps us to keep our values and practices aligned and fosters trust by applying the rules, symbols, and protocol that fit our current value system and strengthen the sense of safety and connection within the community in these times of disruption, insecurity, and constant change.

2.2   Protocol to manage time

The European monarchs have always been aware of the need for a good network, but their personal attention is scarce. The king or queen and their entourage must speak to many people, but they have little time. The European monarchies needed to find the right way to manage the scarce time for personal attention, and protocol gave them just that – an effective way to manage relationships. The rules and guidelines of protocol structure meetings and events with the goal of increasing the effect and the number of meaningful encounters.

"Attention is the rarest and purest form of generosity." – *Simone Weil*

In our world, personal attention has become scarce too. On the one hand, the Internet revolution has brought contact and communication literally within touching distance. On the other hand, this "convenient truth" also created a distance in personal relationships. This makes it even more vital to optimize those few moments of personal contact and use the opportunity to maximize the added value that personalized attention can bring to relationships. In a world where personal attention has become scarce and technology a facilitator for rules and procedures, protocol management as a reference framework provides us with a unique vision in which personal time is the greatest good we can give to someone. It is the modern currency of relationships.

Protocol outside the diplomatic world

Modern protocol is an integral aspect of strategic networking. It is impossible to stage effective relationship meetings without the use of protocol. This is common in the diplomatic world, but the method of protocol is also essential for networking meetings outside governmental organizations, as we discuss in Chapter 13.

At corporate networking events, protocol management increases the number of meaningful encounters between (potential) clients and account managers. Fashion shows use protocol to guarantee commercial success; only clients and potential clients are seated in the first row, and protocol is used to make sure the fashion designer will personally meet these clients at the reception afterwards. The use of segments, or echelons as they are called in protocol, is common practice at large royal events and has been duplicated by many dance festivals; echelons divide the guest list into several groups who each receive their own form of hospitality based upon the goals. Museums see in protocol a unique method to support their sponsorship goals by increasing the number of meaningful encounters during their exhibition openings.

Protocol at Royal Weddings and at dance events

From a protocol perspective, a Royal Wedding and a dance event are equally organized. Both divide their guest list into several segments (or echelons as they are called in protocol) based upon the importance they represent. For each group a level of personal attention and service is determined.

At a Royal Wedding the first echelon is the family, the second echelon are the other Royals and dignitaries, and the rest of the guests represent the third echelon. At a dance event the first echelon is for example the mayor and main sponsors, the second echelon the DJs and sponsor-guests, and the paying visitors are the third echelon. The first echelon will be personally welcomed by the host upon arrival, whereas the second echelon is welcomed by a representative of the host, and the third echelon is not personally welcomed. The first echelon is escorted, not directed. The first and second echelons can park in front of the entrance and for them there is no waiting line for checking coats and getting drinks.

Lack of protocol leads to less impact and little room for networking. There are many reasons why networking opportunities do not offer good possibilities to meet people; overcrowded rooms, loud music, guest lists with no common interest, account managers who are more interested in talking to each other, long-winded speakers, and lengthy dinners that leave no time for meeting people, etc, etc. Just putting a random group of 500 people in one room does not make a networking opportunity. An event only delivers a Return-on-Relationship (RoR) if it is structured and well-executed. Or stated differently; by adding a little extra effort to the preparation and organization of an event, inspired by protocol, the RoR will dramatically increase.

Networking events with little room for networking

A bank wanted to treat their best clients to a special event and invited them to a dinner with interesting speakers and performances. The guests were invited to arrive starting at 7:30 p.m. and the dinner began at 8:00 p.m. The inspiring and unique program lasted until 11:00 p.m.

The result? The account managers of the bank were not able to talk to many of their clients, most guests arrived five minutes before the start of the dinner and left within fifteen minutes after the end of the program. There was no seating arrangement and there were no breaks in the program, so most guests sat next to the same random people all evening which resulted in only two conversations; one on the left and one on the right. This was money not well spent.

Long term

A networking event itself is nothing more than a snapshot; the effectiveness of it hinges very much on good preparation but also good follow-up. Many organizations fail to measure results and ask their employees "Who did you meet and what was discussed?" Experience, however, has proven that most events, when staged and evaluated appropriately, are very effective and bring a lot of useful results.

The future of protocol; how new rituals might modernize protocol in our highly individualized age

by Paul Spies, Director of Stadtmuseum Berlin

Protocol is a term we tend to associate with the complex noble behavior of times gone by. Adopted by the *nouveau riche* of the Dutch Golden Age, it mirrored the courtly behavior of Louis IV in France, offering these parvenus a safe system of routines and rituals to dictate their comportment and ensure they were doing the right thing. A blatant love of art in all its forms belonged to these behavior patterns. Protocol and all it signifies is something we appear to have outgrown these days. Individualized and globalized society requires that "anything goes" in our patterns of behavior. And yet, there is a hankering for the comfort of ritual. The question is then how new and creative rituals might help us in this highly individual and global age.

No coincidence

As a student of art history, and in my very early professional life, I made a study of court life in the late seventeenth and early eighteenth century under William III and Queen Mary, king and queen of Great Britain and Ireland. My studies resulted in the book *The Royal Progress of William and Mary* which took a close look at the palaces and stately homes–their decoration, furnishings, the art selected for display–of the court circle in the Netherlands and Great Britain. It soon became clear that there were numerous similarities in all the residences. It was apparent that amongst all that pomp and circumstance, nothing was there by coincidence. Everything in those houses was placed there by design and had a specific ceremonial function or significance. It was all about covert storytelling. About lineage–showing aristocratic status; about ambitions –showing power play; about virtues– putting the owner-inhabitant in a good light; about belief–in God; and about loyalty–to the king. The houses were there to receive visitors and those crossing the thresholds knew exactly how to interpret the allegory all around them. Likewise, they were fully versed in how to behave in these same surroundings. Protocol, or etiquette, was the order of the day and behavior towards one another in strict accordance with the rules was expected.

In the footsteps of the French aristocracy

During my research on William and Mary, I found a handwritten document in the royal archives giving precise instructions for the handling of the Prussian ambassador's visit to Windsor Castle in 1695. The document describes in minute detail the movements of the ambassador and his entourage. The document suggests that every object in every room was to be presented for its specific function.

The contents of this document show striking similarities with Norbert Elias' description of the culture at the court of Sun King Louis XIV (*The Court Society*, 1969). Elias describes the many daily ceremonies at royal palaces such as Versailles. There was le lever (the royal rising) and *le coucher* (the royal retirement to bed). The ceremonies were attended by the king and queen's favorites who were privileged to be handed an item of royal clothing during the event. These were odd rituals, with no practical application, and which were totally false. The king and queen did not actually sleep in the state bedchambers but in much smaller chambers at the end of their respective private apartments, each apartment being identical to the other as the protocol of a diplomatic marriage commanded. This in turn explains the symmetry of the royal palaces – two identical wings stretching away from a communal center and culminating in the apartment with a cabinet and a wardrobe. This classical style was widely adopted by rich and important subjects and can be admired in many formal homes from that period.

Parvenus and protocol

Later in my career, I was commissioned to write books about the Amsterdam canal houses from the same seventeenth century period. These houses were the domain of the merchant class, wealthy parvenus and first- or second-generation entrepreneurs. Close examination of the houses showed a style very similar to that of the Dutch (copied from the French) aristocracy. What moved this class of wealthy "democrats" to adopt a style so similar to that of the ruling class they despised? Again, the use of a highly symbolic and denotational protocol was an effective way to express power, influence, and wealth. And so we find numerous highly decorative canal houses with painted ceilings, many denoting Aurora, or dawn, a popular bedroom theme. While it is hard to imagine Calvinistic Dutch merchants going so far as to observe the rituals of *lever* and *coucher*, their imitation of the aristocratic way of life will certainly have given them delusions of aristocratic grandeur. Court culture would be familiar to them through their merchant dealings with powerful foreign aristocracy, and some of them were ambassadors at the international courts.

Functional art

A most effective – if indeed not the most effective – instrument of protocol was art. Art in the broadest sense of the term; architecture, painting, sculpture, applied art, park and garden design to name but a few. Even music and theater played their role. Protocol was embellished by art productions of the highest quality. It is interesting to note that though the precise details of a ceremony have been lost over the course of time, the "hardware" of protocol survives in great quantities. We can still visit numerous stately homes and formal houses and admire the often well-preserved or finely restored decorations and furnishings. Here lies the power of art. The beauty (and the value) of these objects has ensured their preservation and survival through the ages. If, in addition, we know the maker, the story, and the background, the value of these relics increases further because we know the history and the meaning of the object.

Interestingly enough, many of the official ceremonies from protocol of times gone by continue to exist in our modern and far less formal society. We all know such traditions as the daily changing of the guard at Buckingham Palace, the annual Trooping the Colour, and the State Opening of Parliament. Most of us are unaware of the true significance of such happenings, but because they fascinate they attract attention, particularly that of tourists.

Ceremonies survive on a much lowlier scale too. What about the ribbon-cutting ceremony to open a new building; the baptizing of a ship with the smashing of a champagne bottle against its side; the arch of family and friends to welcome the newly-wedded couple out of the church? But who nowadays knows exactly what the ribbon, the champagne, or the arch stand for?

Though fascinated by historical protocol, my freethinking and unconventional Dutch nature means I do not practice it at all. I am more of a curious observer, always critical of the function of protocol. And I am not alone in that. Many question the function of ceremonies, the true meaning of which has been lost in the mists of time. It would seem that even protocol specialists are at times critical of traditional protocol, particularly in the Netherlands, where the newly established *Protocolbureau* is seeking to modernize the profession. Perhaps this is thanks to the influence of our king, Willem Alexander, who years ago stated in an interview that he is not "a protocol fetishist." Apparently, he too questions the relevance of "the way it has always been done" if that relevance is lost on people. So, if our highest authority is beginning to question things now, is there any real reason to continue with protocol? Well, even as a critical observer of these conservative traditions, I can think of a number of reasons why we might:

1. Protocol helps with the logistics of ceremonial moments.
   Protocol is the first page of the scenario for an important meeting or event. It gives the rules of the game. This is very important, especially where many people are involved. Clear rules are needed to ensure the event runs smoothly and that its aims are achieved within the timeframe available.
2. Protocol ensures the safety of high-ranking people at public events.
   Employing strict sets of rules, protocol ensures that every act and every movement of every person present is pre-planned such that any departure from the planning is quickly and easily detected.

3. Protocol brings democracy to public ceremonies.
   Protocol determines exactly how people are to behave in a given ceremonial situation. If you stick to the official rules then there will be no risk of offense through improper behavior. Protocol is a leveller, just like British school uniforms.
4. Protocol as immaterial heritage attracts tourist interest.
   As the world shrinks and we all become global citizens, ceremonies begin to be regarded as important elements of national identity and social coherence. While the popularity of institutions such as the church and the family unit is on the decline, that of national ceremonies is on the increase. Quaint protocol with, for many, incomprehensible rites and routines, has a mystical value and hence public appeal. This immaterial heritage is greatly valued, not least for its comical entertainment value.
5. Protocol can lend (symbolic) meaning and value to important moments.
   Protocol is of course not only comical; much of what it contains still has meaning to a greater or lesser extent. Much of what is carried out in the name of protocol represents timeless values that, if correctly understood, lend an extra symbolic value to the ceremony. The meaning may remain hidden and yet still be understood in an abstract way, through a feeling of togetherness, for example.

And this point – the meaning and value of protocol – brings me gradually to my concluding remarks about the modernization of protocol. The central focus should be on "meaningfulness" or "functionality" if you prefer.

Back to togetherness

We have for decades been living in a highly individualistic society. Gradually we are beginning to see the downside of this shift. We lose contact with others, we are alone on an ever-broadening playing field and with an increasingly busier life to manage. There is no togetherness in which to reflect on our own lives and to mirror ourselves in others. Coping with life alone is hard work. Many burn out. Our longing for a sense of community increases. But community in its previous form does not suit; it is outdated and irrelevant. We seek new, more specific, even tailor-made routes to a community far more relevant to our modern selves.

Maybe we should try to look at protocol in the same way; do not (just) follow the traditional, worn-out cliches, but (also) think of specific characteristics or elements that make the ceremony stand out as a unique event. In this age of individualism we need those additions to feel satisfied with the occasion. But also think collective; the moment should be a moment for all, where everybody participates, so that all will feel included. This is the original reason for protocol; doing something together to mark a special moment. So make it special in a modern sense. All you need is an innovative and creative mind...

Protocol is an executor of Strategic Relationship Management

by Tom Verbelen, Director Municipality of Antwerp

In my own experience, I notice that there is wide interpretation and discrepancy in what is commonly described as protocol or protocol services in the public sector. It is somewhat vague in its assets and executive role. An incoming visit to a city as part of a program of a state visit can be a good example of the wide scale of interpretation of protocol. In preparation, but even during the visit itself, too many protocol experts are involved. At least six protocol chiefs claim a role; those of the incoming head of state, the government of the incoming visitor, the receiving head of state, the government of the receiving head of state, the local (province) services, the cities governments. In this type of preparation, it is often difficult to keep track of the various backgrounds of the visit, but it all comes together in the focus, intention and the script of the visit. Bringing us back to the core function.

In government, protocol is mainly ceremonial and covers all habits and rules in what to say, do, how to behave, as it was created in royal households in Europe several centuries ago. As we all know, the prominent example is Louis XIV and his court at Versailles. But even today protocol's role is to make sure there is no chaos in prominent meetings and celebrations. It is a system of rules that explain the correct conduct and procedures to be followed in formal situations. It is the role of the stage manager in theater.

This trend is confirmed in literature. In an article in 1998, Erik Goldstein talks about the development of protocol and the shifting habits of behavior between organizations and the division between ceremonial conduct and the conduct of the relation itself. In *An Expert's Guide to International Protocol* by Gilbert Monod De Froideville and Mark Verheul, the authors write that protocol can contribute to diplomatic and business successes, based on the assumption that it focuses on the executive process.

To conclude this short exploration, I would propose the idea of governmental protocol as a high-quality event management. It is an executor of Strategic Relationship Management, and it focuses on the executive process.

3.   Developing a Networking Vision

Connecting to people and creating meaning are important parts of leadership. People want to belong to something bigger than themselves. They want to build cathedrals, or at least they want to feel connected to an organization that is building one. How inspiring are spreadsheets and short-term roadmaps to you? Most likely they do not make your heart pound faster.

To attract the right network partners, it is important to develop and communicate a clear and appealing vision. Your vision statement is your inspiration, the framework for all your strategic planning. When creating the initial vision statement, you are essentially articulating your dreams for the future. It may apply to the entire company or to a single division of the company such as the department(s) responsible for relationship management which is the focus of this chapter. The vision statement answers the question, "Where do we want to go?"

The vision has an external orientation and relates the present to a goal in the future.[1] An appealing long-term vision with a vivid and concrete description of an envisioned future that lies beyond the narrow focus of short-term results activates employees and stakeholders. It is an aspiration that guides a set of choices about how to best invest time and resources to achieve this vision.[2]

> A strong vision speaks to the heart, hands, and head:
> **Heart** – this relates to the "why"; The vision is inspiring and aims towards a goal that stretches the imagination but still feels possible to achieve.
> **Hands** – this relates to the "how"; The vision is applicable and describes the necessary competences and measurements to implement the vision.
> **Head** – this relates to the "what"; The vision consists of clear language without metaphors (they could be misinterpreted) and is easy to communicate.

Such a vision provides the organization with a framework that is both stable and malleable. The vision is not like a text written in stone – the vision of an organization is the collective sum of the visions of the stakeholders which allows it to create shared value. A vision in society 4.0 is dynamic and adjustable to changing circumstances, open for feedback from stakeholders, and enables the organization to respond adaptively to the changes in its surroundings. It serves as a benchmark to align the organizational strategy and alliances as well as the internal structure and attitude towards the fulfilment of its goals.

It is important to be aware and to communicate "why" Strategic Relationship Management is so important in reaching the overall vision, mission and strategy of the organization and your relationship management goals for the future. As well as "what" should be done to achieve this and "how" this should be executed. This is how the general vision theory of Simon Sinek is translated towards Strategic Relationship Management.

> Simon Sinek explains in his theory of the Golden Circle that "people don't buy what you do but why you do it." According to Sinek "why" is one of the most important messages that an organization can communicate as this is what draws others in and inspires them to action. "Why" is how you explain your purpose and the reason you exist and behave as you do. At an organizational level, communicating your "why" is the basis of a strong value proposition that will differentiate you from others. The stronger an organization can articulate its "why", the better it can attract and involve other stakeholders to join its cause. The "why" correlates with the vision and gives a strong direction to the organizational strategy.[3]

Many organizations start formulating their visions with the best of intentions until the going gets tough and it starts to consume "too much time". That is why it can be tempting to skip this part of the work because people are uncomfortable with this phase of not-knowing, of not-acting-yet, of having more questions than answers. It is hard to resist moving on to the next step; the strategy. Designing and executing a strategy makes us feel like we are actually getting somewhere. It demands wisdom that supersedes managerial thinking, to take a step back and view the context in which the organization is functioning. To let go of quick wins for a while and create some free space and think; what is our place here? What is dearest to our heart and what do we really want to add to our stakeholders in the long-term? What do we want to be remembered for?

> When the solid foundation of a firm vision is missing, the strategy will start to slide.

When this part of the job is not done, and the solid foundation of a firm vision is missing, the organizational strategy will start to slide. The tools and protocols will become goals in their own right, and the direction of the organization will start to fade. And how can an organization that does not succeed in aligning its own internal teams toward a clear purpose be able to inspire, connect, and steer its external stakeholder network? The quality of this first step in creating a clear vision will define the strength of the rest of the process.

> When Jack Ma, the founder of Alibaba, in 1999, delivered his motivational speech to a bunch of friends in a sparsely furnished flat in Shanghai, he knew exactly how to do that; how to touch the head, heart, and hands of his audience. He convinced them to dedicate themselves to start an e-commerce business that would use the Internet to

connect Chinese manufacturers with potential buyers around the globe and to make it bigger than Amazon. A goal that at that time seemed almost impossible to achieve. But he knew how to make the vision look tangible, imaginable. How to help his friends to literally see it happening. At the same time, he stated what they had to let go of. They had to let go of certainty, needed to work harder than usual and give up fixed office hours. They would need to take a leap of faith in a dream that seemed so far away at that moment. And they agreed to do it, because they believed in it. And Ma, with his now famous talent to convince others to back him, persuaded them to commit $60,000 to this new company Alibaba.

At the moment of writing, Alibaba tops Amazon as the world's biggest e-commerce company with a market value of 527 billion US$. And it has expanded its activities to big data and artificial intelligence, crossing traditional sector boundaries and creating an interwoven value proposition to its customers. This motivational speech was made to the Alibaba organization itself; the same ability to create and communicate a strong future vision is necessary to create shared value networks.

The vision is what is carried and practiced and shared by all members of the organization. It is an important part of the organization's identity. Feedback, both criticism and praise, is important to help the organization learn to what extent the vision is carried out effectively and what aspects ought to be improved. This asks for the organization to be open for dialogue with its stakeholders both within and outside the organization. Such feedback loops between the organization and its stakeholders help to (re)shape the vision until it reaches its (temporary) optimum.[4] This approach stands in contrast to the strong need for control and autonomy that characterizes current society in so many ways. To develop such openness with its stakeholders and to show vulnerability demands strong relationship skills. It asks the willingness to cooperate in a transparent manner and the capacity for change (see also Chapter 11).

A Networking Vision contains a common goal; the goal of the other is as important as yours in order for relationships to be reciprocal.

This is where the Networking Vision comes into play. For many, it is difficult to translate the organizational vision, mission and strategy to a Networking Vision for its Relationship Management Strategy. The tendency is to repeat the overall vision which is mainly focused on what the organization wants to achieve and how it aims to do that. A Networking Vision though should contain the following elements:
· The core reason of existence of the network of an organization.
· The reason why your network is appealing to others (how relationships in your network are going to be reciprocal) by describing a goal that is attractive to everyone in your organization's network.

- A challenging goal for its future Strategic Relationship Management (including geographical and time scopes).
- The core values by which it is executed.
- What should be done to achieve the challenging future goal.
- The core competences (present and future) needed to do that.

An example of such Networking Vision is:

- *"The Institute of Strategic Relationship Management (ISRM) trains and advises organizations how to create a meaningful and valuable network that provides the agility and resilience to be successful in society 4.0.*
- *ISRM aims for a strong network with relationship management experts as well as with those dealing with the challenges of relationship management in governmental, non-governmental, and profit organizations in Europe that is doubled and closely connected within two years. In this network expertise and ideas are shared with the goal of bringing relationship management to an even higher level.*
- *We achieve this by being pro-active, trustworthy, and accountable. We want to offer value over the long term."*

While formulating the Networking Vision, try to be as concrete as possible and do not use more than five or six sentences. This helps to keep focus. Important to formulate as well is not only what the relationship management should offer one's own organization and how it can contribute to reaching its own goals, but also how it offers value to its stakeholders and thus why it is of interest to the stakeholders to stay or become part of your network.

Key to a good Networking Vision is to be aware of the importance of reciprocity. What is it your organization wants to offer by its relationship management? Comenius Courses, for example, a well-known Dutch institute in the field of executive leadership development, has a relationship management approach that is highly reciprocal. It is meant to attract more customers, validate the status of Comenius as a renowned and innovative leadership institute, and support the creation of new strategic partnerships. At the same time, its relationship management offers its stakeholders high-quality personal attention, a sense of exclusivity, access to its prestigious network, and a long-term relationship with several free benefits.

A leading organization knows how to inspire and connect others. It is not just people who are inspired and connected – when people are connected, their knowledge is connected as well. When people are inspired, their purposes are inspired as well and the most challenging goals can be reached. That is they way to build cathedrals, by connecting people, bringing their knowledge, skills, and hearts together and collectively building towards realizing a purpose in which the whole is bigger than its parts.

Notes

1. Herminia Ibarra, '*Act like a Leader, Think like a Leader*', Harvard Business Review Press, Boston Massachusets, 2015

2. Herminia Ibarra, '*Act like a Leader, Think like a Leader*', Harvard Business Review Press, Boston Massachusets, 2015

3. www.youtube.com/watch?v=qp0HIF3Sfl4

4. Shelley L. Brickson, '*Organizational Identity Orientation: The Genesis of the Role of the Firm and Distinct Forms of Social Value*', The Academy of Management Review 32(3) × July 2007

Managing Relationships

The Regents of the Oudezijds Huiszittenhuis, Pieter van Anraedt, 1675, canvas, 237 × 425 cm, collection Amsterdam Museum (on loan from the City of Amsterdam)

Upward mobility

by Paul Mosterd, Deputy Director Hermitage Amsterdam

The story is told that at a dinner one evening, Winston Churchill was seated next to a highly decorated young man whom he did not immediately recognize. He asked the Sir with interest how he had earned his knighthood. The young man answered proudly that he was a painter. Churchill replied, "I see! Art is the easiest way up." This is *upward mobility*, an essential premise for networking – if you can not climb the social ladder, networking is effectively pointless. Ferdinand Bol's career is an appropriate example of what Churchill meant. He was an extremely successful and highly respected painter, yet it was only after his second marriage in 1669 that he made a real step upward. Anne van Erckel became his wife, and she was very wealthy. Overnight, Bol went from portraying to being portrayed. He was invited to sit on the board of one of the city's most prestigious charitable institutions.

He is seated at the table in a manner that a true economic regent should. He sits furthest on the left; alert, composed and self-assured. He is a board member, at the mayor's request, of what we nowadays would call a food bank. These positions were an honor for rich citizens. Moreover, it was thought that wealthy board members would be less corrupt, or in any case, would keep less money for themselves. Their pockets were already filled; that was the idea. The regents alongside Bol at the table demonstrate precisely why they are on this board; they are counting money. The motto is "show your virtues." The painting is therefore a depiction of their skills, yet also an open application to more jobs, or perhaps even better jobs. The message is evident; "You can trust us." It is a true testimonial. Of course, Bol knew this like no one else. How many careers had he been able to lift with just one painting?

4.   Relationship Management Strategy

One of the earliest documents on strategy was written by the Chinese general Sun Tzu (or Sunzi, *The Art of War*).[1] Sun Tzu's Art of War says that the greatest generals gained victory without fighting any battles. They would use diplomacy, respect, reciprocity, fear, kindness, or any other psychological means to get what they want. Knowing what to want and what the other side desires increases the chance of bringing a conflict to a good ending by 50 percent, according to Sun Tzu. To achieve this, it is important to collect information about your current position, about the position of the opposite party, and to position yourself in the shoes of the opponent. Sun Tzu also brings in the element of timing – it is not only important to do the right thing; it is also important to act at the right moment.

Sun Tzu considers relationship management an integral component of military strategy. Good relationship management supports the military strategy, and in turn a good military strategy is the basis for successful relationship management. In this chapter, Relationship Management Strategy will be explored as a basis for establishing and strengthening a Strategic Relationship Management competency.

4.1   An active role for the Manager of the Network in the strategy debate of the organization

From an organization perspective, relationship management is an investment and therefore should deliver a return. To assess the return, and therefore the success of the relationship management activities, it is vital to understand how success is defined by the organization. What does the organization want to achieve? To be successful as a Manager of the Network it is important to understand the vision and strategy of the organization. The overall vision and strategy of the organization can be translated into a Networking Vision and a Relationship Management Strategy. The Relationship Management Strategy in turn is executed via the relationship management. This approach is a **top-down approach**. In this approach, it is important for the Manager of the Network to:

- Understand what the ambition of the organization is (one year, three years, and five years from now).
- Understand where (e.g. which markets, which customer needs, what policies) the organization wants to focus.
- Understand how the organization wants to win, be successful within the defined focus area.

The Manager of the Network can translate the understanding of the above into a Relationship Management Strategy by answering these questions:

- What is the ambition of relationship management (one year, three years, and five years from now)?
- Where (e.g. on which stakeholders) does relationship management want to focus?
- What is required for the relationship management to win (be successful)?
- How will relationship management be organized to win?

For example,
- What activities will be conducted?
- What systems are required?
- What organizational structure will be used?

Relationship management; the eyes and ears of the organization.

Next to a top-down approach one can also recognize a **bottom-up approach** of the Relationship Management Strategy. After all, relationships are reciprocal, and relationship management is also the eyes and ears of the organization. Relationship management provides the organization with an antenna on key barriers, opportunities, or connections among stakeholders from which the organization might benefit. Relationship management can provide valuable input to the strategy of the organization such as:
- What are key areas of interest to insiders (those within the network) and what are considered threats by outsiders (those outside the network)?
- What is the current position of the organization as perceived by stakeholders?
- What do stakeholders want to get out of relations with the organization?
- What activities are effective in building targeted relationships?
- What are key requirements to achieve this?
- Which relationships or stakeholder connections are important or have become more important to the organization?
- What are opportunities to fortify and deepen relationships to contribute to the longer-term vision of the organization?

Both with the top-down as well as with the bottom-up approach to strategy, the Manager of the Network ought to claim an active role in the strategy debate of the organization. In the top-down approach the Manager of the Network can provide feedback, identify requirements and limitations, and as such –via an iterative approach– improve the strategy. In the bottom-up approach, the Manager of the Network can actively feed the strategy debate by playing back insights derived from the network of the organization. This role might not come naturally to the Manager of the Network. Daily operational pressures, typical to the role of Manager of the Network, frequently require immediate attention leaving little time for strategic considerations.

Constructive participation of the Manager of the Network in the strategy debate of the organization requires the manager to synthesize the "noise from the network" into valuable insights to the organization. This requires the Manager of the Network to pause, evaluate, reflect, analyze, and ultimately effectively communicate the findings from the network. Lastly, participating in the strategy debate of the organization also requires internal organizational connections (an internal relationship network!). This can be a challenge to the Manager of the Network who naturally will have the tendency to be more externally oriented. However, whenever the Manager of the Network brings the perceptions, attitudes, and responses of stakeholders into the debate, others will consider this as valuable input. After all, the opinions of stakeholders are vital to the success of the organization.

This chapter will therefore explore strategy development in organizations and provide the Manager of the Network with a basic set of tools to actively contribute in the strategy debate. The topics discussed should enable the Manager of the Network to develop a Relationship Management Strategy that is aligned with the organization and provides logic and focus to the relationship management activities. This is in the interest of the Manager of the Network – only on the basis of a well-argued Relationship Management Strategy will the Manager of the Network be able to receive sufficient funding to achieve the defined relationship management ambitions.

4.2 Relationship Management Strategy in the context of a plan or a process

Strategy bridges the gap between policy and tactics. As part of the strategy an ambition, the desired end state, is defined. In the strategy plan the bridge is outlined on how to achieve with the current means the desired end state.

Strategy can be defined in multiple ways. Key components of a strategy are always:
· A solid understanding of the current position (the current means or resources).
· The definition of an ambition (a vision, strategic intent, or end state).
· The definition of a path, an integrated plan based on analyses, which brings you to the ambition.

'Bridging the gap'

Means

Ends

Strategy & tactics
Deploy & employ

Figure 4.2.1 Bridging the gap[2]

Roger Martin and A.G. Lafley bring these in their book *Playing to Win*
together and define strategy as;
"An integrated set of informed choices and timely actions that gives an
organization sustainable advantage over its competitors and provides the
organization with superior returns over the long term."[3]

Many academics have provided various perspectives on the elements of strategy and
the required strategic approach to business challenges. In this paragraph, two
opposing views will be discussed as they also lead to a different perspective on
Relationship Management Strategy; the Intended Strategy approach versus the
Emergent Strategy approach.

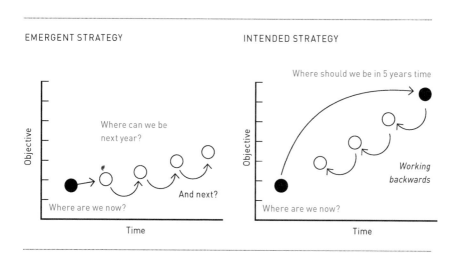

Figure 4.2.2 Emergent versus intended strategy

The Intended Strategy from Michael Porter[4]

The Intended Strategy approach defines the strategic ambition in three to five years. To achieve an ambition, a plan is developed working backwards; "If we want to be at X in year 5, where should we be in year 4, where in year 3, etc.?" The Intended Strategy approach was developed by Michael Porter, one of the founders of the consulting firm Monitor Deloitte. A clear benefit of the Intended Strategy is that it provides a compass, a direction, to the organization. It also provides excitement and energy to the organization. After all, the organization is aiming for a future that is beyond the current state and via a set-based approach it seems feasible! Lastly, the Intended Strategy focuses on the organization. When the organization underperforms in year 2, it is clear that the gap versus the desired future state has widened and additional effort is required to bring the organization back to plan.

The Emergent Strategy from Henry Mintzberg[5]

The Emergent Strategy approach considers strategy to be a process that needs to be continuously rebalanced based on latest developments and insights. Considering the many unknown factors, a five-year game plan is considered unrealistic and at most one can develop a plan for the next year with an indication of the years ahead. The Emergent Strategy approach was developed by Henry Mintzberg, a Canadian academic known for his contributions to organizational theory and books on business and management. Mintzberg promulgates a bottom-up process of strategy development in which different departments provide knowledge and insights and realign with the strategy. Emergent Strategy is the view that strategy emerges over time as intentions collide with and accommodate a changing reality. Emergent Strategy is a set of actions or behaviors consistent over time but not expressly intended in the original planning of strategy. Emergent Strategy implies that an organization is learning what works in practice.

Both strategy approaches have value and shortcomings. Having a clear direction with the Intended Strategy provides for clarity and energy in the organization. However, in times of great uncertainty, it can also lead to frustration and wrong decisions. As an example, during the financial crisis of 2008, most CEOs in the financial industry could not afford to stick to their long-term strategic plans but urgently had to save the company while politicians interfered to ensure the overall financial system did not collapse. In effect, building on paragraph 1.1 of this book, the 3.0 society in which most industries are currently functioning is fraught with ambiguity (e.g. the VUCA world by Robert Johansen). The Emergent Strategy approach addresses the ambiguity and allows the organization to adapt quickly to social and economic reality and benefit from agile response. Many digital start-ups benefit from this approach by continuously testing and improving their propositions and pivoting to new propositions with paradigm-breaking insights. However, an Emergent Strategy can be frustrating for executives who see opportunities that require long-term commitments from the organization. Most business opportunities require an initial investment and a lot of stamina to ultimately reap the fruits of success; Emergent Strategy does not provide the comfort of long-term investments nor certainties for backup when times get rough. Most organizations adopt a blend of Emergent and Intended Strategies in their strategy development and portfolio, although culturally there tends to be a dominant approach.

Relevance to Relationship Management Strategy
The Intended Strategy approach is helpful for the design of a Relationship Management Strategy. After all, organizations that adopt it are clear on their ambition level and have plotted a course to which the Relationship Management Strategy can be aligned. The strategy provides guidance for the identification of important internal and external stakeholders who can contribute to a successful delivery of the strategy. Additionally, by defining the different steps that lead to the ambition level, an accountability framework for Relationship Management Strategy is created. Relationships require investments that most likely will not have an immediate return, but the different steps towards the return can be accounted for in the Relationship Management Strategy Plan. Managers responsible for relationship management in the organization will want to develop the Relationship Management Strategy, including the required budget, and ask for approval of the management board before executing the strategy.

The Emergent Strategy approach is somewhat more opportunistic when translated to Relationship Management Strategy. Expectations regarding a Return-on-Relationship are lower but when successful, the investments and intensity can be scaled up. The Emergent Strategy emphasizes the need to continuously learn and adapt. The networkers of the organization fulfill a crucial role in support of this kind of strategy by being the eyes and ears of the organization and by providing insights gathered from the network quickly back to strengthen the strategy. Managers responsible for relationship management in the organization will want to set up smaller initiatives initially to test the effectiveness before requesting a larger budget to be used to scale up successful initiatives. In addition, the Manager of the Network can consider whether to frequently play back insights derived from the network initiatives by, for example, reporting on the "voice of the market." Lastly, the networking team of the organization is important when pursuing an Emergent Strategy as it facilitates the organization to work in an agile manner beyond hierarchy or fixed organizational structures (see also paragraph 10.1).

For the Manager of the Network it is helpful to identify which approach the organization is pursuing. It will help to identify the contribution relationship management can deliver to the overall strategy of the company and align the strategic intent and expectations for relationship management.

4.3 The strategy paradigm that drives your Relationship Management Strategy

In Chapter 3 we identified the need to develop a Networking Vision. The vision is an important part of the organization's identity. It provides the long-term anchor for the organization's strategy. Strategic myopia is the inability of management to recognize important changes impacting the vision, because people tend to be blinded by usual patterns, convictions, and paradigms. It is most easily recognized when somebody tells you "this is how we do things in this business!" The fundamental response to such a comment being; "What business?" The way we define the business we are in is changing over time and is influenced by changes in technology, society, and consumer behavior.

After the Industrial Revolution in the late eighteenth century, a business would be defined based on the product delivered. Society had moved from an agricultural to an industrial economy. Factories produced products, and scale in the production process made lower costs possible. **Ford was in the car business.**[6]

Theodore Levitt, a renowned former business and marketing professor, changed the paradigm and caused organizations to define themselves based on their customer function. After all, competition developed, and consumers had options to choose from. When travelling from New York to Boston, consumers could opt for driving a car, taking the train, or taking the Greyhound Bus. Ford therefore was not only in competition with other car manufacturers but also with other means of transportation. So actually, **Ford was in the business of transportation.**

As production processes became more specialized and scale increased, it became important to differentiate from the competition. Prahalad and Hamel, authors of the article "The Core Competence of the Corporation"[7] introduced the concept of Core Competence in 1990. A business ought to focus on those elements of the process where it was best. Other elements of the process could be outsourced to those organizations more capable. **Ford was in the assembly business.**

The term "experience economy" was introduced by Pine and Gillmore[8] at the turn of the twenty-first century. Due to advances in technology, increasing competition, and increasing expectations of consumers, products and services are starting to look like commodities. To differentiate in a competitive market and deliver added value to the consumer, organizations are required to deliver memorable experiences. In line with the thinking of Pine and Gillmore Ford "Goes Further" and BMW is the "ultimate driving experience." Nike no longer produces sport shoes or assembles sport shoes but instead is in the business of "experiencing the emotion of competition, winning, and crushing competitors." Defining the business based on the consumer experience allows for a new paradigm and different propositions. Nike generates significant revenue from its digital Nike+ platform and via BMW's

Connected Drive additional services can be purchased while driving the car. **Ford is in the business of "going further."**

The changing paradigm of what business organizations are in has also changed the language. We no longer talk about sales but now discuss customers or even guests. We also no longer refer to products but have changed to propositions being the aggregate of product + service + experience.

Sales   Customers   Guests

Figure 4.3.1 From sales to guests

Interestingly, Robert Pine, coauthor of the book The Experience Economy, claims that we are on the verge of entering a new age of paradigm – the transformational economy (see also paragraph 1.1 of the 4.0 society). When illustrating the transformational economy, Pine uses platform companies such as Airbnb, Alibaba, and Facebook as examples. Applied to what we just discussed, BMW would not be the "ultimate driving experience" but rather an "automotive ecosystem (network)" where different entities connect on the BMW platform to facilitate the needs of the BMW driver. In the age of the Platform Economy we would not refer to customers or guests anymore, but a more appropriate terminology would be... relationships! Pure digital companies use language like traffic or connections, and as a result, as already indicated in Chapter 1, connected values as symbolic representations of the network become more important. Although it is too early to assess the impact of a possible transformation economy, we can clearly see that relationships are taking a more prominent role in everyday life than ever before. How often did you check your mobile device or apps while you were reading this book?

> In the age of the Platform Economy, a more appropriate term for customers or guests would be... relationships!

Understanding how we define the business we are in is crucial for the design of a Relationship Management Strategy. It defines the lens with which we look at stakeholders, customers, and suppliers. It supports the tone of voice we use in our invitation and during our events. It drives priorities and actions.

A company focused on core competency might be dependent on a relationship network providing the strategic capability to the organization of current and future alignment to the production process and needs of suppliers and customers. An organization in the business of delivering experiences might benefit more from consistent incorporation of the experience in the stakeholder encounter. In addition, an organization in the business of delivering experiences might want to focus on regulators and nongovernmental organizations working on legislation regarding data privacy. After all, access to stakeholder profile data is likely to be an important enabler for the delivery of a relevant relationship experience.

4.4 Strategic relationship networks

Digital technology has greatly reduced the cost of information, the speed of information flow, and the access to information. As a result, many organizations no longer operate as part of a value chain but rather a value network. This can best be described via an example from the insurance industry.

In the traditional definition, the insurance sector provides guarantees when times are rough. Insurance is highly dependent on data to calculate a risk premium. Therefore, data collection and the related analytics are a key competency in the sector. Traditionally the sector sold via financial intermediaries who could explain the complex insurance products to consumers.

In the digital age, customers have started to search for insurance products themselves and insurers have responded by simplifying their products. The hunger for customer-specific data combined with the ability to distribute insurance products directly to customers has driven insurance organizations to value networks. Based on specific domains such as "income" or "retirement," partnerships are being established to be more relevant to the consumer. As part of the domain "retirement," customers might be looking at ways to save money via a pension, the purchase of a second home, or other sorts of investments. Customers might want to consult a notary or shop online for information about inheritance. They might approach advisors or their employer for advice on the best tax-savvy setup. Many stakeholders are involved when rescoping the original pension insurance to the network of the retirement domain.

> Relationship management is a critical competency for organizations with sustainable partnerships.

The shift from value chain to value network has significant implications for a Relationship Management Strategy. Relationship management becomes a critical

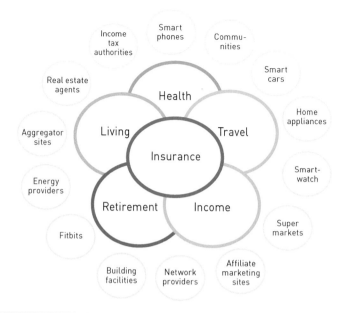

Figure 4.4.1 Insurance value network

competency for organizations that want to establish sustainable partnerships with entities previously not defined as part of their industry. Relationships become an essential and competitive factor in delivering the ability to serve the customer best.

The speed of information flow has also set higher standards of expectations. Stakeholders and customers expect direct feedback. This challenges both the technological infrastructure and the organizational competencies of the company. Resulting from the direct response, not only the speed of the dialogue changes but also the content. Contact centers become customer care centers. Relationship management becomes a data-driven competency enabled by content management to engage stakeholders and customers in a relevant dialogue.

> Digital technology has placed relationship management center stage in strategy development.

Digital technology has placed relationship management center stage in strategy development. It is no longer a competency cherished and explored exclusively by royalty or generals such as Sun Tzu or Von Clausewitz. It is at the disposal of all organizations that are able to effectively elevate relationship management to the strategic level.

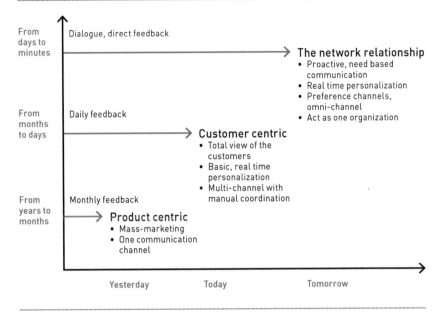

From
days to
minutes — Dialogue, direct feedback

The network relationship
- Proactive, need based communication
- Real time personalization
- Preference channels, omni-channel
- Act as one organization

From
months
to days — Daily feedback

Customer centric
- Total view of the customers
- Basic, real time personalization
- Multi-channel with manual coordination

From
years to
months — Monthly feedback

Product centric
- Mass-marketing
- One communication channel

Yesterday   Today   Tomorrow

Figure 4.4.2 From product-centric to network relationship

4.5   Relationship Management Strategy as an iterative process

Strategy is the foundation that should drive resource allocation, investment decisions, and performance expectations. Strategy provides guidance to the organization and links via a logical set of actions corporate strategy to division, business, and a Relationship Management Strategy.

Roger Martin and A.G. Lafley state that strategy can best be expressed as an integrated set of choices modeled in a Strategy Cascade Model ™.[9]

Key questions to address in the strategy cascade are:
A. **What are our goals and aspirations?** Making the purpose and vision of the organization explicit provides a cause worth fighting for and sets a normative framework for the organization. Quantifying the objectives both financially and non-financially provides the organization with direction.
B. **Where will we play?** A strategy needs to provide focus on what customers to address, in what geographies to compete, and via what propositions to attract the customer base.
C. **How will we win in chosen markets?** The requirements to be successful in the chosen markets need to be explicit in order to allocate resources appropriately. How to win requires a solid understanding of stakeholder

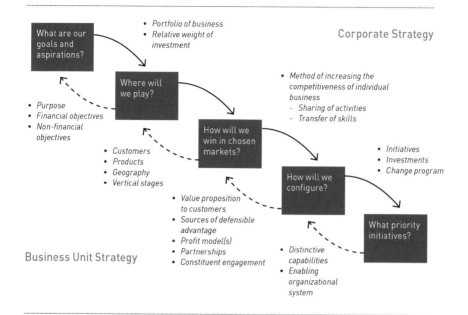

Figure 4.5.1 The Strategy Cascade ™

needs, identifying possible partnerships and relationships in the network that can strengthen the proposition and thorough understanding of the revenue model.

D. **How will we configure?** What systems will enable us to be effective and efficient? What is the appropriate organizational model that fits our chosen market and strengthens our order winners?

E. **What are the priority initiatives?** Sun Tzu highlighted the importance of timing millenia ago. How to start, what to do first? These questions can best be answered by placing them in the strategic context via an iterative development of the Strategy Cascade.

The Strategy Cascade may seem like a really straightforward concept, but making choices is hard to do. Often, choices do not get made due to decision gridlock or choice paralysis. Or choices are made, but decisions were made by individual functions in silos so they do not support one another. As an example, if a strategic choice is made to build strategic relationships with identified stakeholders, the organization ought to also provide the systems (for example, databases and CRM technology) and organization (account management) to support the delivery of the strategic choice.

The Strategy Cascade not only benefits commercial organizations but can also be useful to social sector organizations as described below:

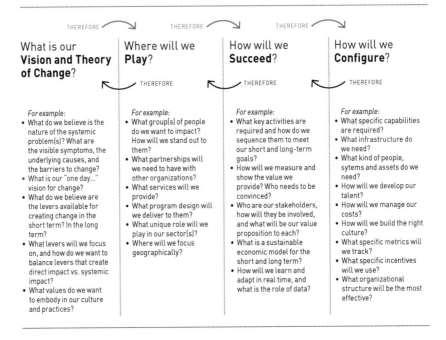

Figure 4.5.2 The Strategy Cascade example in social sector organizations

The Strategy Cascade is not a sequential process but rather an iterative approach. Each question can be supported by fact-based analysis. Each question can be answered individually but is likely to change the answer to the previous and following questions. The Strategy Cascade is valuable in a top-down as well as in a bottom-up process as illustrated in the following visual:

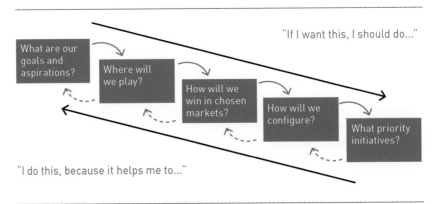

Figure 4.5.3 The Strategy Cascade iterative logic

The Strategy Cascade can be applied in two ways to the development of a Relationship Management Strategy:

1. **Serving as input to the Relationship Management Strategy.** By having a solid understanding of the direction, priorities, and profit model of the overall organization, it is easier to identify how relationship management can contribute value to the organization. When it is clear what markets or segments the organization wants to focus on, more meaningful relationship activities can be developed as opposed to a situation where this is less clear.

2. **As a way to express the Relationship Management Strategy.** The Relationship Management Strategy can be expressed in the form of the Strategy Cascade. For any organization, it is relevant to:
   a. Define the goals and aspirations of relationship management
   b. Identify what stakeholders the relationship management will focus on
   c. Establish how relationship management can be successful
   d. Develop the appropriate systems and organizations that allow relationship management to be successful
   e. Focus on sources and prioritize the most important relationship management initiatives.

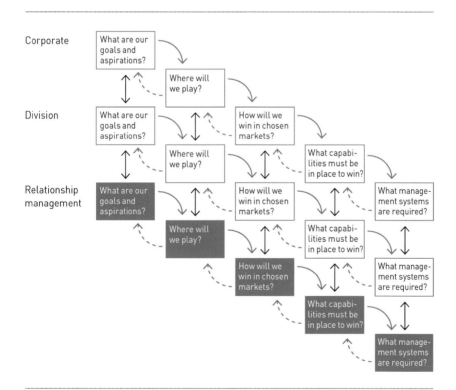

Figure 4.5.4 The Strategy Cascade on different levels

4.6   Making the Relationship Management Strategy tangible

A useful way to map the strategy and translate it into action is the OGSM Framework. OGSM stands for Objectives, Goals, Strategy, and Measurements. It can serve as the basis for strategy planning, strategy execution, and strategy monitoring. The model was first developed and applied by Procter & Gamble.[10] The simplicity of the model is its strength; it forces the user to express the strategy in a short and concise way indicating quantitative objectives.

Objective	Short statements of the objectives of the organization, the program or the Relationship Management Strategy. E.g. the relationship management objective of the organization World Press Photo[11] could be *"to strengthen the worldwide network of photo journalists in order to develop and promote the work of visual journalism."*
Goals	Quantified results identifying what success looks like for the objective defined. Remember that ideally these goals are SMART – Specific, Measurable, Attainable, Relevant, and Timebound. E.g. the goals of the organization World Press Photo could be to *"broaden our network in 10 more countries and with 15 more organizations."*
Strategy	Identifying how you will achieve the goals. There can be 3 or 4 strategies which all support the achievement of the goal. E.g. the Relationship Management Strategies of World Press Photo could be to *"i) Strengthen relationships in 10 countries with governments and nongovernmental organizations on issues related to freedom of the press; ii) Establish a sponsorship network among commercial organizations to enable the funding of activities of World Press Photo; iii) Increase awareness in society of Free Press incidents in 10 focus countries by involving the broader public in all countries."*
Measures	Measurements that help you identify whether the strategy is working. E.g. the relationship measures of World Press Photo could be *"i) In-depth discussions with 10 crisis countries, 5 of which have liberated free press by 2020; ii) Establish a sponsorship network delivering € 15 million by 2020; iii) Have 5 million people visit the exhibitions of World Press Photo."*

1. Relationship Objective	2. Relationship Goals	3. Relationship Strategies	4. Relationship Measures
Overall business objective for World Press Photo, e.g. "to strengthen the worldwide network of photo journalist in order to develop and promote the work of visual journalism"	Quantitative goals for the objective, e.g. "Broaden our network in 10 more countries and with 15 more organizations"	Key strategy 1 to realize overall objective, e.g. "Strengthen relationships in 10 countries with governments and non-governmental organizations on issues related to freedom of press" Key strategy 2 to realize overall objective, e.g. "Establish a sponsorship network among commercial organizations to enable the funding of activities of World Press Photo" Key strategy 3 to realize overall objective, e.g. "Increase awareness in society on Free Press incidents in 10 focus countries by involving the broader public in all countries"	Year target for strategy 1, e.g. "In depth discussions with 10 crises countries, 5 of which have liberated free press by 2020" .... Year target for strategy 2, e.g. "Establish a sponsorship network delivering € 2 million by 2020" .... Year target for strategy 3, e.g. "Have 5 million people visit the exhibitios of World Press Photo" ....

Figure 4.6.1   The OGSM template

4.7   Strategy as an outcome of negotiations at many levels

Strategy is developed at different levels in an organization. As such there is hierarchy in the strategy development process.

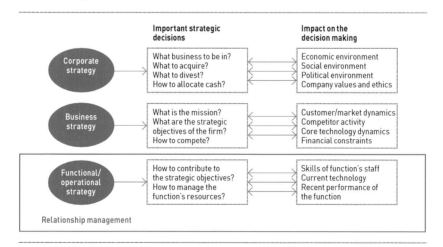

Figure 4.7.1   Strategic decisions and impact at three levels [12]

At the corporate level, the scope is broad and questions relate to the portfolio of investments. At commercial organizations, the questions addressed as part of the corporate strategy tend to be financially biased toward things like shareholder return. At social-profit organizations, the corporate level scope generally is about what policy area to focus on.

The business strategy relates to the competitiveness of the business. For social-profit organizations, the strategy is frequently focused on achieving major breakthroughs in policy or implementation.

> A Relationship Management Strategy ought to be considered as a subset of the business strategy.

The functional or operational strategy focuses on the effectiveness of the relevant functional area. Relationship management can be such a functional area. Impacting on the decision making at functional level are the skills available in the organization, the available technology to support relationship management, and the measurements of the effectiveness of relationship management. A Relationship Management Strategy can therefore not be considered in isolation, but ought to be considered as a subset of the business strategy which in turn is a subset of the corporate strategy.

The outcome of the strategy process determines the allocation of resources. Therefore, in many organizations strategy development is also a negotiation between the different levels in the organization. Frequently the strategy development process is embedded as an integral part (or the starting point) of the budget process. The process is generically called Resource Allocation Planning (RAP).

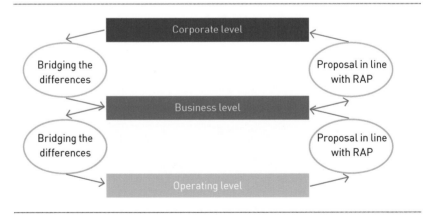

Figure 4.7.2 Resource Allocation Planning (RAP) [13]

The Resource Allocation Plan is meant to ensure that allocation of resources supports the organization's strategic initiatives and priorities. In theory, this process is top-down, but often in practice it is an iterative negotiation where a proposal is submitted by the operating level, for example the Manager of the Network, which is rolled up to a total proposal of the business. When aggregating all proposals, there is likely to be a difference between the resources available and the resources requested. This requires the corporate level to go back to the business and the business to go back to the operating level; the Manager of the Network must bridge the differences in resources available and requested.

This negotiation game, which takes place often annually in many organizations, highlights the importance of the Manager of the Network having a strategy that is logical, aligns with the strategy of the organization, and is measurable and therefore accountable. Only if it is based on a well-argued Relationship Management Strategy can the Manager of the Network receive sufficient funding to achieve the defined relationship ambitions. The negotiation game also highlights the importance of relationship management *inside* the organization by the Manager of the Network. After all, to receive approval for his or her budget requests, it is likely required to receive the support of multiple managers at business and corporate level.

Notes

1. Sun Tzu, *Art of War*, translated by S. B. Griffith, Oxford University Press, New York, 1963
2. Fred Nickols 2012, Distance Consulting
3. A.G. Lafley, R.L. Martin, *Playing To Win: How strategy really works*, Harvard Business Review Press, 2013
4. *What is Strategy?*, Michael Porter. Harvard Business Review (Nov-Dec 1996)
5. *The Rise and Fall of Strategic Planning* (1994). Henry Mintzberg. Basic Books.
6. Markides, Constantinos C., *All the right moves: a guide to crafting breakthrough strategy*, Harvard Business School Press, 1999
7. Prahalad, C.K. and Hamel, G., "*The Core Competence of the Corporation*", Harvard Business Review, May-June 1990
8. Pine, J. and Gilmore, J. (1999) *The Experience Economy*, Harvard Business School Press, Boston, 1999
9. Monitor Deloitte Methodology. See also *Playing to Win: How strategy really works* by Roger Martin and A.G. Lafley, 2013
10. Pepper, John. *What Really Matters: Service, Leadership, People and Values*. Yale University Press, 1 May 2007, pp. 147-148.
11. www.worldpressphoto.org/about
12. G. Johnson, K. Scholes and R. Whittington, *Exploring Corporate Strategy*, 8th Edition, FT Prentice Hall, 2008
13. Based on Johnson, Scholes and Whittington, *Exploring Corporate Strategy*, 8th Edition, Pearson Education Limited 2008

5. Relationship Echelons and Stakeholder Management

In protocol management, stakeholders are clustered in echelons based on their strategic importance and closeness to the royal family. At events, each echelon is treated differently. For example, the top echelons are often seated close to the king, while for other echelons only a meet-and-greet with the king is staged. Modern protocol expands on the concept of echelons and in a broader setting, frequently using the term segments for clusters of stakeholders with similar characteristics. In paragraph 4.4 we discussed that many organizations are no longer operating in a value chain environment but rather in a value network environment, or ecosystem. This implies that the number of participants –potential relations– has increased. The challenge for the Manager of the Network is therefore to define a strategy that allows the organization to focus on those relations that matter most and to identify the approach per stakeholder that is expected to deliver the best Return-on-Relationship.

This chapter will first explore the broader set of participants in the value network in the form of a Stakeholder Management Approach. The stakeholders relate to both the internal and external environments of the organization. In the second part of this chapter, one specific group of stakeholders –customers– will be detailed somewhat further in the context of Customer Segmentation.

> The challenge for the Manager of the Network is to define a strategy that allows the organization to focus on those relations that matter most and to identify the approach per stakeholder that is expected to deliver the best Return-on-Relationship.

5.1 Stakeholders as relationship echelons

A relationship is, according to The Oxford Dictionary, defined as "the way in which two or more people (or things) are connected." Similarly, a relation is defined as "the way in which two or more people or groups **feel about and behave towards each other**." Thus, a relation can improve or be strengthened. In simple terms relationship management is therefore the orchestration of (mutually) beneficial connections between people. We define relationship management in this book from an organizational perspective as a capability facilitating sustainable networks for the mutual benefit of the organization.

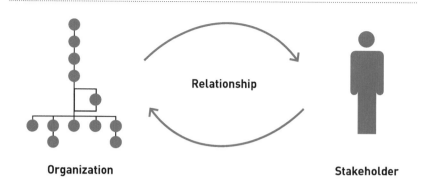

Figure 5.1.1 Relationships as the connection between organization and stakeholder(s)

Where the term relationship or relation describes the connection, the individual with whom the organization has the connection (relationship) is called a stakeholder. A stakeholder is any individual, group, or organization that can affect, be affected by, or perceive itself to be affected by a program.[1] Relationship management is therefore the approach that intends to create positive and constructive relationships with those selected stakeholders who can support the organization in achieving its strategic ambition. This requires:

· A stakeholder framework for the organization.
· Stakeholder analyses.
· Active stakeholder management.

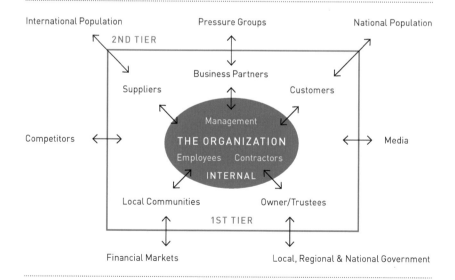

Figure 5.1.2 A stakeholder model for the organization[2]

Stakeholders can be identified on three echelon levels related to the organization:

1. **Internal stakeholders.** These are the stakeholders within the organization. It is the management that has responsibility for and is accountable for different functional, geographical, or customer businesses. They are the employees who might be, like management, responsible for dedicated activities or tasks. But also, frequent contractors can be considered internal stakeholders. Many organizations employ contractors on a semi-permanent basis to conduct activities and tasks or manage part of the business. Although contractors are not on the payroll of the organization, when they fulfil a semi-permanent role as part of the organization they can be considered internal stakeholders. Chapter 10 will further elaborate on the internal stakeholders.

2. **First tier external stakeholders.** These are the stakeholders outside the organization but with direct relationships. Examples of first tier external stakeholders are suppliers, customers, the owners or trustees of the organization, local communities, or business partners such as distributors. With first tier external stakeholders there is a mutual dependency that needs to be managed to ensure the continuing success of the organization.

3. **Second tier external stakeholders.** These are the stakeholders who have an impact on the organization but do not have a mutual dependency. As a result, these stakeholders are more difficult to manage since the success of the organization does not immediately translate into success for the stakeholder. Examples of these stakeholders are media, government, financial markets, pressure groups, national and international populations, and competitors.

Depending on the strategy of the organization, stakeholders within the three echelons can also vary in importance. Therefore, based on a stakeholder analysis, additional specific echelon levels (such as a level 1a, 1b or 1c for the first tier stakeholders) can be identified.

5.2 Stakeholder analyses as input to the Relationship Management Strategy

To define a stakeholder approach, it is helpful to conduct a stakeholder analysis first. A stakeholder analysis delivers insights into:

· The different perspectives, contexts, and values per stakeholder group.
· The different objectives per stakeholder group.
· The different degrees of impact of the various stakeholder groups.

With these insights, it becomes possible to cluster and prioritize stakeholders. After the analysis, it is also possible to define realistic objectives and identify required actions to ensure that important stakeholders either deliver support to the strategic

relationship ambitions or at a minimum are brought to a neutral position.
Four steps can be identified when conducting a stakeholder analysis:

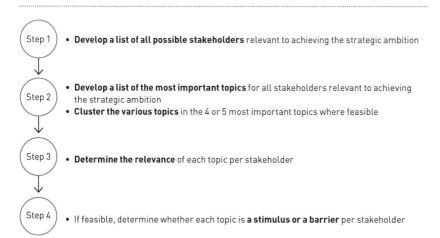

Figure 5.2.1 Step-based stakeholder analyses

Case study Stakeholder Analyses – Aegon N.V.

Aegon N.V. is an international insurance organization based in the Netherlands serving over 30 million customers in more than 20 countries. Trust is a key driver for any insurance organization. For Aegon it is important to be close to its key stakeholders in order to identify potential issues and trends in time. In addition, Aegon wants to serve its customers best and have a sustainable, profitable presence in the markets it serves. To monitor the issues and trends, Aegon conducted a survey among its stakeholders to better understand what they think matters most to Aegon. The survey was conducted with 400 individuals from 33 different organizations. The stakeholders included employees, investors, NGOs, and academics as well as the Aegon Management and Supervisory Board.

The outcome of the survey is a materiality matrix indicating the degree of importance to stakeholders as well as the degree of importance to Aegon. This delivered seven topics that are of the highest importance to both Aegon and its stakeholders. In addition, Aegon has mapped what ability the organization has to influence the topics. The materiality matrix is published very transparently in the Aegon Annual Review as an addendum to the Company Annual Report.[3]

107

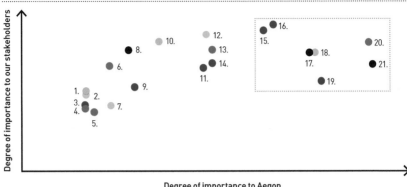

Degree of importance to our stakeholders (y-axis)

Degree of importance to Aegon (x-axis)

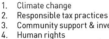

1. Climate change
2. Responsible tax practices
3. Community support & investment
4. Human rights
5. Safeguard standards for intermediaries
6. Social & environmental impact of investments
7. Diversity & equal opportunities
8. Aging & changing demographics
9. Responsible business restructuring
10. Economic & financial uncertainty
11. Internal risk culture
12. Public trust in financial sector
13. Data protection
14. Employee engagement & motivation
15. Transparent products & services
16. Customer service
17. Changing capital requirements for insurers
18. Increased regulation in financial services
19. Attracting & retaining talented empolyees
20. New technologies & digital transformation
21. Low interest rates

Ability to control or influence

● **Direct control**
Issue is entirely within the company's control.

● **Shared control**
Control of the issue is shared with, or exercised through, another company, organization or third party.

◐ **Strong influence**
Company has ability to influence the issue within its own business and value chain.

◐ **Some influence**
Company has ability to influence, but only within its own businesses (not its wider value chain).

● **No influence**
Company has little or no meaningful control or influence over the issue.

Figure 5.2.2 Stakeholder analysis Aegon N.V.

As an example of a stakeholder analysis, consider a pharmaceutical company that wants to introduce a new drug. The company has identified six topics which could be important influences for determining the position of the stakeholders towards the drug: i) seriousness of the disease; ii) competition (alternatives); iii) financing (how the drug will be paid for); iv) product characteristics (for example, potential side effects); v) acceptance by general practitioners (how will GPs respond to the drug), and vi) stakeholder priorities (is the drug a priority for the stakeholder). The pharmaceutical company has subsequently identified three stakeholder groups: the regulator, interest groups (for example, patient organizations), and insurers. In conclusion, for each of the stakeholder groups the company has mapped whether the factor is a stimulus (blue), neutral (white), or a barrier (black).

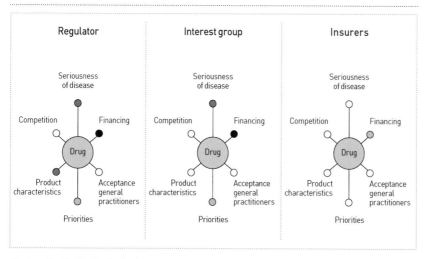

Stimulus ● ○ ○ ◐ ● Barrier

Figure 5.2.3 Stakeholder analysis for a new drug

The analyses show that for two stakeholder groups – the regulator and the interest group – the seriousness of the disease is an important stimulus. To obtain support from these stakeholders, the company should focus on how the drug addresses the seriousness of the disease, although, for both stakeholder groups, the financing of the drug is still an issue. On this topic, the pharmaceutical company ought to identify a mitigating action, especially since for the insurers the financing of the drug is the only relevant topic that defines their attitude towards the drug.

In the above example, the stakeholders were analyzed based on the importance of a topic. However, there are also other elements on the basis of which stakeholders can be analyzed such as:

A. Helpfulness versus potential for damage

Is the stakeholder helpful in achieving the strategic ambition or is the stakeholder potentially damaging in achieving the strategic ambition? The most important stakeholders are those that can be potentially helpful (when their support is given) but at the same time potentially damaging (when they vocalize negative attitudes); the key players.

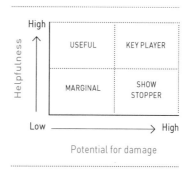

Figure 5.2.4 Helpfulness vs. attitude

B.   Level of information versus attitude

Some stakeholders might have limited information but might still have a positive attitude. Other stakeholders might have a high level of information but develop a negative attitude. The stakeholders to focus on would be those with limited information and negative attitudes. After all, with more information these can possibly be turned into a positive attitude.

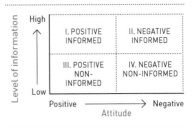

Figure 5.2.5 Level of information vs. attitude

C.   Interest versus power

Some stakeholders might have low interest but also a low power level for contributing to the achievement of the strategic ambition. An example of this could be the general public. Alternatively, some might have very high interest and also a high level

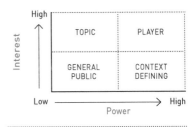

Figure 5.2.6 Interest vs. power

of power. This group of stakeholders we would define as Players; they are key players in the area where the strategic ambition is formulated. These could be competitors, suppliers, or customers. The stakeholders in the segment with high interest but low power are defined as Topics. These are stakeholders who have a content-driven interest but have little influence on the ultimate decision making; they could be employees of the company or academics. The fourth quadrant consists of stakeholders with a low level of interest but a high level of power. These stakeholders are "context defining" such as regulators or politicians. The topic at hand might not be their highest priority, but they might have a decision authority that can change the dynamics.

D.   Summary; impact versus current attitude

The analyses conducted on the basis of these matrices can be summarized in a simple matrix where impact on the organization (a combination of the power, potential for damage, and helpfulness) can be mapped against current attitude of the stakeholders (a combination of interest, level of information, and attitude).

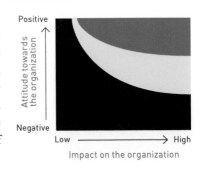

Figure 5.2.7 Impact vs. current attitude

The stakeholder mapping is also relevant to internal stakeholders as is further explained in Chapter 10.

5.3   Strengthening relationship bonds

Sometimes companies define an organization or an institute as a stakeholder. This can be a supplier to the organization or a regulator that is important in the decision making process. However, although the focus of the relationship might be one institute, this does not imply that the scope also includes just one individual stakeholder.

When perceiving one institute as one relationship there is a risk of developing a point-to-point relationship. The risk of a point-to-point relationship is that the organization might lose the relationship if either of the two points leaves the organization, or that reputation might be impacted if either of the two points becomes involved in a dispute. In addition, the insights about the relationship are limited as they are collected via one point only. In practice, many beginning networkers might aspire to such a position as it provides them with control and –at first glance– a position of power as both organizations depend on him or her. However, for the overall benefit of the organization, multiple bonds are stronger than a point-to-point relationship.

111

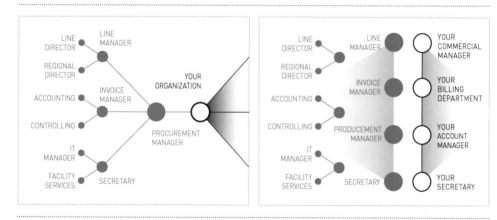

Figure 5.3.1 Point-to-point relationship   Figure 5.3.2 Multiple bond relationship

Consider the above two types of relationships. Figure 5.3.1 is a point-to-point relationship. Figure 5.3.2 is a multiple bond relationship. The latter has a stronger bond with the organization or institute and will be more impactful. The requirements for the relationship management are significant – it requires coordination and planning and all networkers to share information. Most likely there will also be a difference in frequency; it is likely that the contacts between the two secretaries are more frequent than the contacts with the procurement manager. The secretarial contact is to collect information and stage the encounter with the procurement manager in such a way that the encounter is most productive.

5.4   Mapping stakeholders at the individual level

While stakeholder analyses tend to look at entities (such as regulators, media, or suppliers), stakeholder mapping is an approach to assess the individual level. Stakeholder mapping is a visual representation of the key stakeholders and the spheres of influence between stakeholders. A Stakeholder Map:

· Provides information on your own position (within an organization).
· Helps to identify where to focus.
· Identifies who influences whom.
· Provides visual insights into the positive versus the negative stakeholders.

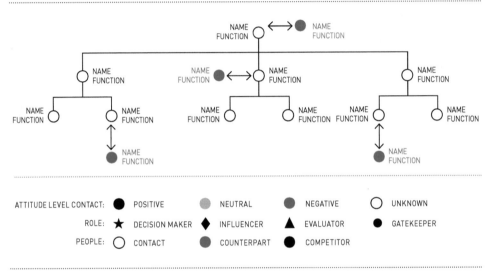

Figure 5.4.1 Example stakeholder mapping

A Stakeholder Map can be helpful in identifying who within the stakeholder entity currently has a positive or negative attitude towards your organization and who is still unknown. As such the Stakeholder Map ideally goes beyond the mapping of organizations to the individual level within the stakeholder organizations—after all, organizations are made up of individuals and individuals have opinions that can be influenced.

Each individual in the organization can be assigned a role; is the person a gatekeeper, an evaluator, an influencer, or a decision maker? Gatekeepers could be assistants who might not have a high-ranking role in the organization, but who are very important in achieving access to key decision makers. Similarly, decision makers could ask evaluators for their opinion in which case the evaluators also ought to be positive towards the strategic ambition defined.

Role	Symbol	Description
Decision maker	★	Person who takes the final decision
Influencer	◆	Member of a decision making unit who influences the decision but is himself not a decision maker. Influences have different degrees of influence dependent on the topic and their relative status in the organization.
Evaluator	▲	An expert within the organization who assesses the content/methodology/quality/price of the proposition.
Gatekeeper	●	Member of a decision making unit who can simulate or frustrate a decision by controlling information or access to key individuals.

Figure 5.4.2 Stakeholder roles

5.5 Stakeholder relationship management

The analyses and mapping described in 5.2, 5.3, and 5.4 can lead to the identification of key actions or events that will help the organization achieve its strategic ambitions. Although the stakeholder analyses can be complex at times, particularly when there are many and diverse stakeholders, in essence the analyses lead to a hypothesis that defines:

·   The current attitude of the stakeholder.
·   The desired attitude of the stakeholder.
·   The identified opportunity.
·   The action concluded to bring the stakeholder from the current to
    the desired attitude.

These steps can be managed with CRM software programs but sometimes a simple overview can be sufficiently transparent and insightful.

Contact	Scope of role	Current attitude	Desired attitude	Opportunity	Action/event
Mr. West	●	●	O	Improve relation	

ATTITUDE LEVEL CONTACT: O POSITIVE   ● NEUTRAL   ● NEGATIVE   O UNKNOWN

ROLE: ★ DECISION MAKER   ◆ INFLUENCER   ▲ EVALUATOR   ● GATEKEEPER

Figure 5.5.1 Stakeholder relationship management overview

The overview of stakeholders and the plan for the related actions and/or events are the essence of the Stakeholder Relationship Management Plan. The overview provides the basis on which the objectives can be defined and results of the actions can be evaluated.

To provide for efficiency, an event can be organized to address several stakeholders at the same time. An event creates the opportunity for a high number of staged encounters in a short time frame. The stakeholders attending the event might have very different opportunities defined. If so, the event is merely the vehicle for establishing contact and conveying key content to the stakeholders. The treatment of the stakeholders during the event, however, can be different to address the specific opportunities identified. A differentiated treatment is the conclusion of the stakeholder analyses and the stakeholder mapping. How the differentiated treatment can be staged during the event will be further described in the last part of this book.

In summary, key elements of successful stakeholder management are:

1. Know your target stakeholders
A solid understanding of your target stakeholders is required for successful relationship management. Collect information to better understand what the perception and context of the stakeholder is, what his or her current attitude is, what the key influencers to the stakeholders are, and what the relevant key topics of importance are.

2. Know your enemies
Do not underestimate the potential of your enemies to influence the outcome or an important decision. Collect insights of non-supporters and explore their relationship and influence abilities.

3. Understand the impact on allies
Understand how your allies are being impacted if they help influence your stakeholders and your organization achieve its strategic ambition. Ensure that they also benefit.

5.6   Customer as relationship echelons

Customers are in essence a specific stakeholder and therefore a relationship echelon. After all, they have an interest in the company performing well and they contribute to its success by paying the bills. Customers are fundamental to the long-term sustainable success of organizations.

For social-profit organizations, customers could be considered those using the services provided. They provide a reason for the organization's existence ("serving a social need"). It is very likely these users will evaluate the performance of the organization directly (for example, by providing feedback) or indirectly (by going to a different supplier).

In the case of for-profit organizations, customers provide revenues and profitability via the exchange of goods, services, or experience. With the revenues received, the organization can invest, improve the proposition, and achieve its strategic ambition. Segmentation forms the basis for differentiating services and attention in order to balance the Return-on-Relationship; the value provided **to** the stakeholder against the value received from the stakeholder.

> Segmentation forms the basis for differentiating services and relationship attention in order to balance the Return-on-Relationship.

When customers are positioned together based on their profile or level of importance, we refer to them as echelons or segments. Customer segmentation addresses three fundamental questions for a Relationship Management Strategy:

1. **Who should we serve?** An organization has a limit to its resources, so investments need to be prioritized; what customer relationship provides the best opportunity for a Return-on-Relationship?
2. **What should we offer them?** What propositions should we offer the prioritized echelons? What type of event would they be triggered by?
3. **How should we serve them?** How best to reach the target customers? What messages or content would be most appealing to them?

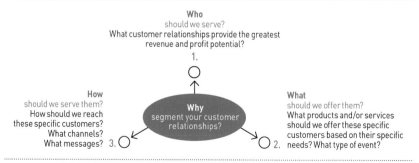

Figure 5.6.1 Customer segmentation

5.7 Customer segmentation criteria

There are multiple criteria to use in segmenting customers. The most obvious is business customers (Business-to-Business: B2B) versus individual customers (Business-to-Consumer: B2C). Within the business or the consumer segment, different segmentation criteria are available.

Demographic segmentation	Attitudinal segmentation	Behavioral segmentation	Number of account(s) segmentation
• Gender	• Image	• Programs watched	• Individual accounts
• Age	• Values	• Pay per view usage	• Family accounts
• Income	• Lifestyle	• Tenure	• Small businesses
• Occupation		• Switching behavior	• Medium businesses
• Education			• Large businesses
• Marital status			

Reason for usage segmentation	Geographical segmentation	Customer profitability segmentation	Decision roles
• Education (school)	• Urban vs. rural area	• High profitability	• Initiator
• Personal research	• Region	• Medium profitability	• Influences
• Business		• Low profitability	• Decider
		• Negative profitabiliy	• Buyer
			• User

Figure 5.7.1 Segmentation criteria

The multiple bases for segmentation as seen in Figure 5.7.1 show different relevant usage for relationship management. Demographic segmentation can be very actionable as generally it is feasible to identify the age or gender in a database. Attitudinal segmentation can possibly be more meaningful and therefore have a larger impact when addressed well. As we have seen in Section 5.5, using decision roles can be effective in complex network relationships or in Decision Making Units such as in the pharmaceutical industry (with academic hospitals, general practitioners, and pharmacists working together in following a patient diagnoses and treatment protocol).

Two elements define successful segmentation criteria for relationship management; actionability and meaningfulness.

Actionability
The criteria need to be actionable. If segmentation criteria are not observable and measurable, it is impossible to use them as a basis for a Relationship Management Strategy. After all, the segmentation criteria must create a cluster of customers that the organization can easily identify, target, and treat as an echelon.

Meaningfulness

The criteria need to be meaningful. It ought to be discriminating and predictive to serve as valuable investment criteria for relationship management. After all, the segmentation criteria must create a cluster of customers that is different in behavior and in motivations to allow for an impactful stakeholder treatment.

By plotting the different potential Actionable and Meaningful criteria in a matrix, the criteria with the biggest potential for serving as a basis for customer segmentation are identified in the area of "highly actionable" and "highly meaningful." On the basis of these criteria a final segmentation frame can be developed.

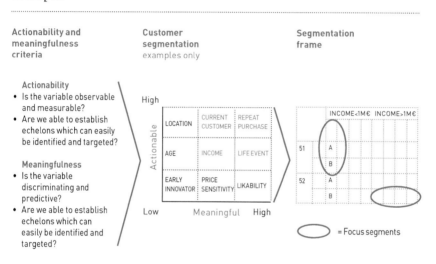

Figure 5.7.2 Action segmentation[4]

The segmentation frame will apply the segmentation criteria to the customer base and bucket the customers into relevant clusters.

5.8   Segment of one

Although the above description of customer segmentation might seem sophisticated, technology has moved on and, in some instances, now allows for a "segment of one". The foundation for segment-of-one targeting is the ability to track and understand individual customer behavior. Thanks to the expansion of data capture opportunities and lower storage costs, such databases are already cost-effective on a large scale. Indeed, technology is now far ahead of the imagination of many Managers of the Network.

The technology that facilitates a segment-of-one approach combines many customer data elements (such as age and income level) with channel data (attended which events), contextual data (internet pages visited) and usage data (previous purchases). Via sophisticated analytical techniques such as cognitive robotics or artificial intelligence, combinations are identified in nanoseconds. On this basis, each individual customer can be served in the most appropriate way as indicated by the system.

Companies such as Netflix, Spotify, Citibank, and Google already use analytical techniques that allow for a segment-of-one approach. As an example, the banner advertising I see when I navigate through Google is different than what is presented to my colleague navigating on the same search terms. In nanoseconds Google has identified my profile, predicted my needs, and served me with an advertising banner on which I am most likely to click.

Relationship management has always been about building personal connections to the benefit of the larger organization. In future, it is likely that technology will support relationship management to increase its efficiency and effectiveness. Technology will also allow for a broader involvement of employees in relationship management. Already personal assistant robots are being developed that can analyze multiple data elements to deliver a personalized response. It could well be that in the very near future you will call a service center and get into a live personal conversation with a software program. It requires little imagination to foresee a future in which a robot is the Manager of the Network's best assistant. Or, as described in the movie Her,[5] we might develop personal relationships with intelligent computer operating systems.

It requires little imagination to foresee a future where a robot is the Manager of the Network's best assistant.

Photo 5.8 Meet Pepper by Softbank Robotics[6]

> **Meet Pepper**
>
> Pepper is a human-shaped robot. During interactions, Pepper analyzes facial expressions, body language, and verbal cues, honing his responses and offering a dynamic and surprisingly natural conversation partner. To date, more than 140 SoftBank Mobile stores in Japan are using Pepper as a new way of welcoming, informing, and amusing their customers. Pepper also recently became the first humanoid robot to be adopted in Japanese homes.[7]

5.9   Differentiating stakeholder treatment

Once all the analyses on segmentation are completed, how to differentiate the treatment of stakeholders to achieve the optimal mutually beneficial relationship? Bill Price, former Global VP of Customer Service at Amazon, created the pragmatic Value/Irritant matrix as a way for companies to manage their customer contact. The matrix triggers the question whether the value you receive from relationships is in balance with the value you bring to the relationship.

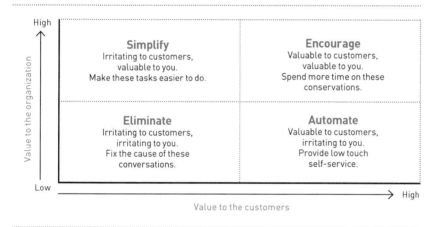

Figure 5.9.1 Value/Irritant matrix[8]

In this matrix, we can see four categories of differentiated treatment:

Eliminate

If no (potential) value is derived from the relationship and no value is provided to the relationship, most likely this activity is not worth investing in. This category of contact should be reduced as much as possible by redesigning the process. This category should move to low-cost relationship activities when they occur. As an example, when customers in this category approach the organization, you might want to refer them to the Internet where information can be downloaded.

Automate

When a lot is invested in the relationship but the value derived is limited, one can consider increasing the efficiency of the delivery of your services. Instead of personalized treatment, you might want to invite these stakeholders to large-scale events. Or instead of visiting these stakeholders in person, you might consider sending them email updates.

Simplify

When the organization derives significant value from the relationship while the investments are minor, you could consider simplifying access to your organization. These are important relationships but they are not getting your proportional attention! It could be that these relationships are currently happy with the low level of attention they receive, but what if a competitor approaches them with a fantastic invitation? These are important relationships for the organization, but you run the risk losing of them as they most likely currently get insufficient attention. You could consider approaching these stakeholders proactively to make them aware of the services available to them or provide them with a direct phone number for your executives.

Encourage

In this part of the matrix, the value to the relationship is in balance with the value from the relationship. These are customer contacts you want to encourage. These treatments ought to be in scope for important relationship events. Maybe providing them with even more attention might lead to even more value!

The Value/Irritant matrix has another level – it can also be applied to the different services offered as part of the relationship approach. As an example, some specific stakeholder encounters might not be appreciated by guests. These encounters would fall into the category **eliminate** and effort ought to be made to reduce these encounters; few stakeholders will appreciate an invitation that contains a lengthy explanation about the logistics of an event. Instead, invitees can be offered a download of an app that will tailor their logistics individually, at the location, and can be used at the convenience of the guest, thereby eliminating the written information on logistics in the invitation.

On the other hand, some encounters might be much appreciated and these ought to be **encouraged**. An encounter with the host of the event could be one of those. If so, the program of the event ought to make it easy for the host to meet as many invitees as possible and maybe even frame the encounter by taking a personal photo.

The Value/Irritant matrix is a simple version of differentiating stakeholder treatment. When moving to a segment of one, more sophisticated treatments become possible frequently called Next Best Service or Next Best Action. With these treatment approaches next steps are defined based on previous behavior. As an example, when a stakeholder has visited an important event where he or she has personally met the host, a Next Best Service could be to send a photo of the encounter with a personal note from the host as a follow-up as soon as the stakeholder contacts the organization. This will no doubt strengthen the relationship. However, if the objective of the organization is to raise money for a charity, it could be a good idea to include a request for donations when sending the photo. These forms of Next Best Actions are in larger organizations frequently supported by technology and we will address that topic further in Chapter 8.

Notes

1. Sowden, Rod; Office, Cabinet (August 30, 2011). *Managing successful programmes. Stationery Office.* p. 59.
2. G. Johnson, K. Scholes, R. Whittington, *Exporing Corporate Strategy*, 8th edition, FT Prentice Hall, 2008
3. Aegon Annual Review 2015 - www.aegon.com/Documents/aegon-com/Sitewide/Reports-and-Other-Publications/Annual-reports/2015/Aegon-Annual-Review-2015.pdf
4. Monitor Deloitte, customer strategy
5. *Her*, Warner Brothers, October 13, 2013.
6. Softbank Robotics designs and produces interactive humanoid robots. Its first personal emotional robot was launched in 2014: Pepper.
7. Source: SoftBank robotics, December 2016; www.ald.softbankrobotics.com/en/cool-robots/pepper
8. Price, B., Jaffe D, *The Best Service is No Service*, Josse-Basse, 2011.

6.   Developing a Relationship Management Plan

Once defined, the Relationship Management Strategy needs to be implemented. This can be done based on a Relationship Management Plan. This might seem obvious, but it is no easy task to document the complexity of relationship management in a simple list of activities. In this chapter we will discuss from a practical perspective how relationship management activities are an integral part of the overall activities of the organization. Strong relationships are built across the silos of the organization where the Manager of the Network provides the strategic context and is the orchestrator or facilitator of relationship building and maintenance.

6.1   Cascade of objectives

Establishing a relationship is never an objective in and of itself; each project and every resource invested ought to contribute to a business objective. A Relationship Management Strategy and the related Plan can therefore be considered as parts of a cascade of objectives.

The organization might pursue a strategy to increase sales to existing customers. To achieve this, the company sets up a program called "Loyalty". As one of its components, a loyalty card is introduced. One of the features of the loyalty card is an invitation to a music event where the customers with many loyalty points are treated as VIP customers and meet the CEO of the company.

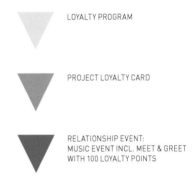

LOYALTY PROGRAM

PROJECT LOYALTY CARD

RELATIONSHIP EVENT:
MUSIC EVENT INCL. MEET & GREET
WITH 100 LOYALTY POINTS

Figure 6.1.1   From program to initiative

As we see here, many different initiatives can be set up within the same program working ultimately on the same strategic objective. On a continuous basis one needs to assess whether the initiatives still contribute to the overall strategic objectives. This underscores the need for the organization to have a shared understanding of the vision and mission of the organization and therefore what the strategic objectives are (see also Chapter 1 and 4).

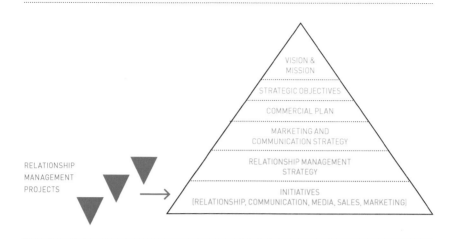

Figure 6.1.2 A cascade of objectives (example)

Relationship projects can therefore be visualized as part of an organizational pyramid of objectives starting with the Networking Vision of the organization which is translated into strategic objectives and a commercial plan. The marketing and communication strategy supports the commercial plan. Similarly, the (Networking Vision and) Relationship Management Strategy supports the marketing and communication strategy.

The above pyramid is only an example. The pyramid can also be defined from a corporate strategy perspective where relationship management might be a cascade of objectives flowing from the strategy of the executive office rather than, as in this example, the marketing and communications strategy.

6.2   Relationship Management Plan

After the Relationship Management Strategy is defined and documented, the conclusions of this strategy form the basis of the Relationship Management Plan. This Relationship Management Plan is ultimately the document that will guide the allocation of resources (time, people, money). Simply stated; "Now, what are we going to do and who will do it?"

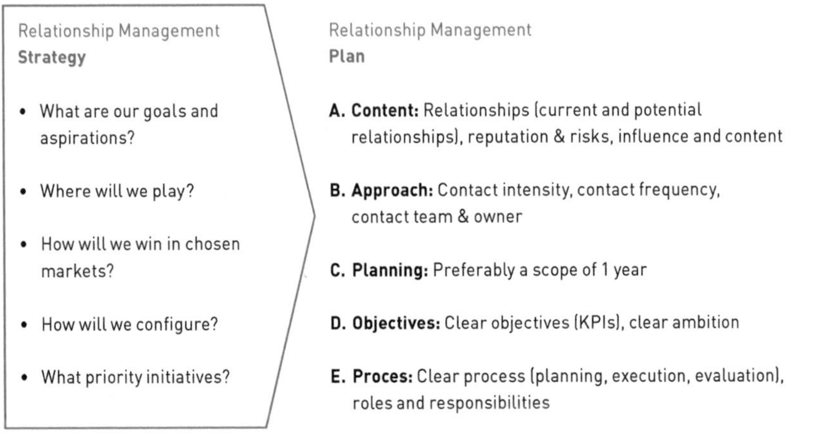

Relationship Management **Strategy**	Relationship Management **Plan**
• What are our goals and aspirations?	**A. Content:** Relationships (current and potential relationships), reputation & risks, influence and content
• Where will we play?	**B. Approach:** Contact intensity, contact frequency, contact team & owner
• How will we win in chosen markets?	**C. Planning:** Preferably a scope of 1 year
• How will we configure?	**D. Objectives:** Clear objectives (KPIs), clear ambition
• What priority initiatives?	**E. Proces:** Clear process (planning, execution, evaluation), roles and responsibilities

Figure 6.2.1 Components of a Relationship Management Plan

The Relationship Management Plan overall consists of:

A. Key **content components** of the plan such as:
    a. What relationships to focus on (Chapter 5).
    b. What reputation to establish, how to establish reciprocity, and what risks to mitigate (Chapter 1, 3, and 4).
    c. What topics have been prioritized to influence and what content of mutual interest to produce or leverage for doing so (Chapter 1 and Chapter 5).

B. What **approach** to follow as an organization to building and strengthening relationships? Elements to consider as part of the approach are:
    a. What contact intensity to adopt. Are the relationships treated on a personal basis or are they primarily contacted via phone or large-scale events?
    b. What contact frequency to adopt. Is an annual event enough or would a monthly contact point be more productive?
    c. The networking team (networkers) and the owner. As part of the plan it needs to be clear who is the relationship owner and who is on the team with which the owner will build or deepen the relationship (Chapter 10).

C. The **initiatives** to be **planned** in a timeline to allow for optimal allocation of available resources and communication to others. Ideally the plan is linked to the overall planning calendar of the organization. Although a strategic plan might have a horizon of three years or longer, considering the dynamics of relationship management, stakeholders will change jobs or attitudes, thus a one-year plan is often more practical.

D. **Clear objectives** defined to provide focus on the activities and assess their success. These ideally are in the form of Key Performance Indicators (KPIs); these will be further explained in Chapter 9.

E. To avoid crisis management or impulsive allocation of resources, a predefined **process and governance** for relationship management should be documented in the plan. This allows for more focus and sharing of materials as the process will align the various activities. At its highest level, the process has three phases: i) planning of initiatives; ii) execution or delivery of the activities and iii) evaluation of the initiatives to serve as input for the planning. As part of this process it is beneficial to identify upfront the roles and responsibilities of the individuals involved in relationship management.

A structured way of providing input to the relationship management activities is to funnel from a broad perspective (value areas and echelons) to the individual level profiles and related initiatives. This approach ensures that the strategic criteria applied to identify value areas and priority echelons are translated to the individual level. This approach also facilitates a level of concreteness as the networker in the organization will relate to the identified individual stakeholder, while the Manager of the Network has the overview to orchestrate the bigger–relationship–picture.

A. Define focus echelons						
Strategic Relation Management Plan	A. Relationship echelons		B. Echelon profiles			
Value area	Relationship echelons	Name	Category	Objective	Order winner	

↓

B. Identify relationship profiles						
C. Individual relation profiles						
Key individual	Organization contact pers.	Level (operational, medium, top)	Impact on the organization	Reputation	Individual objective	Order winner

↓

C. Plan relationship activities	
D. Relationship action	
Contact intensity	Initiatives

Figure 6.2.2 Funneling from focus echelons to relationship initiatives

The networker in the organization will relate to the individual relations identified while the Manager of the Network has the overview to orchestrate the bigger relationship picture.

After completing the required homework to develop a Relationship Management Strategy, the Relationship Management Plan is now a very systematic approach to organizing contact management. It can be visualized as in Figure 6.2.3

Strategy	Relationship strategy	Initiative
Reduce the cost of distribution.	Improve relationships with suppliers by jointly investing in digital initiatives to reduce costs across the supply chain network.	Organize an event on 'Opportunities of the digital supply chain in our industry'.

↓

Relation	Importance	Our reputation	Category
Jensen	Significant	Negative	Category A

↓

Relation	Contact intensity	Contact frequency	Contact owner (networker)
Category A	Executive level Management level Operational level	2x year executive 6x year management 12x year operational	Mr. Kramer
Category B	Management level Operational level	4x year management 24x year operational	Mrs. Jacobovits
Category C	Operational level	24x year operational	Mr. Punit

Figure 6.2.3 Example relationship management contact planning

In Figure 6.2.3 the overall strategy, the Relationship Management Strategy, and specific initiatives have been defined and serve as input for the Relationship Management Plan. On the second layer we detail one relationship as it is currently; Mr. Jensen is a "significant"–important– stakeholder but unfortunately our reputation with Mr. Jensen is negative. Considering the type of stakeholder he is, he is categorized as an A stakeholder. In the third layer, we see that A customers are treated with the most executive attention; twice a year an executive encounter is scheduled, six times a year management contact is staged, and on a monthly basis operational contact is sought. Most likely in this situation the executive contacts benefit from the other contacts held prior, so these encounters can be very productive in strengthening the relationship and improving our reputation with Mr. Jensen. Mr. Kramer is the overall contact owner for category A contacts. As can be seen in Figure 6.2.3 each category is treated with a different contact frequency and intensity.

Figure 6.2.3 is a simplified example of a **Relationship Management Contact Plan**. But we can see that multiple contacts take place at various levels to build strong relationships. This requires a systematic approach which can be supported by an excel spreadsheet. However, as the organization becomes more complex, as the number of relationships increases, or as the importance given to relationship management increases, an investment in Customer Relationship Management (CRM) software might be worthwhile (see also Chapter 9).

Ultimately the Relationship Management Plan is constrained by one common factor across the organization; time. Therefore, a practical template for documenting the Relationship Management Plan is a simple Gantt chart as seen here in Figure 6.2.4.

Relationship Management Plan		2019 TARGETS	TRAFFIC LIGHTS	Q1					
				JAN		FEB		MARCH	
				PLAN	ACTUAL	PLAN	ACTUAL	PLAN	ACTUAL
Objective 1:	1. Number of ...								
Objective 2:	2. Number of ...								
Objective 3:	3. Number of ...								
Objective 4:	4. % of ...								
Objective 5:	5. Number of ...								
TOTAL BUDGET									
BUDGET	KEY ACTIVITIES								
	CAMPAIGNS								
	EVENTS								
	DIGITAL INITIATIVES								
	REGIONAL ACTIVITIES								
	RELATIONSHIPS ECHELON SPECIFIC ACTIVITIES								
	ONGOING PROGRAMS								
	OTHER								

Figure 6.2.4 Example Relationship Management Plan

Public sector Strategic Relationship Management - The Municipality of Antwerp's story of facilitating benefits for the community

by Tom Verbelen, Director Municipality of Antwerp

Strategic Relationship Management and governance

Are strategic relations and their management for the public sphere a working combination? Is it a task of the government to build and maintain strategic relations? To obtain what type of profit exactly? These questions could arise in the public debate on the core business of governments. The integrity of leaders is often the center of attention.

Strategic Relationship Management and development of a network of contacts for governmental purposes does not seem at first glance to be something of direct benefit. This is different from a commercial environment where the contacts often lead to a direct result in extra commercial orders, more sales, or a higher profit. However, there is "no role in a lean and mean government organization for a wide range of strategic relations", as we hear often, because it could raise questions in the press or from the opposition about integrity issues or misconduct with taxpayer money, or obscure lobbying work with a negative impact on democratic transparency.

I consider the contrary to be true. Maintaining relations is part of the very existence of public officials. A democratic government is forced to communicate and build relationships to achieve its communal goals. On a national level, it is obvious how international relations are organized – a ministry of foreign affairs manages the contacts with other countries and international organizations. The diplomatic world is a perfect example of Strategic Relationship Management for governments. It covers many of the features that define the know-how of relationship management; building long-term relations, communicating with stakeholders who have an interest in the matter, having a certain goal in the objective and personal attention by a stable representative (the network of ambassadors, embassy staff).

On a national level, governments are constantly seeking coalitions or partnerships to rule a country or act on a supranational level (such as EU networks), both with internal and external stakeholders. The techniques of relationship management apply brilliantly to this ecosystem.

The angles become more complex when looking at it from a local perspective. This complexity is not only within the system and boundaries of the governmental levels – nowadays, in a globalized world, keeping relationships and maintaining international contacts is also fashionable. The volume of incoming visits of cities, provinces, and regions, and outbound initiatives (of Flemish and Dutch) provinces and regions has grown substantially. Most of them focus on specific domains such as economic growth or foreign aid for development cooperation.

In general, balances in international relations are shifting. Pressure on national identity in a continuously globalizing world, the future, and leading positions of supranational levels are uncertain; for example, Britain leaving the EU (Brexit).

On a local level, the role and importance of cities and metropolitan areas are growing. More people live in urban areas; in 2014 54 percent of the world population was living in cities, while in 1950 it was only 30 percent and estimates are that by 2030 60 percent and by 2050 nearly 70 percent will live in cities. *Homo urbanus* is a fact! In literature, this effect was first picked up by Jane Jacobs in *Death and Life of Great American Cities*; more recently Benjamin R. Barber talked about the effects in his book *If Mayors Ruled the World: Dysfunctional Nations, Rising Cities.*[1] This growing population and the related importance of cities' impact has a significant influence on the way a government must cope with its relationship management. But it seems that the transparency and the strategic approach of a well-structured and inclusive relationship management is not common.

The Antwerp approach
Antwerp is Belgium's second largest city (beta city). It is a pocket-sized metropolis of 205 square kilometers, with approximately 550,000 inhabitants of 175 nationalities. The city is the international leader in the diamond trade, it is one of Europe's main ports, and Antwerp is inextricably connected to fashion.

Antwerp relationship management
In previous decades, Antwerp's relationships were built around declarations and memoranda of understanding, in temporary sister-cities relationships, and were based on representation in European and international networks to obtain subsidies for city development programs. In 2013, new legislation created the opportunity to rethink the strategic approach of our external relations and a new department was reinforced. The crux of the idea was to define measurable added value for Antwerp.

On an organizational level, we chose a mild form – evolution instead of revolution in the centralization of the means, contacts, and knowledge. Between 2013 and today, different modifications have been put in place, and the structure has been updated several times. As in a modern approach to Strategic Relationship Management, this type of process is in my opinion a normal one. Just like society itself, government relations are subject to evolution and must adapt to current affairs, so agility is important to the success of Strategic Relationship Management.

For government organizations, international (external) relationship policy and management are not always a matter of marketing and sales, although image building and positioning are important concerns. There is not a highly output-oriented goal. Strategic Relationship Management for government organizations is meant to use their core value to create long-term commitments and stable relationships where sharing and the exchange of (negative) messages as well as the seeking of positive and project-based collaboration are made possible. It is an extension of the administrative force.

Starting in 2013 some assumptions were made:

The **perception of Antwerp** in its relations varies by time and distance. The closer to the center of the city, the more knowledgeable relations are about our identity; on a national, European, or global level, Antwerp's image is more vague. As a metaphor, we use a pebble thrown in a pond; it causes the water to ripple and the circles to widen as the distance grows. We can use this as an advantage when we work together to take partners and Antwerp stakeholders along in our international relations.

I have **defined stakeholders and partners**, where partners are other governments or related organizations with whom we interact and stakeholders are the largest-scale of the organizations (private and NGOs) that have an interest in Antwerp. Both stakeholders and partners play a crucial role in the development of relationships for the city actions we take; for example, they contribute substantially to the city's annual international mission, one of our main products.

We **manage and update data on our contacts**; we introduced a central IT system to register information about stakeholders, contacts, etc. This is crucial for us to be able to organize personalized and accurate follow-ups.

In its strategic translation, the Municipality of Antwerp formulated the following mission statement for its external relationship management:

International and external relations management is one of the objectives of a well-organized city framework. The Municipality of Antwerp is committed to good and trusted long-term relationships with external stakeholders, to the well-being and prosperity of its residents, visitors, businesses, and our knowledge and creativity ecosystem – in short, the Antwerp community.

The use of Antwerp's physical and mental opportunities, the physical assets of our location, especially the creative city of fashion and diamonds, innovative city of start-ups and digitalization, *city-to-stream with a world port and metropolis on a human scale, lead to more synergy and trust with our partners. External relations management means conveniently connecting to these partners and using this connection to strengthen ties and organize ongoing follow-up.*

An evaluation was made after three years of external relationship management experience, and the results were positive. It concluded that with the use of the RACI model,[2] instruments we were using were functioning adequately and we will continue on this path (time and context).

Different products to operationalize relationship management were developed:

An annual **city mission** led by the mayor: a broad-based delegation of participants – stakeholders and Antwerp companies and organizations – undertakes a mission to a relevant city or set of cities to learn and exchange a wide range of topics with a city-oriented interest. This product is a high-scale example of a multi-layered form of relationship-building and conduct toward a relevant content.

Working visits: more frequent visits with smaller formal delegations led by a member of the board of mayor and aldermen, focused on a modest set of policy themes.

As follow-up to both of these visits, we organize return visits.

A **diversified diplomatic approach**: we organize several annual events for diplomatic representatives. Some focus more on the promotional level of the qualities of the Municipality of Antwerp, others on substantively ad-hoc exchange with heads of missions. We make sure we have an approachable board and administrative delegation.

Apart from stakeholders and partners, we build and maintain a **network of partner cities**; on the basis of an acquisition profile, Antwerp seeks collaboration with cities (both European and global) with which specific programs and memoranda of understanding are developed.

In the future these general products, which were mainly developed as an overlay, will be supplemented with a more internal and detailed scheme of strategic implementation plans for every department of the city's administration.

Notes

1. https://yalebooks.yale.edu/book/9780300209327/if-mayors-ruled-world
2. RACI is an acronym derived from the four key responsibilities most typically used: Responsible, Accountable, Consulted, and Informed. A responsibility assignment matrix.

7.   Relationship Management Capabilities

The complexity of managing relationships is increasing rapidly as more relationships are generated and they mutually reinforce each other. For an individual to manage a personal relationship, skills and the right attitude are required. For an organization to manage the complexities of multiple relationships, capabilities are required in addition. The critical capabilities required for effective relationship management are described in this chapter.

First we will cover the data management capability. Data allows the organization to steer, monitor, and improve relationship building. Having the ability to collect relevant data, draw insights from the data, and act upon those insights is a valuable capability allowing the organization to effectively develop relevant relationships with stakeholders.

As concluded previously in paragraph 1.12, to build trust in the relationship it is important to deliver on commitments made and be consistent in communication to stakeholders. However, when managing multiple (communication) channels it can be challenging for the organization to ensure consistency let alone allocate the best message to the most appropriate communication channel. Therefore, omnichannel management is included in this chapter as a key relationship management capability.

Lastly, as reputation is a fundamental building block for establishing sustainable relationships, the capability of managing communication and media is briefly discussed. In the last paragraph we provide examples of how to strenthen relationships via earned media versus paid or owned media.

7.1   Data management

At a Tourism and Travel event, a journalist told the story of his visit to a boutique hotel in the Sahara Desert. It was a small hotel, not part of one of the larger hotel chains, and would occasionally be visited by international guests although it catered primarily to the local market. When he stepped out of the taxi, the bellboy took care of the luggage. The journalist approached the reception desk and, when he gave his name, the journalist was warmly welcomed "Ah, Mr. Baker, welcome back to our hotel. It is so good to see you back after such a long time!" The journalist, Mr. Baker, was very pleased although also somewhat astounded–he had stayed in the same hotel probably ten years previously. How did this small hotel keep up with his records? They must have a great database. It was only when he turned around to check the whereabouts of his luggage that he understood. He saw the bellboy still standing beside his luggage signaling a thumbs-up to the receptionist. Then Mr. Baker remembered; during the little interchange with the bellboy when taking his luggage out of the taxi, the bellboy had asked whether Mr. Baker had been at the hotel before. He had said something like "Yes, many years ago." The hotel was running a smart script where the bellboy was instructed to inform the receptionist about returning guests. A warm welcome to Mr. Baker!

That is how human interaction and good scripting can provide a very effective (and low cost) form of data management. After all, a critical data point was whether the guest had stayed in the hotel before and this data point was obtained by the bellboy via a cleverly scripted dialogue when welcoming the guest. The data point of the guest having stayed in the hotel before was quickly communicated into an insight (Mr. Baker is a returning visitor) via a thumbs-up to the receptionist. Finally, the receptionist translated the insight into action; "Welcome back, good to see you after such a long time!"

A well-staged encounter is applicable in many sorts of relationship events. Organizations wanting to conduct effective Strategic Relationship Management will need to develop a similar capability in customer data management. As organizations get bigger over time, it becomes more and more challenging to remember all the different visits, preferences, and life events of stakeholders. As relationship management grows into a strategic capability, the stakeholder knowledge itself becomes a strategic asset that ought to be owned by the organization and not be only in the heads of the organization's employees (with the risk the knowledge leaves the organization as employees leave). Lastly, to effectively manage and grow relationships, the organization needs to be relevant. This implies that the organization needs to anticipate the needs and desires of its relations. Data analytics can support the organization in anticipating stakeholder needs and allowing the organization to deliver value to its relationships. Therefore, data management is vital for any organization that wants to implement Strategic Relationship Management.

> Data management is vital for any organization wanting to conduct Strategic Relationship Management.

Consider the amount of relationship data that can be collected and analyzed. Figure 7.1.1 is an illustration; the volume of data quickly becomes large and difficult to navigate.

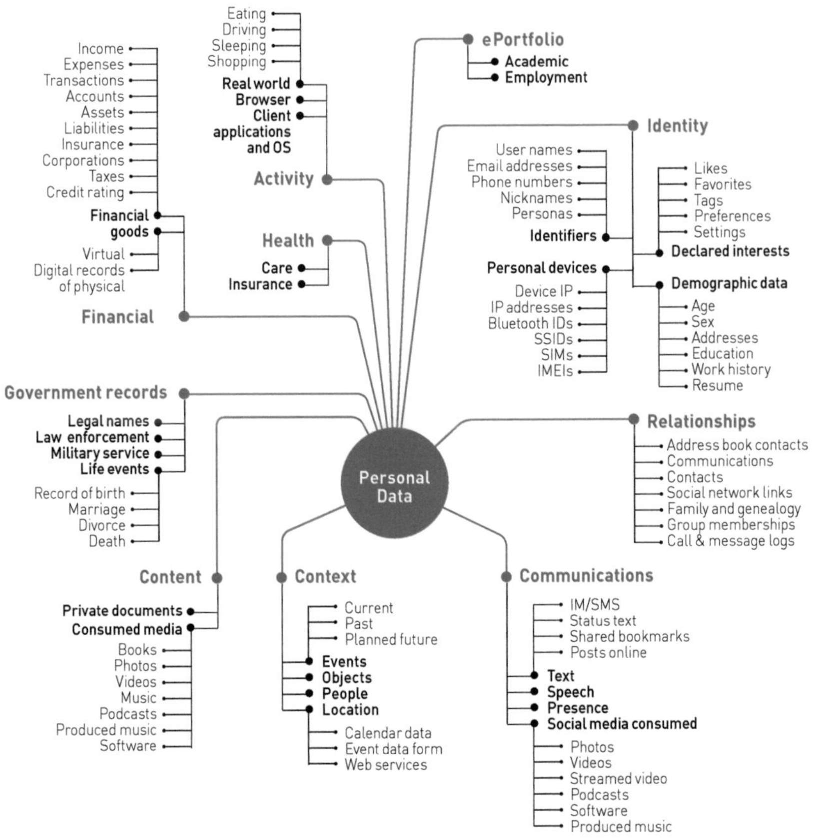

Figure 7.1.1 Types of personal data

Activity
- Eating
- Driving
- Sleeping
- Shopping
- Real world
- Browser
- Client applications and OS

Financial
- Income
- Expenses
- Transactions
- Accounts
- Assets
- Liabilities
- Insurance
- Corporations
- Taxes
- Credit rating
- Financial goods
- Virtual
- Digital records of physical

Health
- Care
- Insurance

ePortfolio
- Academic
- Employment

Identity
- Identifiers
  - User names
  - Email addresses
  - Phone numbers
  - Nicknames
  - Personas
- Declared interests
  - Likes
  - Favorites
  - Tags
  - Preferences
  - Settings
- Personal devices
  - Device IP
  - IP addresses
  - Bluetooth IDs
  - SSIDs
  - SIMs
  - IMEIs
- Demographic data
  - Age
  - Sex
  - Addresses
  - Education
  - Work history
  - Resume

Government records
- Legal names
- Law enforcement
- Military service
- Life events
  - Record of birth
  - Marriage
  - Divorce
  - Death

Relationships
- Address book contacts
- Communications
- Contacts
- Social network links
- Family and genealogy
- Group memberships
- Call & message logs

Content
- Private documents
- Consumed media
  - Books
  - Photos
  - Videos
  - Music
  - Podcasts
  - Produced music
  - Software

Context
- Current
- Past
- Planned future
- Events
- Objects
- People
- Location
  - Calendar data
  - Event data form
  - Web services

Communications
- IM/SMS
- Status text
- Shared bookmarks
- Posts online
- Text
- Speech
- Presence
- Social media consumed
  - Photos
  - Videos
  - Streamed video
  - Podcasts
  - Software
  - Produced music

Data management is a discipline growing in importance and scope. Data management has many different facets of which the following will be described in this paragraph:
- Stakeholder data acquisition.
- Stakeholder data management.
- Stakeholder data analytics.

7.1.1 Stakeholder data acquisition

Before identifying what stakeholder data to collect, it is best to define the purpose of the data first. For example, when serving dinner to stakeholders, it is useful to know whether anyone has any allergies or cannot eat certain dishes for religious reasons. Better even would be to understand your stakeholders' meal preferences to be able to please or surprise them. More broadly, some relationships might be governed by a corporate policy where it is not allowed to accept invitations for events with a ticket value of, say, more than € 65. By knowing these corporate

1. Define key objectives

Questions to address
- What is the strategic ambition?
- What is the relationship strategy?
- What are the key objectives to be achieved?

Example
- Increase the number of "friends" of the organization
- Strengthen the buyin for strategic investments

2. Identify required data elements

Questions to address
- What data can help me be (strategically) relevant?
- What data element provides a predictive value?
- What data helps me build stronger relationships?

Example
- Small life event data (birthdays, new job)
- Key concerns regarding strategic investments

3. Assess available data collection points

Questions to address
- What costumer touchpoints can I use?
- Where can I collect and store the data?
- How can I best aggregate and analyse the data?

Example
- Account managers
- Social media (e.g. LinkedIn)
- Event invitations

4. Define data acquisition strategy

Questions to address
- What data will I structurally collect where?
- What is required to do this?
- How will I translate data analyses to action?

Example
- Data acquisition strategy

5. Define data acquisition strategy

Questions to address
- Execute the activities defined in the data acquisition strategy

Example
- Instructions to account managers
- Investments in data management
- Investments in data analytics

Figure 7.1.2 Steps to develop a data acquisition strategy

policies, one can tag the policy to the individual relationship and ensure he or she will not be invited or has the opportunity to pay for participation. As there is a lot of potential data to collect, it is important to understand upfront what the organization wants to achieve and on what basis the data to be collected can be prioritized (see also Chapter 6). Figure 8.1.2 highlights the steps to take when developing a data acquisition strategy.

On the basis of the defined objectives, it becomes obvious what data can support the objectives. When the objective is to increase the number of "friends" the organization has, it seems relevant to know about small life events; after all, you would expect a friend to say happy birthday on that particular day. Similarly, when a stronger buyin for strategic investments is required from relationships, it seems evident that key concerns regarding the strategic investments should be identified with each relationship, so the relevant follow-up can be set up. Now that it is clear what data is relevant to collect, the logical next step is to identify where to collect the data.

There are multiple data sources. The most relevant are described below:

- **Public data sources**

Relevant data can be retrieved from public sources. As an example, data available from the Chamber of Commerce lists key responsibles at an organization, size of the organization, and addresses. Annual reports provide additional information on profitability, important individuals in the organization, and the strategic objectives of the organization.

- **Web behavior**

Most organizations have websites and other forms of digital communication (social, apps). These platforms can be a rich source of data on stakeholder behavior and preferences. Data on click behavior, stakeholder feedback, or download requests can be collected and inform the organization about stakeholder preferences and opportunities for improvement.

- **Employees of the organization**

Employees who work at customer touchpoints (e.g. Contact Center Agents, Account Managers, Secretaries, Account Receivables/payables, Event hosts) are frequently in touch with stakeholders. The data gathered at a minimum is transactional data (ordering information, confirmation of attendance). In addition, profile data can be collected (meal preferences, areas of interest). However, just like in the story in the introduction of this paragraph about the bellboy, employees of the organization can be instructed to inquire about strategic data of stakeholders (available budget, key concerns, priority setting).

- **Partnerships**

Partnerships with other organizations can provide an opportunity to enrich stakeholder data already available or expand the relationship base. When organizing a charity event with a well-known charity, the relationship base of the charity provides an opportunity to reach out to prospective stakeholders currently not in scope of the organization.

The data acquisition strategy bundles the key findings from the above steps and translates them into an action plan. This is different for each organization and each stage of data maturity, but most likely the following topics will be described in the data acquisition strategy:

1. *Content*
   a. Purpose of the data.
   b. Data elements to collect.
   c. Touchpoints where data is collected.
   d. Data storage and maintenance.
   e. Data analytics and resulting actions.

2. *Support*

   a. Key IT requirements and priorities for capturing, storing, and analyzing the data.

   b. Budget requirements and priorities to support the data acquisition strategy.

   c. HR initiatives and priorities relevant to support the data acquisition strategy.

7.1.2   Stakeholder data management

The stakeholder data collected needs to be stored and maintained; the rule of thumb is that 20 percent of data not regularly maintained is not relevant after one year because contacts change organization, email, or preferences. In addition, data collected at different touchpoints needs to be combined. This data can be contradictory (one touchpoint indicates it is Mr. James while another touchpoint indicates Mrs. James). Therefore, rules need to be established for what touchpoint has priority. Or other means of data quality management need to be put in place, for example, via a so-called golden record which is a data element with the highest priority and known to be true.

As data becomes increasingly important in most organizations, the area of Stakeholder Data Management also takes center stage. Although originally data management was a key responsibility of the IT division, several organizations have elevated the role of data management to a chief data officer who has oversight on the broad spectrum of data management across various disciplines ranging from IT to business divisions.

For the Manager of the Network it is important to be aware of the area of data management to provide relevant input as well as derive sufficient support. Figure 7.1.3 provides an overview of the different components of Enterprise Data Management.

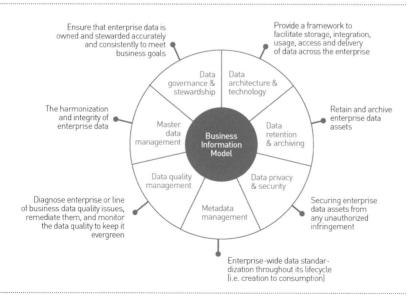

Figure 7.1.3 Enterprise data management areas [1]

The involvement of the Manager of the Network will be important in the area of Data Governance and Data Privacy. The Manager of the Network covers key aspects of customer data where it relates to relational data; therefore, the manager can be assigned a stewardship role as part of the overall data governance. As a data steward, the Manager of the Network ensures the appropriate data is collected, data integrity is protected, and the data is applied in line with the policies of the organization. Data privacy is another area that is likely to become part of the responsibility of the Manager of the Network. Penalties from government agencies for violation of data privacy laws can threaten the survival of the business. The Manager of the Network should be careful not to violate the privacy legislation and industry codes. In practice this implies that as part of the data acquisition strategy, a check must take place concerning the applicable privacy legislation and relevant codes. In addition, when starting a new campaign or sending out invitations for an event, a check concerning the privacy legislation ought to be part of standard procedure.

7.1.3   Stakeholder data analytics

The value of relationship management can be greatly enhanced by applying data analytics. The data collected ought to lead to insights and actions. This implies that the data needs to be analyzed. The receptionist in the hotel anecdote described in the beginning of this chapter used a simple, human form of analytics. When the bellboy gave her a thumbs-up, the analysis conducted led to the insight that the guest has been at this location before, triggering the script "welcome back to this hotel!" This was a reporting form of analytics.

Generally, there are three levels of data analytics that involve an increasing level of volume, velocity, and variety of data. In Figure 7.1.4 the three levels of Stakeholder Data Analytics are described.

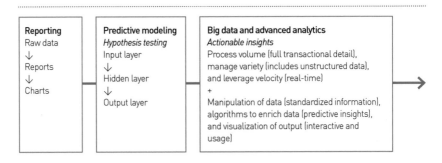

Figure 7.1.4 Increasing levels of sophistication of customer data analytics

Reports are the simplest form of analytics. They could be lists of attendees at an event or reports on the frequency of stakeholders attending a company event in the previous three years. Reports look back on previous actions and as such provide an overview of what happened; they are based on more operational data of limited variety. Although reporting is a straightforward analytics technique, it can be very effective in supporting Strategic Relationship Management. Reports (or dashboards) can provide useful insights into what the relationship priorities ought to be or what the level of investment per relationship has been (concluding the Return-on-Relationship).

Predictive modeling techniques are a more sophisticated form of analysis. This analytics technique combines data and determines a Next Best Action or Next Based Service based on the profile developed. Predictive modeling techniques can be used to determine whether stakeholders are likely to accept an event invitation, the amount they are likely to contribute to a donation event, or to establish what next relationship activities ought to be proposed (Next Best Activity) to strengthen the relationship.

The most sophisticated level of customer data analytics, **advanced analytics**, combines structured data (data which can be clustered such as stakeholder profile data) and unstructured data (data which is not clustered such as voice or visual data). Advanced analytics is used for ambient technology and leads to artificial intelligence useful for operating robotics (drones, chat bots, service robots). Although currently not a common practice in relationship management, it is easy to imagine a future in which service robots will play an important role during events to stage the experience and deliver relevant personalized services (see also 5.8).

7.1.4 Relationship data privacy regulations

Any work on data management in the context of relationship management would not be complete without a word of warning regarding the importance of the privacy of the data of an organization's relations. Considering most regions have their own data privacy regulations, it is impossible to elaborate on all legislation in this book. However, the basic rule always is to only collect, store, and use data for which the contact has given his or her (prior) consent. In addition, an additional benchmark always is to look into the mirror and ask yourself whether you would appreciate another organization collecting, storing, and using similar data about *you*. Or your children.

Although each region has its own regulations about privacy, it is useful to take the European General Data Protection Regulation (GDPR), introduced in May 2018, as a proxy. GDPR encompasses all organizations and their staff members in Europe, Iceland, Lichtenstein, and Norway. In addition, non-EU businesses working with EU citizen or employee data within the EU zone (via branch offices) must be compliant with GDPR regulations. The GDPR regulation is in many aspects more stringent than the regulations that apply in the USA and in many other countries. Acting in line with the GDPR therefore allows your organization to operate in the

European Union and is a good indication whether the organization is likely to be in compliance with relationship data privacy rules in other regions.

The objective of the GDPR is to better protect personal data and to prevent abuse of personal data. GDPR serves to ultimately create a safe environment (digital and otherwise) in which handling of personal data is governed by strict standards. Each individual in an organization must handle relationship data with great care. A failure to comply with GDPR comes at a hefty price; the penalty is 2–4 percent of an organization's worldwide revenues, never mind the considerable reputational damage your organization will then incur. The regulation involves the use of all data that can be traced back to personal data (relationship and staff details) as well as keeping this data in a central, secure environment. Relationship managers and members of the relationship staff are responsible for accepting, using, keeping, and protecting personal data. Examples of data that GDPR considers personal are names, addresses, dates of birth, and email addresses. Other data, too, is included if this can be traced to individual persons. This includes IP addresses, client numbers, and other information.

Dos and Don'ts of GDPR

GDPR is an elaborate piece of legislation and requires detailed study and an assessment of the internal practices regarding relationship data management to ensure the organization is fully compliant. However, there are some clear dos and don'ts that can be helpful as a start in case of doubt. They are listed below.

DOS	DON'TS
Data minimization Only collect and process data that is absolutely necessary for the purpose of the activity. Avoid using a unique identifier as much as possible.	Don't collect all kinds of data because it might facilitate the relationship. You are responsible as soon as you accept the data and thus, liable for everything that happens with it.
Controlled processing environment Save privacy data in secured archiving systems.	Avoid saving data on your own hard drive. You're not only responsible for the usage of the data but also for the storage.
Deleting data Make sure that relationship data is deleted as soon as the data has served its purpose.	Don't keep confidential relationship data when the activity for which the data was collected has ended. Keep as little data as possible and remove anything that you don't need.
Incident reporting Report a data breach incident immediately inside your organization so appropriate measures can be taken.	Don't ignore an incident when it happens. It won't resolve itself.
Minimize printouts / downloads Use online dashboards and tools instead of local files and printouts.	Don't print or download all kinds of documents when you don't absolutely need them.

Figure 7.1.5 Dos and don'ts of GDPR

One of the steps GDPR requires, before one is allowed to send relationships commercial communications, is to obtain demonstrable consent ("opt-in"). These opt-ins must be registered, too. An organization must always be able to show how these opt-ins have been collected, so their legal validity can be proven.

Dear Madam/Sir,

As a valued friend of our organization, your personal data is processed in a database controlled by us. This database allows us to keep up-to-date contact details and, as we are keen to share our knowledge with you, to keep you up to date on legal developments relevant to you via newsletters and the like.

In view of the entry into force of the EU General Data Protection Regulation 2016/679 (*GDPR*) on 25 May 2018, we as "data controller" take the opportunity to update the information about the personal data that we process in this respect. Furthermore, in accordance with applicable e-privacy laws, we may only process your data if you have consented thereto. With this email, we are seeking your consent.

Your personal data processed by us may include your name, gender, postal address, email address, phone number, language preference, job title, function, information about the sector you work in, your jurisdiction of interest, reports of our contacts with you, and mailing lists. We do not distribute this data to third parties, except where explicitly permitted by the new rules (for example, in order to enable suppliers to maintain the database). The sharing of personal data with our office is subject to the EU Commission's standard contractual clauses.

Under the GDPR you have the right to know what personal data we collect and store, and you may request a copy at any time and/or receive this information in a commonly used format. You are also entitled to have personal data corrected, you may request us to delete your personal data, and/or you can object to certain personal data being used or, where applicable, ask us to restrict the processing of personal data. You further have the right to lodge a complaint with the competent supervisory data protection authority.

By clicking the Consent button below, we will register your consent to our collecting and storing your personal data and you can change your preferences. We will store your personal data until your consent is explicitly withdrawn in writing. Please keep in mind that limiting or deleting your personal data might result in us being unable to send you any business related information

Consent   Withdraw Consent

Of course, we hope that you give us your consent, so that we can continue to add value to your business.

Figure 7.1.6 GDPR consent template

Impact of gdpr on the relationship manager

GDPR distinguishes two roles related to the collection, processing, and use of personal data; the Data Controller and the Data Processor. As a Manager of the Network or an event's organizer within your organization, you would be designated as the Data Controller. You decide and are responsible for communicating the purpose for which you are collecting personal data from attendees, speakers, and any other event participants. If you outsource the event registration to a technology provider, the technology provider would be considered the Data Processor in the context of your business relationship.

This paragraph should not be seen as a substitute for legal advice. But it is useful to understand the impact on Relationship Management on the basis of the areas described below:

- **Know where your contact data originates.** Many relationship managers do not know what the origins are of the relationship contact data. It might come from previous events, business cards collected, or purchased email lists. Under GDPR this is no longer acceptable–the Data Controller is required to have the origination of the data documented and should be able to prove that the people in your database have opted in to have their information stored and used by you.

- **Collect relationship contact data with clear consent.** GDPR requires that requests for consent "must be given in an intelligible and easily accessible form, with the purpose for data processing attached to that consent." It is therefore required to have an upfront understanding of what the data is going to be used for. In addition, the format of collecting the data (such as via registration portals or website) should allow for contacts to opt in or opt out.

- **A privacy policy available.** Any organization is required to have a privacy policy and a privacy notice. Your relationship management's privacy policy is a document that tells your team how they should handle the personal data you have collected. In contrast, a privacy notice is the document you share with your relationships that informs them what personal data you are collecting and why.

- **Ensure a data secure practice in your organization.** Most likely many employees in your organization work with personal data and all employees ought to know how to approach the collection and use of personal data moving forward. Also it is required to define in advance with your employees how to respond to any potential data breach or requests for access to data or data deletion. Some simple examples to illustrate the impact on day-to-day activities:

  - *Sending out emails.* When sending out emails to multiple relationship contacts, the email addresses should not be typed into the To: space. After all, when sending the email to multiple people they will be able to identify the email addresses of the other people you have mailed. GDPR would consider this a data breach. Therefore, emails to multiple contacts should always be sent via the BCC: box so no one can see the other recipients.

– *Using Excel.* GDPR prohibits individuals from using Excel to store personal data or other confidential data that is shared with others. The sole exception to this is your personal work file, for which you are still allowed to use Excel. Sharing with other colleagues is not an option, as this is contrary to GDPR. And, last but not least, an important addition; an Excel file should be deleted as soon as you no longer need it. Excel does not meet the GDPR requirements such as i) avoiding duplicates ii) setting authorizations to access the data; iii) central storage of data; iv) monitoring the data and deleting it after it has been used or when the retention period has expired.

– *Acquire consent before taking photos.* You might want to take photos during an event which will be shared with others, for example on your website. You will need to have upfront consent for taking photos of individuals at the event. In this case best to request this consent when people sign up for the event.

· **Working with outsourcing partners or technology providers.** As a Data Controller, you are responsible for providing guidelines to Data Processors, generally your external partners. Therefore, you will want to validate with them whether your partners are able to:

– Publish your privacy notice.

– Enable you to collect consent to use personal data.

– Document that consent to use personal data.

– Allow participants to control that consent over time.

– Respond in a timely manner to requests for data access.

– Act on requests for data rectification or destruction.

– Demonstrate that they hold and process your participants' data securely.

After reading paragraph 7.1.4 it is understandable that you might feel like all your investments in building a relationship database are at stake. And indeed most likely your contact list will shrink significantly as a result of GDPR. However, please also consider the upside:

– There will be less waste in your customer database. The contacts that remain in your database have explicitly given their consent and are open to deepening the relationship.

– Across the organization there is an increased attention to the value and risks of relationship data. This can strengthen the (strategic) position of the relationship manager.

– Practices giving a bad reputation to relationship management, such as spam or superficial contact attempts, will be reduced. GDPR will bring a new level of professionalism to relationship management and enhance the quality of the profession as well as of relationships overall.

7.2 Omnichannel management

A challenge for many Managers of the Network is the multitude of channels via which stakeholders communicate with employees of the organization. Stakeholders might contact the organization via letters, email, a contact center, Twitter or WhatsApp. Across all of these channels they ought to receive a consistent messaging. The treatment of the Strategic Relationship Management is to be managed consistently (see Figure 7.2.1). It is the nightmare of any Manager of the Network when a stakeholder is treated badly during a simple transactional touchpoint while the Manager is investing significant resources in hosting an event for this stakeholder in light of his or her potential.

> The nightmare of any Manager of the Network; a stakeholder is treated badly during a simple transactional touchpoint while the Manager is staging a major event for the stakeholder in light of his or her potential.

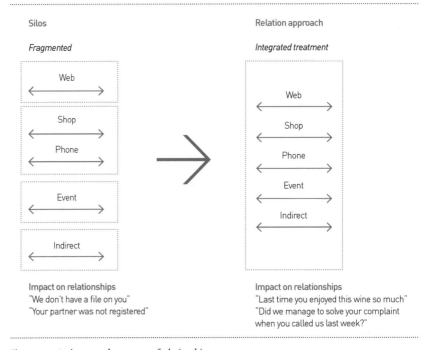

Figure 7.2.1 An integrated treatment of relationships

Applying a process approach as described in the beginning of this chapter, facilitates consistency and logic in the organization regarding relationship communication. It ought to help employees at different touchpoints with how to communicate and what messages to deliver. As an example, when a strategic stakeholder is approaching the customer contact agent for a simple transaction, the agent can identify via a classification such as Gold Customer on his or her screen that this is an important stakeholder who is invited to an important event and is to be given a higher level of service support. In addition to the process, a model coming from the world of advertising agencies can also be useful in providing consistency to the service delivery; see the so-called flower model and Big Idea (below).

The flower model centers the core of the communication concept – called in advertising the Big Idea. It is an exciting communication concept that triggers energy and creativity and can be applied to many types of execution. The flower model connects the communication idea with different (communication) channels and objectives. It is the starting point for creative development. As all developments are based on the core Big Idea, it highlights the essence, increases differentiation, and promotes consistency across the organization. In Figure 7.2.2 an example of the flower model is provided based on the 2016 IKEA "The Dream" Big Idea.

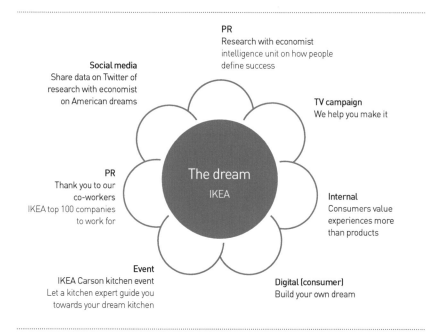

Figure 7.2.2   Flower model inspired by The Dream of IKEA [2]

As we see in the IKEA example, the Big Idea (the dream) is developed in various formats. There are even multiple events included in the overall campaign. In this case, the events relate to stakeholders coming to hear experts highlight how to transform a kitchen into your dream kitchen. Although multiple forms and channels of communications are used, all communications are centered on the Big Idea. A certain level of consistency is provided for.

7.3   Customer communication and media

An event provides media in itself since attendees will talk to others about the event and the message of the organization will be distributed to a larger audience via word of mouth. Although this might seem like it is "free" media, the organization of an event was required to trigger word of mouth – as such free media does not exist. However, in general three types of media can be distinguished as illustrated in Figure 7.3.1.

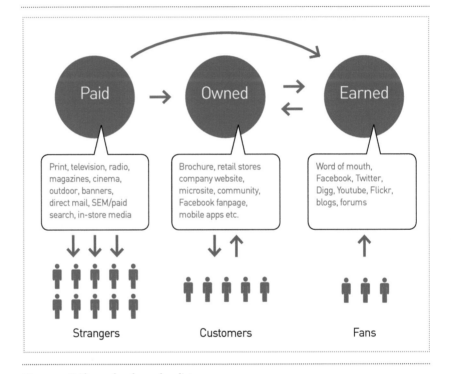

Figure 7.3.1 Paid, owned, and earned media[3]

> Organizing an event provides earned media and has a big impact on the reputation of an organization.

Paid media is considered traditional media, published content which is paid for. Owned media is media that the organization controls itself via its website or when invitations are sent to the attendees of an event. Earned media is word of mouth media, it is not controlled by the organization and it is not paid for. It is distributed by others and impacts the reputation of the organization.

Interestingly enough, earned media tends to have a bigger impact on the reputation of an organization. This is established in research done by Ganesan and Hess (1996).

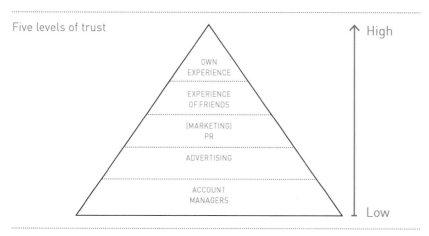

Five levels of trust

OWN
EXPERIENCE

EXPERIENCE
OF FRIENDS

(MARKETING)
PR

ADVERTISING

ACCOUNT
MANAGERS

High

Low

Figure 7.3.2 Five levels of trust[4]

Research indicates that people have difficulty trusting account managers.

Much research indicates that people have difficulty trusting account managers. After all, account managers are paid by the organization for achieving sales or relationship targets. Also, advertising is not trusted as it is clear the key objective is to promote a certain product or service. At the top of the trust pyramid are experiences of friends or best of all; my own experiences. When friends tell me I should try a service, their reputation is at stake. I trust my friends and they would not want to damage that trust. Experiences of friends therefore are perceived as sincere and have a high influence on behavior.

Applying this knowledge to Strategic Relationship Management places a high value on initiatives that drive positive word of mouth. After all, the media value of word of mouth delivers a broader reach than only the attendees of an event (earned media) and delivers a very high-level of trust (experiences of friends). However, the risks associated with an investment in Strategic Relationship Management initiatives are significant; word of mouth is not controlled by the organization. Positive word of mouth can greatly facilitate the organization achieving its relationship objectives, but negative word of mouth can have the opposite impact. A prominent case study on the latter is "United breaks guitars."

United breaks guitars[5]

Musician Dave Carroll said his guitar was broken while in United Airlines' custody. He alleged that he heard a fellow passenger exclaim that baggage handlers on the tarmac at Chicago's O'Hare International Airport were throwing guitars during a layover on his flight from Halifax to Omaha. He arrived at his destination to discover that his $3,500 guitar was severely damaged. Carroll filed a claim with United Airlines, who informed him that he was ineligible for compensation because he had failed to make the claim within its stipulated "standard 24-hour time frame." Carroll wrote a song and created a music video about his experience. The song's refrain includes "I should have flown with someone else, or gone by car, 'cause United breaks guitars." The YouTube video was posted on July 6, 2009. It amassed 150,000 views within one day, prompting United to contact Carroll saying it hoped to right the wrong. The video garnered over half a million hits by July 9, 1 million by mid-August 2009, 10 million by February 2011, and 15 million by August 2015.

The benefits and risks associated with earned media trigger many debates on how to apply this media to relationship management. Generally, two approaches can be seen in practice:

1. A defensive approach

Some organizations are reluctant to facilitate the distribution of word of mouth. Often there are corporate communication policies that forbid employees to use social media while they are at work. Employees are instructed to be careful about posting to social media as they represent the company and could be dealing with confidential information. Some organizations even have penalties for employees who violate the code of conduct on social media. When a defensive approach to earned media is taken, the role of the Manager of the Network or event manager is to conduct the communication related to a relationship event.

2. An offensive approach

Other organizations pro-actively facilitate word of mouth. They offer social media channels or content to their employees or external stakeholders. Playbooks with templates and social media analytics might be offered to employees. There is a form of social status derived from being one of the top publishers of the organization. At events, participants are invited to take photos and a hashtag (#) is introduced, so the event can become "trending on Twitter" and as a result get picked up by traditional media, increasing the reach to a broader audience. In this context the role of the Manager of the Network or event manager is to facilitate the communication conducted by the networking teams or stakeholders.

What approach to apply depends on the objectives of the Relationship Management Strategy, the industry worked in, and the preferences of the stakeholders. The Manager of the Network ought to be aware of the potential and risks of earned media as part of the overall Customer Relationship Management approach.

Notes

1. Deloitte Consulting, 2017
2. https://www.adweek.com/brand-marketing ikea-says-american-dream-about-more-just-buying-stuff-173683/
3. With inspiration from mec, Starbucks and Forrester
4. Ganesan and Hess, Dimensions and Levels of Trust: Implications for Commitment to a Relationship, A Journal of Research in Marketing, 1996
5. Caroll, D., United Breaks Guitars: The Power of One Voice in the Age of Social Media, Hay House Inc., 2012

8. Assessing the Return-on-Relationship (RoR)

Relationships require investments that most likely will not deliver an immediate return. After all, building true relationships requires trust and acts of kindness such as delivery of favors with uncertainty both of return and timing. Although it takes some of the romance out of relationships, organizations need to measure progress. Once the Relationship Management Strategy has defined clear objectives, the Manager of the Network can be made accountable for the investments.

Chapter 8 will explore the economics of relationship management. The impact can also be visualized in a network with social network analyses (digital) techniques, which we will discuss briefly. After describing the variables that define the economic value of a relationship, this chapter will conclude with the cascaded approach from Relationship Management Strategy to a defined Relationship Management Plan.

8.1 Return-on-Relationship

Successful relationships are pleasant, authentic, and durable connections with another individual. As discussed in Chapter 2, royalty leveraged relationships to strengthen kingdoms and safeguard future generations' siblings. There was little romance in arranged encounters of nobility; they were highly staged. Similarly, in current business, relationships serve a purpose for the broader benefit of the organization.

> Balancing reciprocity; balancing the value **to** the stakeholder with the value derived **from** the stakeholder.

As mentioned earlier, a sustainable relationship has a mutual benefit that is continuously (re)balanced; it is balancing the value **to** the stakeholder with the value derived **from** the stakeholder. Stephen Covey[1] even uses the term emotional bank account as a metaphor for the balance in a relationship. He defines the emotional bank account as "the amount of trust that has been built up in a relationship." One can make a deposit into the emotional bank account (via an act of kindness, for example) or a withdrawal from the emotional bank account (by asking for a favor). Covey has identified six ways to deposit into the emotional bank account:

1. **Understanding the individual.** Listen to what the other person is saying and empathizing with how they may feel.
2. **Keeping commitments.** Arriving on time, following through on promises

however small helps build up credit in the emotional bank account.

3. **Clarifying expectations.** Being transparent about expectations builds a higher level of trust.

4. **Attending to the little things.** Little things are small acts of kindness that "we didn't have to do." The additional effort builds trust and delivers an element of surprise in addition to the consistency delivered when keeping commitments.

5. **Showing personal integrity.** Acting with a transparent moral compass makes it easier for others to trust us.

6. **Apologizing** when we make a withdrawal. When we make a mistake, apologizing sincerely counteracts the damage done to the emotional bank account.

These six ways of making a deposit into the mutual relationship also highlight how difficult it is to achieve this from a managerial perspective – they all relate to individual behavior. Orchestrating and influencing individual behavior in an organization requires a vision, a strategy, and consistent execution.

"You can design, create and build the most wonderful place in the world. But it takes people to make the dream a reality." – *Walt Disney*

The RoR ought to be mutual in order to be sustainable and survive crises of confidence. The benefits delivered by investing in relationships can come from multiple perspectives such as:

· **Defensive**; the relationship reduces risk by providing early warning signals on things like regulatory changes, market trends, competitive activities, or public opinion; Investments in relationship management can prevent the organization from making a mistake or can cushion the crises (damage control) when times are rough.

· **Offensive**; the relationship supports growth of the organization, for example, by strengthening its public image, enhancing customer loyalty, or building employee satisfaction. The investments in relationship management lead to lower costs, increased sales, and potentially to growth in profitability.

· **Societal**; in multiparty relationships (networks) where mutual benefits are created, societal benefits are frequently delivered. These can originate from a common purpose of the relationship and can have an economic rationale such as building the reputation (social recognition) of the stakeholders involved in the relationship. Examples of this are fundraising activities or political lobby groups.

Considering the fact that relationship management
· has a long-term focus...
· delivers mutual benefits...
· and frequently benefits a larger stakeholder group (network effect)...
... it can be concluded that the RoR is by definition bigger than the Return-on-Investment (RoI). Or in mathematical terms; **RoR > RoI**.

After all, the RoI has a fixed period time horizon to measure the Return-on-Investment, such as sales revenue. If two projects are conducted and one of them was conducted with better relationship management, it will have added benefits such as customer loyalty, employee satisfaction, or reputation delivering a long-term value to the organization. Interestingly enough an investment in relationship management usually does not require a dramatic increase in budget; after all, understanding the individual, keeping commitments, or attending to the little things require investments in effort and attitude rather than euros or dollars.

> Return-on-Relationship > Return-on-Investment.

8.2   Calculating the Return-on-Relationship

In a business context the economic value of relationships can be established for the organization. Albeit only looking at one side of the relationship value balance, calculating the economic value can be useful when conducting a strategic due diligence during the acquisition of an organization, when evaluating the effectiveness of the investments in relationship management, or when building the case for additional investments in relationship management activities.

> The economics of a relationship, at its basic level, has three drivers: the value of a relationship, the number of relationships, and the duration of a relationship.

As such, in a mathematical formula, the RoR looks like this:

$$\text{Return-on-Relationship (RoR)} = \frac{\text{The value of relationships}}{\text{Relationship investments}} = \frac{\text{The value of relationships} \times \text{the number of relationships} \times \text{the duration of a relationship}}{\text{Relationship investments}}$$

More important than the actual outcome of the formula are the different drivers of value and how to influence them:

1. **The value of the relationship.** What benefits (or in financial terms; profitability) can the organization obtain from the relationship? The value of the relationship can be quantified on the basis of things like
   a. Number of services or products acquired.
   b. The profitability of the service or product.
   c. Promotions or discounts provided.
   d. Acquisition costs.

   If the relationship is financially less immediate, benefits could be quantified in terms of the profitability of the personal introductions (the leads) generated, the financial impact of successful policy-making (via a relationship lobby), or the premium value (incremental margin on the proposition) or additional sales derived from the endorsement of a relationship.

   The higher the profitability, the more (economically) valuable the relationship at its basic level is.

2. **The number of relationships.** How many relationships is the organization involved in or how many customers is the organization serving? The number of relationships can be quantified on the basis of factors such as
   a. The number of established relationships within the target echelons (see Chapter 5). This provides an indication of the volume of relationships.
   b. The share of wallet (the value spent on the organization's propositions by the established relationships within the target echelons). This number provides an indication of the value or depth of the relationship.

   The more relationships are established within the target echelons, the higher the potential for an economic return on the relationship management.

3. **The duration of the relationship.** This is the length of the relationship in time. The longer the relationship, the higher the (potential) profitability of the relationship.

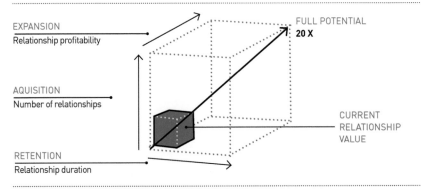

Figure 8.2.1 The economics of the relationship

On the basis of the above variables, the economic value of the current relationships can be calculated – the RoR . Within a strategic context, targets can also be set on the desired level of relationship profile. Herein lies the economic potential of the relationship. As an example, if the organization is able to double the duration of the relationship (from two to four years), the RoR will also double. This argumentation is the basis for many organizations investing more in their existing relationships than on relationship acquisition. After all, increasing the average duration (retention) often provides for better economics of relationship management than focusing on relationship acquisition.

> Increasing the average duration of a target relationship often provides a better RoR than focusing on relationship acquisition.

Although the mathematical approach to calculating the RoR might seem abstract, the drivers facilitate making the Relationship Management Strategy tangible. Frequently it is identified that investing in maintaining targeted relationships is a solid business case, as it might prolong the duration of the relationship. Additionally, positive stakeholders might function as ambassadors for the organization and thus can be an efficient approach to customer acquisition or reputation management.

When calculating the RoI, it is important to differentiate between lagging indicators and leading indicators. **Lagging indicators** are for example those used in accounting to describe the financial results. By definition, lagging indicators look backwards on the performance over the previous period. **Leading indicators** however look at results that have a predictive, causal relationship with future financial results. Leading indicators are often used in marketing, servicing, or sales. By definition, leading indicators have a forward view. Relationship investments might not have an immediate RoI in the form of profitability or revenues, but they are likely to impact leading indicators such as number of relationships, intensity of the relationships, or the duration of the relationships. The Relationship Management Strategy would gain in strength if leading indicators were included as measures to assess progress. If a causal connection between the leading indicators, the RoR and the financial results of the organization can be established, the organization participates in the Champions League of relationship management!

8.3 Factors influencing the Return-on-Relationship

The variables which drive the Return-on-Relationship should not be considered in isolation as they have a mutual impact on each other. When the profitability on a relationship is very high, increasing the number of relationships might diminish the exclusivity and as such reduce the profitability of the individual relationship.

Increasing the duration of the relationship might require additional investments in loyalty which also lowers the profitability of the relationship.

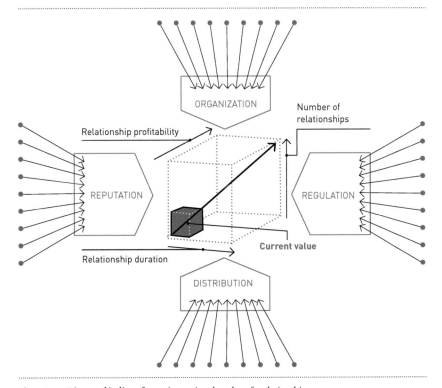

Figure 8.3.1 Direct and indirect factors impacting the value of a relationship

As can be seen in figure 8.3.1 there are both direct as well as indirect factors influencing the value of a relationship. This ought to be taken into account when defining a Relationship Management Strategy or analyzing the Return-on-Relationship.

1. Reputation

The reputation of an organization can have a direct impact on the costs and revenue of a relationship. A positive reputation will reduce the effort and cost required to build a relationship. After all, many stakeholders will want to be associated with a successful organization. A positive reputation also facilitates building the duration and the value of a relationship. A negative reputation will have the opposite effect; more investments will be required to build a relationship which results in a lower Return-on-Relationship.

Reputation is in turn influenced by many factors and (in)direct stakeholders (see chapter 5). Considering the importance of reputation for building strategic relationships, Reputation Management is therefore frequently a key component of a Strategic Relationship Management Plan. It impacts the list of desired relationships (e.g. the list of invitees for an event), the format of building the relationships (e.g. the content presented during the event) as well as the process of relationship management (e.g. the etiquette followed during an event). Investing in reputation and the relations which contribute to a positive reputation, is therefore likely to have long term positive impact on the Return-on-Relationship.

2. Distribution

The distribution, or reach, will impact the value of relationships. If we are limiting the scope to a regional area the number of relationships targeted will be smaller than when we increase the scope to a national or international level. Similarly, with TV advertising for acquiring relationships, our reach will be larger than when we call upon existing customers to bring a friend. Relationships themselves can also facilitate distribution. When we have high profile relationships (e.g. key opinion leaders) who publicly endorse the organization or initiative, it will increase reach to a broader audience and lower investments in distribution, thereby improving the Return-on-Relationship. Although already important in medieval times, having royalty on your side would be a guarantee for a big turnout at an event. Celebrity endorsement has become more professional in the current digital age and is coined as a discipline by itself; Influencer Marketing. Influencer Marketing focuses at building relationships with key opinion leaders, influencers, who can help the organization achieve its strategic objectives. Frequently influencer marketing focuses at the new digital celebrities. As an example, one of those artists is PewDiePie, a Swedish commentator with his own YouTube channel with over 95 million subscribers (July 2019) and earnings over 12 Mio USD per year.[2]

As part of relationship management, distribution is considered when discussing the scope of an activity (e.g. an event) and the channels used for building the relationship (e.g. online or endorsement).

> Celebrity endorsement as part of relationship management is coined as a discipline by itself; Influencer Marketing.

3. Regulations

Regulations set the conditions within which relationships are developed. In many industries such as the pharmaceutical, accountancy or the financial industry, regulations limit the amount spent annually per relationship. Frequently, all investments in relationships (dinners, events, travel) need to be documented and accounted for. This requires quite an administration for the Manager of the Network.

Regulations also influence the revenue and profit potential in an industry. Regulators are in many Relationship Management Plans earmarked as important stakeholders as they can influence the rules of the game.

4. Organization

The organization itself is a key driver in delivering a positive Return-on-Relationship. The ability to recruit talent, to train employees and deliver with passion is essential in developing and maintaining successful relationships.

In Chapter 5 and 10 the internal stakeholders are discussed. The internal stakeholders are in turn influenced by external factors such as the labor market, competitive activities and relationships which deliver competencies and capabilities to the organization. Sometimes the organization of components of the Relationship Management Plan, such as the event organization, are outsourced. Talent recruitment might be a critical activity for organizations requiring a highly skilled labor force with large turnover. In these cases, building effective relationships with event organizers or universities allows for the organization to build and maintain critical capabilities required to deliver a successful Return-on-Relationship.

8.4   Social network analyses

The value of relationships becomes even more fascinating when considered in a network perspective. Six Degrees of Separation is the idea that all people in the world are six or fewer steps away from each other. A chain of "a friend of a friend" statements can be made to connect any two people in a maximum of six steps. The concept of Six Degrees of Separation was introduced by Frigyes Karinthy in 1929, but now, in the digital age with social media at our disposal, the concept of Six Degrees can be validated with a mouse click.

Digital tools can support the analyses of our relationship network. For example, we can identify which stakeholders are network brokers and provide a bridge from one community to another community. These stakeholders have a gatekeeping function, possibly based on their specific knowledge. Similarly interesting are Influencers in the network. These are the stakeholders that are the fewest degrees away from all others in the network. Influencers have the highest closeness scores, a measurement that reflects relative proximity to the whole network. They often have the best overview and insights in how to get things done.

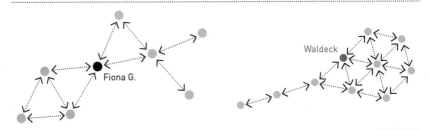

Figure 8.4.1 Fiona G. is a Broker   Figure 8.4.2 Waldeck is an Influencer

On the Internet, social network analyzer tools (e.g. socilab) are available to map your own social network. Challenge yourself to identify the key brokers and influencers in your network.

Social network analyses can also support relationship management and add additional considerations when calculating the value of a specific relation. Consider Figure 8.4.3 which is the network of general practitioners (GPs) in New York. Each dot is one GP. The size of each dot is proportionally equal to the volume of prescriptions written. The color of each dot relates to the relationship spend of company A per GP – blue dots are GPs frequently visited. GPs who are considered opinion leaders, for example because of their relationship with an academic hospital, are white. Each connection between GPs is a mutual shared patient or organizational affinity (for example, working with the same pharmacist or hospital).

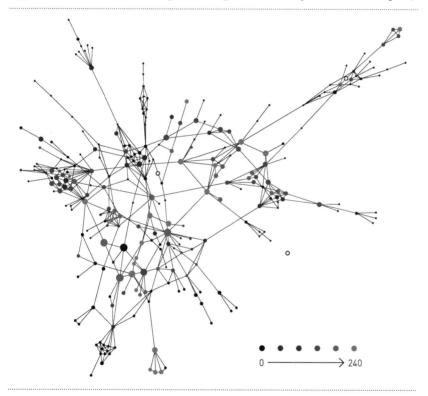

Figure 8.4.3 Network of General Practitioners in New York[3]

In the network of New York GPs, smaller local networks or clusters can be identified with multiple connections. Targeting these clusters seems like an efficient approach. Also, we see green dots in the network that have relatively few connections. These seem to have little network impact and most likely deliver a lower RoR.

How the social network analyses can be used effectively for relationship management can be demonstrated by visualizing the viral effect of relationship investments in the New York GP network over a period of three years.

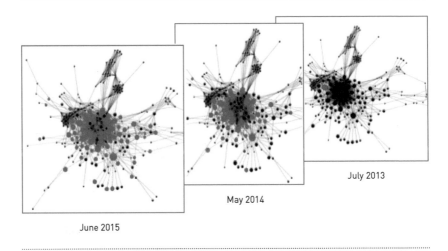

July 2013

May 2014

June 2015

Figure 8.4.4 Distribution of a new drug as a prescription in the New York network of GPs[3]

The blue dots in Figure 8.4.4 represent the number of prescriptions of a specific new drug written in New York by GPs. As we can see, in 2013 the new drug was adopted by only a few GPs. However, in 2014 many more GPs had prescribed the drug to their patients. By June 2015 the drug seems to be well established among the New York GPs. The social network analyses demonstrate a clear viral effect of the investments in relationships. By analyzing the viral effect – in this case the adoption of a new drug – mathematical models can be developed to predict the probability of influence and (speed of) adoption of the network. It is fascinating to think how this can become a new tool for the Manager of the Network to improve the targeting and effectiveness of the relationship investments.

Notes

1. Covey, *Seven Habits of Highly Effective People*, Free Press, 1989
2. Pewdiepie Youtube channel: https://www.youtube.com/user/PewDiePie
3. Deloitte Consulting & Deloitte Consulting analyses 2015, 2017

9.   Relationship Performance Management

In Chapter 4 we discussed the Relationship Management Strategy development process. The focus of the organization was established and success for Strategic Relationship Management was defined. In Chapter 5 we narrowed the strategic objectives to focus areas by exploring relationship segmentation. In Chapter 8 the term Return-on-Relationship (RoR) was introduced as a measure to quantify the benefits of relationship management.

Success can have different perspectives depending on the objectives defined. To enable alignment and focus across the organization, it is critical to define what success means before investing valuable time and resources in relationship management. Ideally the definition of success is somewhat more than "strengthening our relationship"; it ought to be quantified in the form of Key Performance Indicators (KPIs). Once strategic objectives are quantified, management is able to monitor progress and therefore manage investments in relationship management. In this chapter we will look more closely at performance in the context of Strategic Relationship Management.

9.1   Performance management models

Different performance management models are available to the Manager of the Network to monitor the results of investments. Some of these models have a more financial bias. Another trade-off between the models is the degree to which they drive behavioral change in the organization. Key models are plotted in Figure 9.1.1, and we can conclude that the Balanced Scorecard is a practical tool for the Manager of the Network to steer behavior on the basis of both financial and non-financial indicators.

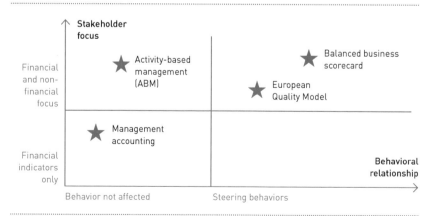

Figure 9.1.1 Performance management models

Management accounting is a performance management model applied in most organizations by the financial discipline. Budgets are made available to departments, expenses are administered, and periodically costs versus the available budgets are reported. This level of performance management has a strong financial bias and tends to have limited impact on relationship behavioral change in the organization other than making people cost conscious.

Activity-based management (ABM)

Activity-based management allocates different cost components (including overhead costs) of the organization to activities or to relationships. It helps the organization get a better understanding of the costs required to develop and maintain a relationship. So this type of performance framework is often used to improve the efficiency of an organization or in strategic decision making regarding the prioritization of relationships. An example of an ABM approach would be the costs required for handling inbound call volume from customers at the contact center. Possibly some of the inbound requests can be managed at a lower cost via the website (like subscribing to an event). Another example could be the calculation of a Customer Lifetime Value (the total value derived from a relationship versus the total investments in the relationship).

Examples of frameworks that include both financial and non-financial focus as well as driving behavior at the organization include the European Quality Model and Business Scorecards.

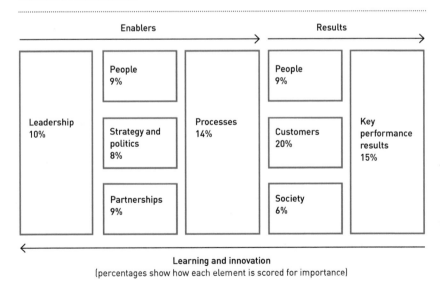

Figure 9.1.2 European Quality Model[1]

The European Quality Model originates from the discipline of Quality Management from the domain of Operations Management. The definition of quality in this context is "delivering a consistent output with no defects." The European Quality Model assesses various aspects of the organization (both enablers and results) and allocates weights to each cluster, resulting in a quality audit score or index (to a total of 100). In addition to providing an overall index on quality, the model is a diagnostic tool allowing the organization to understand in more detail cause and effect of investments. The model assesses the health of the organization on components such as leadership, people, and processes. The Quality Model can support the organization in defining priorities and allocating resources to those areas of the organization with the biggest impact. It can help to identify possible root causes for why our relationship delivery is not meeting our strategic objectives. As such it can be suitable as an audit tool for relationship management, although the Balanced Business Scorecard (BSC) has a more actionable and immediate impact as a performance management tool.

The Balanced Business Scorecard (BSC)[2] was first introduced in the *Harvard Business Review* by Kaplan and Norton.

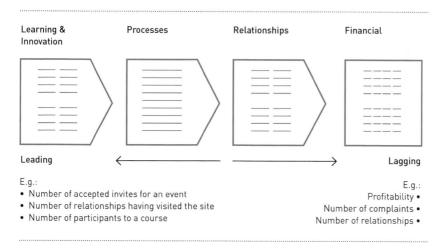

Figure 9.1.3 Balanced Business Scorecard

The scorecard clusters four areas: Learning & Innovation, Processes, Relationships, and Financial. The areas have a hierarchy; Learning & Innovation is considered to be the most leading indicator area while the Financial cluster contains the lagging indicators. Leading indicators are those that have a predictive value. Lagging indicators look back at what happened and report on the resulting status.

- The **Learning & Innovation perspective** monitors the investments in people, systems, and innovation. It allows for investments required to ensure the long-term sustainability of the organization for the various stakeholders and shareholders.
- The Learning & Innovation perspective provides input to the **Process perspective**. The processes conducted by the organization influence the deliverables, relationship output, and the financial results of the organization.
- The output of the Process perspective serves as input to the **Relationship perspective**. This perspective monitors relationship acquisition, relationship engagement, and relationship retention. Key Performance Indicators frequently tracked in this perspective are market share, stakeholder complaints, Return-on-Relationship, or customer profitability. Also, the Net Promoter Score (NPS) is an indicator that many organizations monitor.
- Lastly, the Relationship perspective serves as input to the **Financial perspective**. This perspective assesses the longer-term financial viability of the organization. It is easy to see how the Financial perspective incorporates more lagging indicators while the Learning & Innovation perspective incorporates more leading indicators. After all, financial indicators look back on what happened; Learning & Innovation indicators ought to have a predictive value on what will happen in future.

The NPS[3] methodology asks stakeholders to answer the question; how likely is it that you would recommend this company or proposition to family and friends? The responses can be given on a 10-point scale where 10 is "very likely" and 1 is "not likely at all." Stakeholders who respond with a 9 or 10 are called promoters. Stakeholders who respond with a 0 to 6 are classified as detractors. Those who respond with a 7 or 8 are considered to be passives. The NPS formula is: (Total number of promoters – total number of detractors) / (total number of respondents) x 100. With this formula, the NPS therefore ranges from -100 to 100. A negative NPS indicates more detractors than promoters of the organization.

9.2 Relationship performance measurement

Organizations can measure the performance of relationship management by identifying quantitative Key Performance Measures (KPIs) that support the strategy. In 9.1 the difference between Lagging Indicators (looking backwards) and Leading Indicators (looking forward) was established. Another way of differentiating KPIs is to identify objectives that closely connect to the Relationship Management Strategy ("long-term indicators") versus KPIs that monitor the short-term performance albeit in the context of the long-term ambition ("short-term indicators").

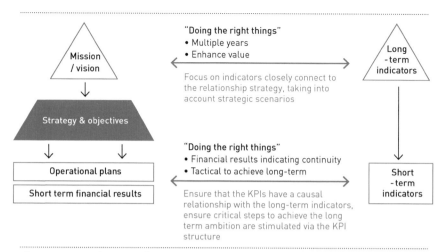

Figure 9.2.1 Key Performance Indicator philosophy

Long-term indicators are used to establish whether the vision is being achieved. These KPIs track whether the organization is "doing the right things"– is the organization focused on the right relationships? Is the organization delivering the right messaging? Are we able to mobilize important stakeholders for our cause? Are we increasing our market share with our strategic clients? Short-term indicators on the other hand focus on "doing things right"– is the event within budget? Are we meeting the desired contact frequency with our key segments? Is our Net Promoter Score increasing? Short- term KPIs measure whether the strategy is executed correctly, not whether the strategy itself is successful.

Designing a measurement framework requires a fundamental reflection on what the organization really wants to achieve in combination with diligently working through the details. Here is a suggestion of steps to follow when designing a measurement framework to monitor a Relationship Management Strategy.

1. Define the Relationship Management Strategy
This step is described in Chapter 4; defining the Relationship Management Strategy requires spelling out answers to questions such as:
a. What are our ambitions?
b. Where do we want to play?

2. Identify the winning capabilities of the Relationship Management Strategy
Or as formulated in Chapter 4, what is required to win? Some activities might be required as qualifier; without those activities the organization is not considered a serious option for its stakeholders. Organizing a Christmas event for employees is such an example. It is likely that there are a few relationship management capabilities that make the organization unique, that position the organization to

win and achieve its vision. These can be highlighted to stakeholders by relationship management initiatives. They could be related to some unique strong relationships, to the unique company culture, or to specific stakeholder echelons.

3. Define and standardize KPIs

In order to enable monitoring, benchmarking, target-setting, and clear communication of KPIs, it is vital to define and standardize them across the organization. These KPIs should be directly related to the identified winning capabilities on the basis that they are the ones that will drive success for the organization.

Ideally KPI definitions have the following components:
a. Objective of the KPI; What does the KPI intend to achieve?
b. Description; A description of the KPI
c. Measure; What is the measurement (%, Euro, or absolute number)?
d. Calculation; How is the KPI calculated?
e. Frequency of reporting; Weekly, quarterly?
f. Responsibility; What department or individual is responsible for the KPI?
g. Data source; Where does the data to calculate the KPI come from?
h. Process; What is the process for calculating and reporting the KPI?

4. Build the scorecard

Scorecards come in many forms. They range from a simple spreadsheet or table to cockpit overviews with traffic lights. The latter are more challenging to make as they provide not only the actual score of the KPI but also a value judgment on when the KPI is green (on target), amber (in the danger zone), or red (alarm!). To build a traffic light scorecard you must have an understanding of the zones and not just the absolute numbers.

5. Set KPI targets.

Monitoring a KPI is less meaningful if targets are not formulated for the KPI. More positively stated; you can only celebrate if everyone knows that a target has been achieved. Targets can motivate the organization but can also be a source of frustration if not realistically defined. Target setting can become political at many organizations as they can be translated to available budgets or individual performance targets. Although sometimes a painful process, it is worth going through as good targets provide focus, alignment, and motivation to the organization.

9.3 Relationship target setting

In essence there are three types of relationship targets on the basis of which performance can be measured and compared.

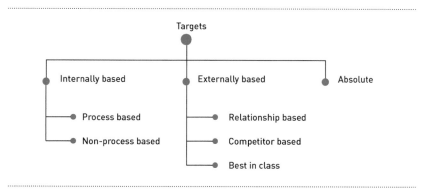

Figure 9.3.1 Target setting

Internally based targets are defined based on the previous performance of the organization. Targets can be related to processes (such as on-time delivery) or to non-process activities (more attendees at the event than last year).

Externally based targets are either relationship based (a Net Promoter Score, of, say, +10), competitor based (as in higher market share), or Best in Class (win an award).

The third and last type of target is the **absolute target**. This is often a number that speaks to the imagination (like organize an event with 1,000 stakeholders attending).

A good test to validate whether targets are defined properly is to assess whether it is possible to communicate the targets in the following structure:

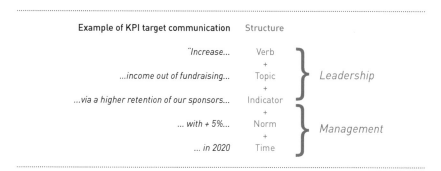

Figure 9.3.2 Example of KPI target communication

The first three components are the leadership elements: define the relationship direction (a verb), the topic to focus on, and the indicator. The next components reflect management of the Relationship Management Strategy: the norm (what is feasible) and the time (by when).

In many organizations, a lot of debate serves as input for this simple sentence structure. It is worthwhile to validate one's own Relationship Management Strategy based on this structure. Are your targets properly set?

> KPIs and scorecards are tools to support management in achieving the strategic relationship ambitions.

9.4 Closing the loop

As indicated in the previous paragraph, KPIs and scorecards are tools to support management in achieving the strategic relationship ambitions. These tools should be used actively in the organization. They are the monitor to assess whether the Relationship Management Strategy is executed well and/or whether the right Relationship Management Strategy is executed. The relationship performance management process, where KPIs and scorecards are used in practice, is frequently called "closing the loop" or Listen, Learn, Act.

Listen
Firstly the KPIs or the scorecard need to be populated. This is often based on market or internal data or based on relationships. In addition to the data, feedback can be collected from internal and external stakeholders. In many organizations, this is done via customer panels, customer arenas, or by asking the Manager of the Network to document feedback received from stakeholders after an event. Managers of the Network are therefore also the antennae of the organization to listen and document the "voice of our stakeholders."

Learn
It is important to take time to analyze, reflect, and draw insights from the data and feedback collected. What is going well? Where are there issues? What is causing these issues? Insights get deeper when they are discussed with colleagues or even with external stakeholders. After getting a clear view on the causes of underperformance, the causes can be prioritized and assigned an owner to develop an action plan for improvement.

Act
Action plans can be developed per cause and aligned with each other to ensure they do not contradict. The alignment of all actions is at times also called portfolio

management. As a last step, the prioritized actions are communicated to the organization and executed. This is followed up by measuring the results of the actions in the next step of the circle; listening.

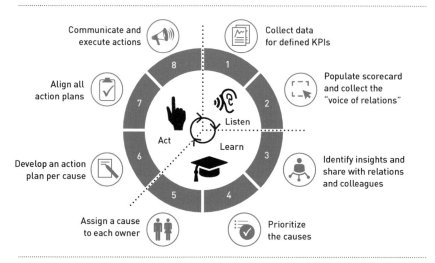

Figure 9.4.1 Listen, learn, act

9.5   Supporting CRM system

The story about the Travel and Tourism journalist in the Sahara Desert (in 7.1) was used to illustrate how human interaction and good scripting are effective alternatives to heavy investments in data management and Customer Relationship Management (CRM) technology. In fact, protocol and etiquette provide many scripting clues to optimize the customer encounter. Consider the many titles and forms of address used, medals of honor pinned on as decorations, or dress codes applied when nobility stages a major event. All of these subtle (and less subtle) clues make it easier to approach a stakeholder with the appropriate level of respect and honors. Or, as we would say in more modern terminology, the Managers of the Network are provided with visual clues to quickly understand what treatment strategy is applicable for the encounter!

> Protocol and etiquette provide Managers of the Network with visual clues to quickly understand what treatment strategy is applicable for the encounter.

Unfortunately, the visual clues applied in protocol are generally not applied during less formal events or at business events outside of protocol. In addition, as organizations have grown in scale, relationships have grown in complexity. With

167

larger organizations, therefore, it can be very useful to have a supporting CRM system that facilitates the storage of relationship data, analyzes relationship data, provides performance scorecards on relationship developments, and flags the required relationship treatment strategy to the employees working at a specific relationship touchpoint.

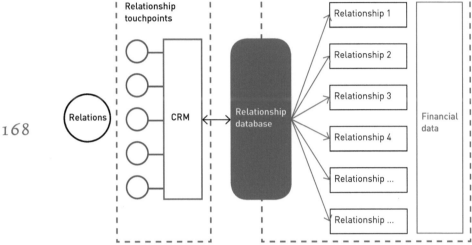

Figure 9.5.1 CRM system supporting relationship touchpoints

A CRM system in essence is a spreadsheet with pre-programmed algorithms to run the analyses and to visualize the scorecards. The CRM system is based on a database with relationship data. To enable rich analyses, the relationship database or the CRM system is sometimes linked to other data such as financial data. This allows prioritization and definition of relationship treatment strategies based on stakeholder potential or customer lifetime value. It takes a bit of the romance out of relationship management but ensures a higher Return-on-Relationship investments.

9.6   Example Relationship Key Performance Indicators (KPIs)

The relationship management KPIs should support the Relationship Management Strategy and therefore a good scorecard is unique to the organization. To assist in the brainstorming, here are some relationship KPIs to consider.

Return-on-Relationship	The financial return generated by the relationship minus the investments in the relationship.
Investment per relationship	Total costs invested in a relationship.
Customer lifetime value (CLV)	The total value (incl. potential value) derived from a relationship minus the total costs (incl. potential costs) invested in a relationship.
Relationship equity	Relationship Equity is the total value of all new customer relationships created in a given period. It is equal to the number of new customers acquired in a given period, multiplied by the CLV of those customers.
Net Promoter Score	Based on a 10-point scale; the % of promoters (who gave a rating of 9 or 10) minus the % of detractors (who gave a rating of 0 – 6).
Total relationships	Total number of relationships of the organization.
Total stakeholders	Total number of stakeholders of the organization.
Total prospects	Total number of individuals/stakeholders with whom the organization would like to build a relationship but which are not currently relations.
Relationship coverage	Total number of active stakeholders of the organization divided by the total number of potentially active stakeholders.
Relationship intensity	Total touchpoints with a relationship weighted based on the impact of each touchpoint.
Drop-off rate	Total number of stakeholders who unsubscribed from newsletters or did not respond to invitations.
Response rate	Email response rate, invitation response rate. The % of responses versus the total invitations sent.
Number of complaints	Total number of complaints during an event.
Number of compliments	Total number of compliments during an event.
Top-of-mind brand awareness	% of relevant individuals (target audience) mentioning the brand first when asked what brands they know in a specific category.
Service employee retention	% of employees staying with the organization for one, two, or three years (depending on the definition of retention).
Number of stakeholders per event	Number of relevant contacts (stakeholders) attending an event.
Number of touchpoints	Number of touchpoints with a relationship over a year.
Relationship data coverage	% of data elements stored in the database per relationship in relation to the total number of data elements desired for all relationships of the organization.
Email coverage	% of email addresses of stakeholders in relation to the total number of stakeholder relationships of the organization.
Relationship actions conducted	% of actions per relationship followed up from the total number of actions identified.
Employee Net Promoter Score	Based on a 10-point scale; the % of employees promoting the company (provided a rating of 9 or 10) minus the % of employees with a rating of 6 or lower.
Social media mentions	Total number of mentions of the organization on social media.
% Social positive	% of positive social media mentions in relation to the total number of mentions on social media.
Unique views on site	Total number of unique views on the internet site.
Total number of downloads	Total number of downloads of reports or event agendas from the Internet site.
Number of media impressions	Total number of impressions of the event or organization in the media.
PR Return-on-Investment (RoI)	Total media generated minus the total costs invested in public relations efforts.
Attendance show	% of attendees coming to an event compared to the total number of stakeholders who had indicated they would attend.
No-shows	% of attendees not coming to an event in relation to the total number of relationships who had indicated they would attend.

9.7   Reflections on relationship performance management

In this chapter, we discussed relationship performance management and stressed the importance of closing the loop. Let us close the loop for this chapter and end with reflections on four key questions:

1. Is it clear what success of the Relationship Management Strategy means and what the relationship management KPIs are?
2. How is data on relationships currently being collected and relationship management monitored?
3. How are new insights on relationship actions and results generated and shared in the organization?
4. Are relationship action plans developed and executed based on the relationship insights generated?

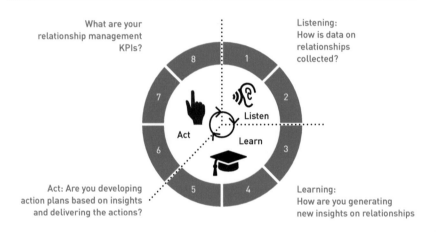

Figure 9.7.1 Reflections on relationship performance management

Notes

1. EFQM Excellence model, European Foundation for Quality Management, Brussels, Belgium
2. The Net Promoter Score is a registered trademark of Fred Reichheld, Bain & Company, and Satmetrix Systems and first introduced by Reichheld in his 2003 Harvard Business Review article 'One Number You Need to Grow' (December 2003).
3. Robert S. Kaplan, David P. Norton (1992). "The Balanced Scorecard - Measures that Drive Performance". In: Harvard Business Review. 1992, Jan-Feb, pp.71-79.

Making relationship marketing more valuable

by Marike Dragt, Head of Relationship Marketing at ING Wholesale Banking

ING Wholesale Banking meets all the banking needs of large corporations, multinationals, and financial institutions. With a history that stretches back 200 years, ING has made its name by helping clients build successful businesses. Within ING Wholesale Banking, relationship marketing is defined as the one-to-many (live) contacts with clients and prospects, mainly through sponsorships and events.

A personal relationship is one of the key drivers for ING clients to choose ING

Relationship marketing is the most important marketing channel for ING Wholesale Banking. It contributes to strengthening relationships and earning a primary relationship. It also makes it easier to get in contact with prospects and position ING Wholesale Banking as the European network bank (thought leader, international, sustainable and innovative bank). Relationship marketing is beneficial to ING Wholesale Banking's brand recognition and it stimulates cross selling. The personal relationship is one of the key drivers for ING clients to choose ING.

Relationship marketing team

The role of the central relationship marketing team is to oversee and align the relationship marketing activities from a strategic perspective by engaging in a strategic dialogue with business sectors and countries and safeguarding a consistent and one-bank client approach.

The main purpose of the global relationship marketing team is to make relationship marketing as relevant and valuable as possible for ING and its clients. We want to keep getting better every day by ensuring that all relationship marketing activities are in line with a clear strategic focus, target group focus, and communication focus, by monitoring and evaluating according to these focus areas.

Target group focus

To be sure we invite the right audience to our activities, we target clients for our events on different criteria:

1. *Prospects versus existing clients*

Nurturing and maintaining relationships is a key objective of relationship marketing. However, in markets where ING needs to gain territory, relationship marketing can also be used for attracting new clients. Depending on ING Wholesale Banking's strategic objectives, the relationship marketing focus should distinguish between targeting existing clients and targeting prospects.

The type of business strategy (from acquisition to loyalty) per country and business line should form a starting point for Strategic Relationship Marketing planning, for example, to determine what events ING wants to participate in. This requires continuously measuring and monitoring the impact relationship marketing activities are having on our existing clients/prospects.

In one of our growth countries, we initiated a virtual round table with a mix of existing clients and prospects, where existing clients acted as ambassadors for ING with the prospects who took part.

2. *Client value and potential*

Whatever ING's current year growth ambitions, we need to look at which clients are most valuable and represent high potential for ING. These clients need to be nurtured. From this perspective, relationship marketing should play a key role where it can develop a marketing program for these client groups or ensure they are invited to the most exclusive ING Wholesale Banking events.

Using a segmentation model, we define our top value clients and high potential growth clients based on preset criteria and algorithms. The team measures and monitors the relationship marketing activities by these clients' value/potential. For example, third-party sponsorships are analyzed and evaluated on the value and potential criteria of the segmentation model. This means we know exactly what the potential of the clients attending the event is.

3. *Industry*

Industries in which ING Wholesale Banking wishes to grow form a starting point for strategic relationship marketing. This requires measuring and monitoring activities by industry type. For example, lending in high-potential industries is a key strategic focus for relationship marketing, such as the automotive sector in Germany. We initiate events based on generated content and research.

4. *Decision making unit*

After targeting our clients, we carefully research the decision makers, influencers, and profiles within the organization on which we should focus our activities. For example, in the Netherlands we initiated an event for supervisory board members who are relevant for influencing decision makers within our client portfolio.

ING started a partnership with the junior company of the Dutch National Ballet focused on supporting talent and the joint ambitions we have for the next generation who will be our future clients.

Communication focus

All our relationship marketing initiatives are aligned with the broader ING/ING Wholesale Banking positioning and communication objectives in three areas:
- Our ING-wide purpose "Empowering people to stay a step ahead in life and in business."
- Our customer promise "Clear and easy, anytime, anywhere, keep getting better, empowering."
- The three key themes of ING Wholesale Banking:
  - *International business*; positioning ING Wholesale Banking as the banking partner that can truly support and enhance daily as well as strategic international financial management of multinational businesses.
  - *Sustainability*; communicate, develop, and strengthen our sustainability profile.
  - *Innovation*; positioning ING Wholesale Banking as a forward-thinking bank that embraces innovation as a means to better serve our clients.

We have defined key principles for relationship marketing activities, and our objective is that all events create a link with at least one of these three selected themes. This can be done by ensuring the event is a natural fit with one of ING's themes, the event host emphasizes one of the themes in an introductory speech, and the manner in which ING presents itself at the event fits one of ING's themes. Some other examples; We are launching a campaign with a focus on sustainability where events play a key role. From an innovation perspective, we initiated a round table for the sector food and agriculture on the future and developments in this sector, based on external research.

Making relationship marketing more valuable

To be as relevant as possible as a relationship marketing team, our main ambition is to continuously improve the value of relationship marketing activities and the way we operate. We do this in the different focus areas mentioned above (strategy, target groups, and communication), connecting with our main stakeholders and following the internal and external developments that are relevant for our expertise. Some examples of how we make relationship marketing relevant are:
- Pro-active advice on content, based on client intelligence
  - Collect and analyze client data for events to better target on the relevant content.

- Insights into results of relationship marketing activities
  - Measuring and continuing unlocking marketing intelligence.
- Optimize online and offline relationship marketing activities
  - Improve digital experience and communication for events
  - Further develop an integrated communication approach of sponsorships
  - More differentiating approach on paid and owned relationship marketing activities, depending on market positions.
- Share knowledge and best practices
  - Roll out and share knowledge and best practices on Wholesale Banking relationship marketing with ING country organizations.

Data is key to relationship marketing optimization; by collecting data from relationship marketing activities (client insights), we understand and can better define the customer needs. Within marketing we can use this data to optimize the customer journey with ING. It enables us to continuously improve the relevance of strategic relationship marketing. We call this "closing the loop" by strategic relationship marketing.

Increase client value by closing the loop with strategic RM

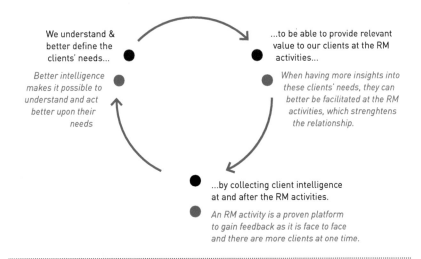

We understand & better define the clients' needs...

Better intelligence makes it possible to understand and act better upon their needs

...to be able to provide relevant value to our clients at the RM activities...

When having more insights into these clients' needs, they can better be facilitated at the RM activities, which strenghtens the relationship.

...by collecting client intelligence at and after the RM activities.

An RM activity is a proven platform to gain feedback as it is face to face and there are more clients at one time.

Figure 9.7.2 Closing the loop

10.   The Responsibility for Strategic Relationship Management

This part of the book focuses on the internal responsibility for relationship management by starting to describe what a network organization is. The second paragraph is about mapping and managing the internal stakeholders, followed by a part about designing the structure of the responsibility for the relationship management and the formation of networking teams. The last paragraphs focus on the competencies and tasks of a networker.

This book distinguishes two different roles:
· **The Manager(s) of the Network of an organization**; those responsible for the facilitation and management of the entire network of an organization as described in this book. *Please note; a manager as used here is not meant to be a controller, but rather a facilitator and enabler of the networkers.*
· **The networkers**; those internal stakeholders building and/or maintaining a network (this is a role and can be almost every employee within an organization).

It is often said that employees are responsible for building and maintaining their own networks because relationships are mostly based upon personal likings or functionalities. That is true, however, from an organizational perspective there is also a need. Organizational networks should be sustainable and remain after the employee leaves the organization. By nature, all relationships can be seen as personal, but they are also crucial to and an inherent part of an organization.

As professionals, we are all networkers, and we all have different ways of being part of a relationship. We all have different kinds of working relations (internally and externally) and also one or more networks we participate in to a greater or lesser extent. People always know other people, in formal or informal relationships, while doing official tasks, but also during breaks or on a social occasion.
   This can lead to complications; the information that is shared can come from different perspectives but also with different purposes. Roles might be unclear or overlapping, and the information that is shared might be lost because of that.

In general, we do not learn *how to be* in a working relationship; it is mostly trial and error. From an organization's perspective, trial and error is not an ideal situation. The reputation and success of the organization is at stake and organizations would rather strive for efficiency and effectiveness in building and maintaining a network. Networks should not be shaped randomly but in such way that they contribute to the goals of the entire organization. To achieve this, a network should be structured and transparent, and access to networks should be shared among colleagues and the organization should benefit from everyone's relationships.

So how should the responsibility for relationship management be organized internally?

Once an organization has chosen to implement a Networking Vision and a Relationship Management Strategy, the next step is to prepare the organization to be able to deliver. This means a structure must be set up, a team should be formed, and the tasks and responsibilities should be divided. Guidelines should be set on how employees should operate to ensure their activities contribute to the Networking Vision and Relationship Management Strategy.

Organizing all this starts with a clear understanding of the goals and objectives (Networking Vision and Relationship Management Strategy) as described in Chapter 1, 3, and 4. The activities need to be organized or structured in such a way that they contribute to achieving these goals, as described in Chapter 8 and 9.

Furthermore, the structure will have to be aligned not only with the goals and objectives (strategy) but also with the culture of an organization; the implementation of a Relationship Management Strategy needs to be consistent with the way the tasks and responsibilities (the structure) are normally implemented and the way the organization normally works together – the culture of the organization. Strategy, structure, and culture will have to work toward the same goal, following similar processes, and in a similar way. Developing a Relationship Management Strategy leads to a different structure and a new way of working. It is important to engage employees and it is important to plan this carefully.

10.1   A network organization

In this chapter, we will discuss the characteristics of a network (or networked) organization and what it means to implement one. A network or any other new way of (self) organizing and the implementation of a Strategic Relationship Management Plan go well together.

In the world we live in, change is the common factor. An organization is constantly influenced by its surroundings, its customers, and new technology. It needs to change its structure, roles, and responsibilities constantly. This change also applies to employees, and the network of an organization should thus be independent from the professionals that are part of it. The good relationship should remain after the employee has left the organization.

Most large organizations as we know them have their origins in the eighteenth or nineteenth century. The Industrial Revolution required organizing principles such as control and rules. The paradigms regarding organizations now need to shift. The changes in society, technology, and communication ask for transformations of organizations into so-called 2.0, 3.0 or even 4.0 business models, as described in paragraph 1.1.

As Frederic Laloux wrote in his book *Reinventing Organizations*,[1] many people sense that traditional organizations are stretched to their limits. The current way of organizing only seems to patch up bits and pieces instead of providing a solution. More administration, bureaucracy, meetings, and management seem to be leading to less decision making power and vigor. It leads to more frustration in the workplace.

Modern business models have a big impact on how employees are motivated to work harder and to be loyal. In a new approach (starting from the paradigm of highly trained professionals), employees are motivated by the content of their work and the freedom to organize their work themselves. Decisions and choices are increasingly made by employees working in self-directed teams.

Especially in relationship management, where the relationship is built and managed by individual employees on several levels, it seems to be crucial that the networkers/employees have the power and the autonomy to deal with their stakeholders in an independent way, though fitting within the Networking Vision and Relationship Management Strategy of the organization, as discussed by the CEO of the Nederlands Dans Theater, Janine Dijkmeijer, in paragraph 1.7.

A network organization is an organization where responsibility, authority, and accountability are put at the lower levels. The needs of the network sometimes ask for roles that are not always clear and need to be defined on the spot.

Management lets go of their control, and "old-fashioned ways" of performance evaluation, task division, and job descriptions are revaluated. Members of a network organization must be cross-trained and have variety in tasks and responsibilities, which are assigned to the team. They can have managerial tasks as well.

In Chapter 1 we noted that the desire to move toward a more heterarchal (meaning less ranking and more flexibility) organization instead of hierarchical organization can lead to struggles between the old and the new. For decision makers (but also for many others in the organization), the step toward a heterarchal organization is often a difficult one to make.

> "You never change things by fighting the existing reality.
> To change something, build a new model that makes the existing model obsolete." – *Richard Buckminster Fuller in the book Reinventing Organizations by Frederic Laloux*[1]

A network organization does not automatically mean that we envision a leaderless organization. General McChrystal, in his book *Team of Teams*,[2] explains how he changed the way his team worked without changing the formal structure. The informal structure, the communication lines, and the importance of a shared vision can be changed without changing the formal structure.

Researchers like Paul Milgrom and John Roberts[3+4] concluded that organizing tasks in a modern way can only be successful if the total system is transformed with consistency. The CEO of Zappos, Tony Hsieh, came to the same conclusion. He wrote his famous memo to his employees; "Having one foot in one world while having the other foot in the other world has slowed down our transformation toward self-management and self-organization."[5] Consistency, perseverance, and courage seem to be crucial in implementing new organizational principles.

Autonomy for employees, in this case for the networkers while they are interacting with (external) stakeholders, will be more effective if it is consistent with the strategic goals that are set at the corporate level. The more aware the networker is of the Relationship Management Strategy, the Networking Vision, and the core values of the organization, the more effective and autonomous his or her networking activities can be. Awareness of the core values is key to the success of network organizations. Organizational identity and vision should always be translated into meaningful objectives for employees.

A network organization must find a balance between autonomy and consistency; to what extent is a team independent of the overall goal? How much efficiency can an organization gain from autonomy? The organization must choose wisely between freedom and restraint, autonomy and interdependence, and steering and self-organizing. The team should operate in a consistent way with the overall strategy, structure, and culture.

> *Network Organizations; the value discipline Customer Intimacy*
> *Treacy and Wiersema[6] (1995) state that an organization needs to decide on the "value discipline." This means that a choice must be made regarding the core competency that must be consequently implemented into the organization.*
>
> *There are three fundamental choices possible according to this model: Operational Excellence, Product Innovation, and Customer Intimacy. The first one focuses on delivering products/services at low cost to a large public and in the second one, innovation is key. The third one means acting as a business partner to the customer. A business partner is specialized in serving the specific needs and wants of customers. They can do that because the organization knows exactly what the customer wants; optimal solutions and value.*

A Relationship Management Strategy from a network organization could be implemented in combination with all three value disciplines. Implementing a Relationship Management Strategy is a way in itself to become more conscious and more focused on the needs and wants of the stakeholders, as earlier described in Chapter 4 and 5.

The networkers' skills, knowledge, and attributes will give the organization a clear focus on external stakeholders, leading to more added value for the stakeholder base or accounts. The organization will become more of a business partner to the customer than a supplier of products and/or services.

According to Laloux's theory,[7] organizations can keep the traditional hierarchical structure while at the same time pushing the majority of decision making down to the lower levels within the organization. The lower level employees are in direct contact with their stakeholders and know what needs to be done. Value-driven cultures are more and more working from a community culture. Tapping into the social architecture of a company makes it easier to inspire people to work together toward a goal and initiate change in terms of continuous learning and development/ improvement. It will unlock our collective potential[8] and will lead to more empowerment (employees can come up with solutions without management approval). This is quicker, and solutions are likely to be a better fit.

179

If/when empowerment is combined with a more value-driven culture and an inspirational purpose like creating authentic relationships with customers, it is possible to implement a more network-focused organization. This includes a clear stakeholder perspective that can cost more in the beginning but will deliver more Return-on-Relationship in the longer term. The link needs to be made to the Key Performance Indicators (KPI's) mentioned in Chapter 9. The KPIs that are set for the company or larger departments should be translated to more team and individual KPIs, so accountability and result orientation will be made easier. The performance management cycle has to be as followed:

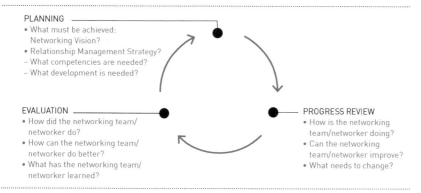

PLANNING
• What must be achieved:
  Networking Vision?
• Relationship Management Strategy?
– What competencies are needed?
– What development is needed?

EVALUATION
• How did the networking team/
  networker do?
• How can the networking team/
  networker do better?
• What has the networking team/
  networker learned?

PROGRESS REVIEW
• How is the networking
  team/networker doing?
• Can the networking
  team/networker improve?
• What needs to change?

Figure 10.1.1 Performance management cycle

The conclusion of this chapter seems to be obvious; a network and the implementation of a Relationship Management Strategy go well together but implementing one influences an organization at a strategic, tactical, and operational level. Without adapting the strategy, structure, and culture of the organization, the implementation of a Relationship Management Strategy will not be successful. To quote Peter Drucker; "Culture eats strategy for breakfast."[9]

10.2 Mapping internal stakeholders

This chapter is focused on internal stakeholders. External stakeholders are those outside the organization, but internal stakeholders are part of the organization itself. The goal of defining the internal stakeholders is to determine:

- Who are the networkers and who are the Managers of the Network?

- What networking teams need to be formed? What networkers operate in the same network?
- Who will be directly or indirectly involved in implementing the Relationship Management Strategy?

It is easy to underestimate how important it is to analyze internal stakeholders, for structuring purposes as well as for implementation purposes. To be able to structure the organization, it is important to know who formally and informally has what roles and responsibilities regarding the relationship management tasks:

- *Formally* based on the tasks and responsibilities part of the formal job description.
- *Informally* based on the tasks and responsibilities in practice.

It might be that employees have taken over some tasks and responsibilities that originally did not fit into their formal roles, so it is important to know who we are dealing with and whom to address for certain responsibilities. Not knowing the internal stakeholders may lead to issues. If stakeholders feel left out, it could lead to (unintentional) resistance. It is also possible that the influence of some of the stakeholders is underestimated and their informal power or influence is so much bigger than thought. Getting stakeholder prioritization wrong is also a cause of issues and the wrong people are given too much (or too little) attention. Also, the influence of a stakeholder could change during the implementation and the attention should be given to other stakeholders.

Once it is decided that Strategic Relationship Management is important for the future of an organization, it is crucial to include the internal stakeholders involved in this process. A systematic process for mapping (and leading) internal stakeholders is advised. In general, the process of mapping stakeholders described in this paragraph can be used for both types of stakeholders, internal and external. The focus in this paragraph is however on the internal stakeholders; the external stakeholder approach was discussed in Chapter 5. In the following chapters we will describe how to determine who is/are the facilitators or Manager(s) of a Network and how to form networking teams.

The goal is to have a clear picture of the people within the organization with a stake in the Relationship Management Strategy. Initially this will help to determine the requirements of the responsibility for the relationship management and ultimately it will help to lead and communicate with the stakeholders effectively.

> According to Lynda Bourne (2009), stakeholders are extremely important to the success or failure of projects or other organizational endeavors. Her stakeholder mapping model involves five steps (identify, prioritize, visualize, engage, and monitor). [10]

What are stakeholders?

In Chapter 5 we talked about stakeholders with a focus on external stakeholders. Looking at an internal stakeholder we can say that anyone that has an interest in the outcome of a project or process can be seen as an internal stakeholder. Stakeholders fall into two main types – those who *contribute* to a project and those who are only *affected* by it, and some stakeholders fit into both categories. So, in this case we are talking about all employees who are involved in the implementation of a Relationship Management Strategy.

The Lynda Bourne "stakeholder mapping model": [10]

1. *Identifying* **your stakeholders is the first step:**
   This step will result in a list of employees, based upon their importance for and their expectations of the new Relationship Management Strategy. The more detailed this information is, the easier it will be later on in the process.
2. **The second step is to** *prioritize:*
   Which internal stakeholders will be involved the Relationship Management Strategy the most? Who will be most engaged in managing the relationship management? Who is involved in a positive way and who in a negative way (formal and informal power and influence may be used, so it is important to anticipate on this)?
   This information may change along the way, so it is advised to update on a regular basis.
3. **The third step is to** *visualize:*
   Present the data via lists, graphics, pictures, tables, excel sheets or mind maps. This will help to get insights and convince others to make use of the information. *Another example of visualization is shown in picture 10.2.1, influence/interest matrix. This visualization helps in the next step 4, engage.*

4. **The next step is to** *engage*:

   In the end, certain colleagues need to give their support and they must understand what the future situation will be like. Engage them in plans, encounters, meetings etc. by presenting the new future in a clear and motivating way. *By using the influence-interest matrix (figure 10.2.1), it is easier to engage your internal stakeholders in the way that fits best.*

   It is important to keep in mind that people have certain feelings, perceptions and framework of references that might have an influence on the way they receive a message of change. Some people are by nature more willing to move into changes than others. The better you are prepared to an expected attitude or mind set, the easier it may be *(see the next part about empathy mapping)*.

5. **The last step is monitoring:**

   This step is important to see if the activities are leading to effective internal relationships. Monitoring will lead to a continuous review of the (internal) stakeholders.

   Examples of monitoring use the performance management cycle, performance appraisals (more individually) and Key Performance Indicators (at team and employee level).

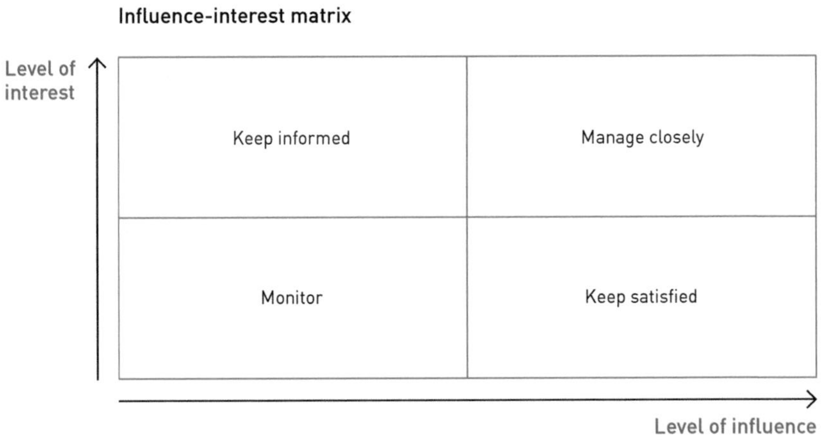

Influence-interest matrix

Figure 10.2.1 Influence-interest matrix

Empathy mapping

To prepare for the above-mentioned "engage" phase, one needs to obtain an even clearer understanding of the stakeholders and Empathy Mapping could be a useful tool. Empathy mapping can help to determine the responsibility; who will be most successful in which role? The empathy map can be used while defining roles (paragraph 10.5) and it is a useful tool during the implementation process, during change (paragraph 11.1 and further).

Empathy mapping[11] is an easy way to get to know stakeholders better and to anticipate people's thoughts and/or behavior by understanding the other's mind and feelings better before entering a conversation or negotiation.
For example:

· What does someone think of the idea to implement the Relationship Management Strategy? What actions or behavior did you see happening that might lead to that assumption?
· What does he or she feel about the new relationship management? Does he/she feel uncertain or uncomfortable about the new skills he/she needs to learn?
· What emotions might someone be feeling? It might be that thoughts/beliefs and feelings/emotions cannot be observed directly, so you could pay attention to body language, tone, and choice of words?
· What does he or she hear when you talk about this change in the roles or responsibilities?
· Did you hear him or her talk in a positive or more negative way about this new approach?

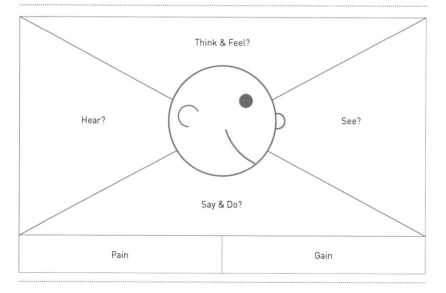

Figure 10.2.2 Example of an empathy map, as shared by Solutionsiq.com[12]

10.3 The relationship management structure

> "The business strategy selected by the management determines the structure most appropriate to the organization." – *Gomez-Mejia* [13]

A structure needs to be aligned with and supportive of achieving the goals of the organization.

In this chapter, we discuss what choices need to be made when choosing a structure for the internal organization, management, and responsibility of the relationship management approach. After developing a Networking Vision and Relationship Management Strategy and after defining the relationship management goals, the external and the internal stakeholders, and all the activities that need to be carried out, developing an efficient structure for relationship management requires the following steps:

Choosing a Relationship Management Organization Model
1. As soon as the external and internal stakeholders are mapped, they can be linked, and networking teams can be built around the plan. Networking teams are the internal stakeholders who operate in the same network.
2. Secondly, the networking teams need to be linked with the formal coordination of the relationship management, the Manager(s) of the Network.
3. In line with the corporate strategic direction, the networking goals need to be connected to the Relationship Management Organization Model.
4. Also, decisions need to be made about what resources (budget, people, systems) are given to the Managers of the Network and the networking teams and what their decision making authority is.

This is how the structure should be organized when the external stakeholders (or customer or client) are in the lead. Other examples of organizing are the grouping principles of accounts (like city councils, schools within a region, or size of expected revenue/sale) or line of business (when the organization model is based on specific knowledge or competences).

In order to thrive in a competitive environment, organizational structure should evolve to unlock the potential within enterprises and unleash the latent power in networked teams. Under this new model, predictable efficiency gives way to rapid adaptability. Smaller is actually better. Focused teams with resources, air cover, and real decision authority will generally be faster to market than heavily structured groups that require approvals before each step. [14]

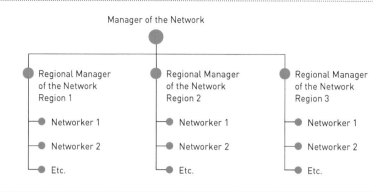

Figure 10.3.1 Example of an organizational chart of a social-profit non-profit organization

A social-profit non-profit organization whose activities were divided into several regions structured their network. They chose a matrix structure for their relationship management. Within the regions the networkers were informed, trained, and given the responsibility to carry out the Relationship Management Strategy. Each region was assigned a regional Manager of the Network who was made responsible for supporting the networkers in the region and aligning the regional activities with the Relationship Management Strategy set out by the management at the head office. The development of the Relationship Management Strategy became a responsibility of the (overall) Manager of the Network at the head office. The functional input had to come from the segments.

10.4   The Manager(s) of the Network

How to coordinate the responsibility for the management of the network in an organization? Is one person or one department responsible for all relationship management? The ideal situation does not exist, for in most organizations the networking activities and the management of a network are scattered over several departments or business units; to achieve success though, there needs to be at least some form of centralization and coordination.

Figure 10.4.1 is an example of a Relationship Management Department that has the central role of linking the necessary departments within the organization. In this setup, those departments work functionally together within the goal of achieving the Relationship Management Strategy. The head of the Relationship Management Department (the Manager of the Network) is the central figure and has the final responsibility for the management of the organization's network.

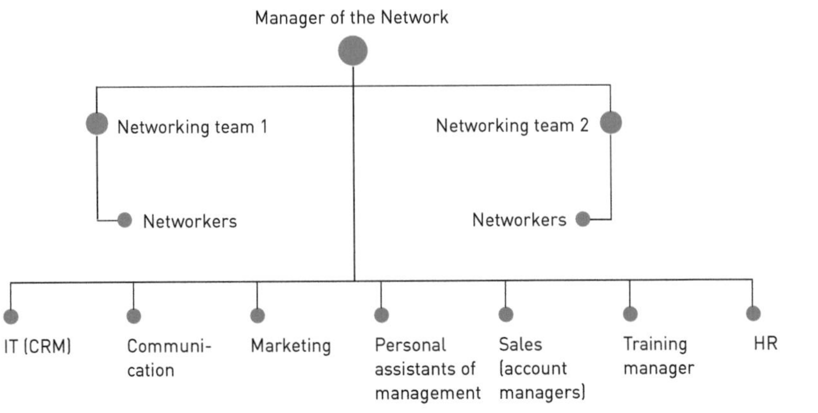

Figure 10.4.1 Relationship Management Department organization chart

The Relationship Management Department is there to support the overall goal and purpose of the organization. The department is among other things responsible for:

· Translating the overall strategy of the organization into a Networking Vision and Relationship Management Strategy and communicating this vision and strategy in the organization.

· Mapping and managing the internal stakeholders, defining roles/responsibilities, and assisting the networking teams in mapping and managing external stakeholders.

· Forming the networking teams; linking the networkers within the organization to the external stakeholders, those operating in the same network.

· Measuring results, formulating the KPIs, and calculating the RoR.

· Supporting the networking activities by making sure the CRM system works well to support the relationship management activities and is used properly by the networkers, by developing routines for mapping and managing external stakeholders, and by developing a training program for the networkers.

· Keeping an eye out on data management and all social media activities.

· Developing networking activities such as networking events and newsletters.

· Keeping track of the external networking activities the organization is involved in.

To manage and facilitate a network in a coordinated way, the Managers of the Network stimulate the networkers toward certain goals by dividing roles and tasks. A so-called transactional leadership transforms the networkers by focusing on the importance of relationship management and its purpose, as well as the added value of the networkers when working toward the relationship management objectives.

The Manager of the Network should also have certain competencies. He or she needs to support, coach, and stimulate the networkers. Authentic and self-conscious leaders are driven by values and communicate a clear vision. The Networking Vision creates and protects the reputation of the organization and its long-term and short-term goals. The Manager of the Network should also be able to let go; the responsibility for handling the network belongs with the networking teams. Furthermore, the Manager of the Network should be a conceptual and analytical thinker, should be result-oriented, and should have clear sight of what is happening in the organization regarding Strategic Relationship Management and what information is important to the network and the networkers.

In addition to these hard competencies, the Managers of the Network should also be able to lead their teams in a relational and engaging way. The leaders of the network should be value-driven and able to build authentic relationships with their networkers.

Paragraph 4.3 referred to the transformational economy. With every connection encountered in the future, something will transform us and has an impact on us. We will continuously have to learn and develop new competencies.

10.5   The profile of a networker

The goal of this chapter is to define the profile of a networker. What are the knowledge, skills, and attributes of a great networker? What should he or she be able to do?

What is a networker?
Networkers are those internal stakeholders who are in need of a meaningful network. For the success of their job, knowing the right people is essential. Building and/or maintaining a meaningful network is part of their job, preferably supported by professional relationship management.

Who are the networkers?
Almost all employees are in need of a network, but some more than others. For account managers and diplomats, building and maintaining a network with external stakeholders is daily business, but for others this is less the case.

What is the goal of a networker?
The goal of a networker is to build and maintain a reciprocal relationship with those external stakeholders who are important to the success of the networker and his/her organization.

In this chapter, we will present a set of competencies, but these competencies could be different per organization depending on the values and specifics of the Relationship Management Strategy in the organization.

For new employees, the profile can be used in the selection process. For current employees, the profile might not fit (yet); for them the profile can be used as input on how to develop and train for the new role.

Unfortunately, not everything is trainable. Networkers must have a talent for building relationships. To recruit and select people who already fit the profile of a networker saves the organization time and money for training. This requires a good, profile-based recruitment and selection process.

A goal and result-oriented organization should be supported by a suitable performance management system, through which individuals, departments, and self-directed teams are kept accountable for the results that were agreed upon: performance management, reward systems, training and development, recruitment, and selection. This should all create a setting where Strategic Relationship Management is made possible and leaders and employees can hire and train the right people for these tasks – today and in the future.

The competencies of a networker

The Managers of the Network should to be able to provide tailor-made support. The competencies of a networker need to be defined; what should he or she be able to do?

What are competencies?

Competencies exist of knowledge, skills, and attributes (Merriam Webster, since 1828):

· The acquired **knowledge** will be defined based upon to the task and the responsibility of the networker. Tasks and responsibility can be found in a job description.

· **Skills** are defined as the ability to use one's knowledge effectively and readily in execution or performance.

· **Attributes** are defined as "[a] quality, character, or characteristic ascribed to someone or something."

Competencies that entail empathy, communication on various levels, and the ability to build and sustain a good relationship are a good starting point for a networker. These are examples of competencies that are useful:

Empathic competency

Empathic people take other people's feelings and thoughts into consideration by anticipating and asking questions. Even though empathy is difficult to learn, training could be helpful for networkers. It can improve their skills in building relationships.

According to Daniel Goleman[15], empathic accuracy is defined by your own understanding of your own cultural background. And there are various levels of awareness to be acknowledged so the networker should not only be supported in understanding diversity and how to make use of that understanding, he or she should also be supported in trying to understand his or her own background and upbringing.

Cross-cultural competency

In this modern globalized world, the need to be able to embrace cultural differences has also developed. It is of crucial importance to develop cross-cultural awareness and skills to be able to build and sustain a relationship with people who are different from yourself. Handling diversity well is of the utmost importance for networkers.

The more international your stakeholders are, the more important it will be to develop an intercultural communicative competence. Bennett[16] created a developmental model of intercultural sensitivity. The six stages a person needs to go through start with denial and lead to integration. It could be important for a networker to realize in what stage he or she is and to create the possibility to develop into the next stages. Also interesting and not to be missed is Hofstede's[17] Cultural Compass as a helpful tool to develop more cultural awareness.

Ethical competency

Ethical awareness should be part of the tool kit too. This can easily be aligned with the concept of social intelligence; the element of social cognition (understanding how the social world works) is important to be able to attune to the values of one's organization, oneself, and the other in the relationship. This ethical competency should be part of the tool kit of the networker but also of their employer.

> Researches like Martha Nussbaum (2011) wondered whether citizens can deal with all the responsibilities that government is shifting on to them. Nowadays in collective labor agreements, the pressure on employees increases, and the responsibility for being employable is shifting toward employees. But are we ready and able to develop ourselves toward that society?

In the context of Strategic Relationship Management, we could ask the same question. Employees are asked to build a network and sustain relationships in the light of the organizational vision and strategy. Implementing a new Relationship Management Strategy requires a lot from employees. This should be acknowledged by employers, and employees need to be supported by all kinds of means to be able to handle this.

Social intelligence competency

Daniel Goleman[19] made a fundamental revelation in the new science of human behavior; "We humans are wired to connect." Relationship management is built upon the use of social intelligence. As was published in McKinsey Quarterly,[20] social intelligence can guide decisions (Martin Harrysson, Estelle Metayer, and Hugo Sarrazin). Behavioral aspects can and should be part of the considerations that play a role in the decision making process. Leaders in any organization who play a part or lead by example in a Strategic Relationship Management should be aware of this. All the described competencies for networkers should be part of the profile of a leader too.

What does this mean for networkers? It is not just (potential) clients who are wired to connect but the networker is too; both should participate. A potential blessing and a potential threat are revealed in technology and social media trends; they signal a slow vanishing of opportunities for people to connect in person. Research reveals that how we connect to others has enormous significance, so we must be intelligent about our social world and its possibilities.

Social Intelligence can be organized into two broad categories (Daniel Goleman, 2007):

Social awareness is what we sense about others to understand the feelings and thoughts of the other. It helps us understand complicated situations. Social awareness is showing empathy, listening, and understanding other people's feelings, but also understanding the unspoken norms of the social world and knowing how to anticipate.

Social facility is what we do with that awareness, how we make use of effective interactions. Social facility is also reflecting compassion for others.

Communication competency

Networkers should be able to communicate, verbally and nonverbally, in such a way that existing and potential relationships feel respected and listened to. There are two facets to every message. On one hand, there is the content of the words or the gestures that give the conversation size or direction. On the other hand, there is the relational aspect; how should the content be interpreted, how to see the relationship with the other, and how to respond? The tone of voice or other, nonverbal aspects might influence how the recipient of the message will interpret it. The ability to communicate well is a way to gain influencing powers, so crucial in relationship management.

Nonverbal

Prof. Albert Mehrabian did his main research in the 1960s and 70s and established that three core elements make up communication: nonverbal communication, tone of voice, and the literal meaning of the spoken word.[21] Nonverbal communication has been researched often ever since because the outcome of Mehrabian's research was that nonverbal communication is significantly more important than verbal communication. It gives an extra layer to the spoken word that can make the absolute difference.

The meaning or feelings behind the spoken words (angry, loving) accompany the message in such a way that they either support or contradict the content of the words. You can emphasize or support your verbal message by using your hands, eyes, shoulders. You can show distance by taking a step back, and when you move forward, you make the conversation more intimate or even too intimate if you enter someone's personal space.

People follow communication patterns they learn in school and in their upbringing, so intercultural aspects have a big influence. Also, group dynamics influence the communication and the effect of it, as well as different channels and communication networks.

By being more aware of your own communication style, you become more aware of your own influencing behavior. You can use this for preparing the conversations you have with your colleagues or clients to achieve the desired outcome more quickly and easily. Leary's Rose[22] has proven itself to be very helpful for these preparations.

In paragraph 1.11 we described how symbols and gestures add to the credibility and strength of the message. This is as true for organizations and entities as it is for individual networkers; why do we do the things we do and how credible and trustworthy are we in the way we express our message or build our relationships?

Listening

Listening skills are crucially necessary in order to catch what is said and perhaps even more important to what is not said. To focus on what the other tells you is often hard work. We all know the examples of bad listening habits; people who are more focused on themselves, or who show distracted behavior, looking away while you talk or picking up only what they want to hear!

Figure 10.5.1 The Chinese character for listening

The Chinese character for listening is reflected in the picture.

Listening with your eyes and feeling with your ears without prejudice in order to create space for engagement and to really hear and see each other is different from the bad listening habits mentioned above.

Trust

The importance of trust was discussed in paragraph 1.12 on authentic relationships. Trust and being able to build trust are important factors in communication. It is a condition to have effective communication, but also to have an impact. One needs to be sure of oneself to be honest or vulnerable, especially with someone you do not know well. If the other person responds in a similar open and honest way, effective, good communication can be a result. A conversation that can build mutual trust is a climbing spiral; all factors enforce and stimulate the communication as such.[23]

In paragraph 1.12, Prof. René Foqué's work on functional and moral trust was mentioned. Regarding trust from a teamwork and competency perspective, we want to elaborate on that a bit more. The pyramid of trust is similar to the idea of Maslow's pyramid of needs. In relationships, individuals must have their basic trust needs met before being able to progress.[24]

PYRAMID OF TRUST

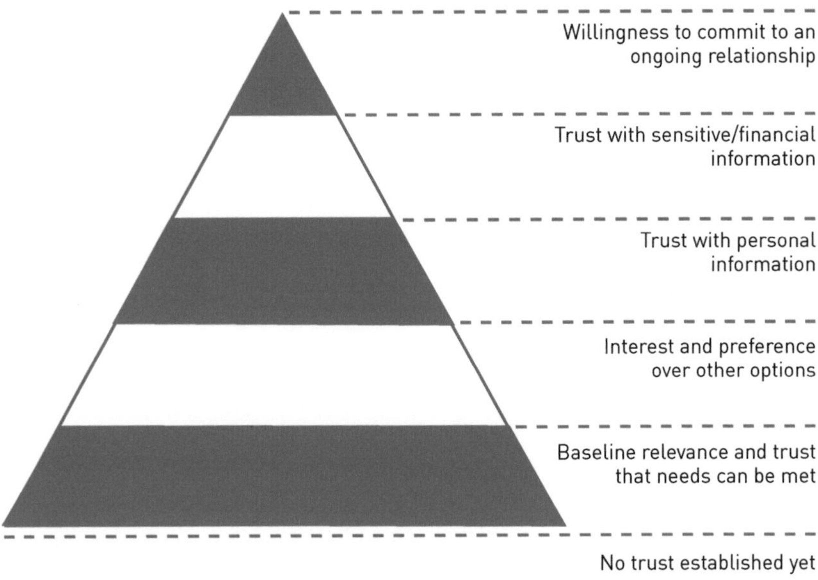

Willingness to commit to an ongoing relationship

Trust with sensitive/financial information

Trust with personal information

Interest and preference over other options

Baseline relevance and trust that needs can be met

No trust established yet

Figure 10.5.2 Pyramid of trust[24]

In addition to the distinction of the functional (reliability) and moral (integrity of the person or organization) trust that Prof. René Foqué uses, we could say that the levels as shown in the pyramid will lead to different types of relationships and also can require different competencies to be used.

To be able to deal with the constant changes and the complexity in the world, we need to be flexible and know that we can rely on the people we build relationships with. Professional trust is important to have not only when we work closely together but also when we build relationships with customers and colleagues. Frank J. Barrett used the analogy of playing jazz in *Yes to the Mess* for how to work in a team and the necessity to be able to trust your teammates.[25]

Networking skills

Not everyone is a born networker; some people lack the necessary experience, knowledge, or skills. During the evaluation, it will become clear if a networker is effective. If this is not the case, the networker will have to be supported with the appropriate training or coaching.

To determine the effectiveness of a networker, it is important to have a clear definition of the competencies of a professional networker as described above. This is not only useful for monitoring/evaluation purposes but also for the development of an effective training program and for the recruitment/selection of the best networkers for specific events or meetings.

Networking skills can be trained, but this takes a repetitive approach over a longer period of time. The more you practice, the more you gain experience. However, not every networker can be trained to the same level and to the same extent. And for some people it may take longer than for others, and some might have to go through a more intensive development than others. Effective networking skills training requires a personal approach.

Examples of networking skills trainings would include the above-mentioned skills but also table manners and other etiquette, practical diplomatic skills, ethics, integrity, and so forth. In addition, it is important to train people how to compose a guest list for a networking event, how to prepare such a meeting, how to determine goals, welcome guests, make introductions, introduce conversation topics, how to process the information gathered during the meeting, and how to determine the follow-up. Last example of a training topic could be how to make use of a CRM system.

There are some different sorts of trainings for these different topics, in group sessions or individually, onsite and online, and by making use of different methods like role-playing, personal coaching, or observation.

10.6 Defining the role and responsibilities of the networking teams

When an organization has decided on the relationship management structure, it is time to define the roles and responsibilities of the networking teams. They begin with the organization's needs and wants and those of the stakeholders, which should be translated into roles and responsibilities depending on the stage the relationship is in. Based on these roles and responsibilities, the competencies, knowledge, and skills that are needed for each role need to be specified.

To bring some order to all the activities that will lead to the defining of the roles and responsibilities, it is important to decide:

1. To what extent are the relationship management activities focused on the core business of the external stakeholder?
2. Or to what extent are they focused on the person or the organization of the stakeholder?

Kwakman & Burgers[26] defined the 4 P's of relationship management and while defining the roles and responsibilities of the networking teams, it can be useful to have a look at the activities from this perspective.

Relationship management activities	Core business	Non-core business
Stakeholder as individual person	**Project focused** Exceeding & managing expectations	**Person focused** Strengthening the personal relationship by giving attention and recognition
Stakeholder as an organization	**Partnership focused** Adding to successful business & assuring sustainability & continuity	**Process focused** Strengthening relationships between networkers and employees of the stakeholder organization (client)

Figure 10.6.1 Example of relationship management activities; roles and responsibilities networking team[26]

Based on the roles, the responsibilities become clear and questions that can be asked are: What are the responsibilities when building long-lasting relationships versus new relationships? Do these different responsibilities require different skills to be used by the employee and different objectives or targets? In paragraph 5.6. we argued that customer segmentation, needs, and wants can become clear from that segmentation. Those needs and wants can be used to define the networking teams' roles and responsibilities.

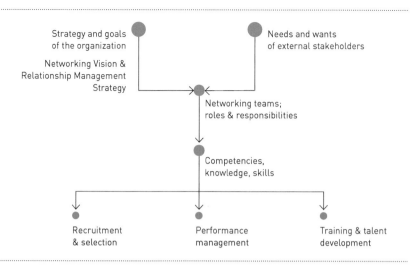

Figure 10.6.2 Needs and wants of external stakeholders translated into roles and responsibilities/HR tools

The clearer the roles and responsibilities within the team are, the easier it will be to develop new skills in a talent development program. It will also make performance management easier and it will be easier to hire the right person if there is a vacancy. This will mean an alignment between the strategic choices and the use of Human Resources management tools as well as more consistency in the implementation of the Relationship Management Strategy.

Roles can best be described when linked to the scope of their relations (strategic/ tactical/operational, business units, other relations) but also to specific characteristics needed in a certain phase of a relationship.

> The theory of Kwakman & Burgers[27] can also be useful in dividing roles and responsibilities:
> - **The creator of commitment**; exceeds expectation, can make the client committed to your organization.
> - **The confidant**; creates long-lasting relationships, creates ambassadors.
> - **The developer**; acquires new clients for existing products and services.
> - **The innovator**; able to create new products and services with new partners.

The Relationship Management Strategy will lead to certain relationship management goals and every networking team will derive their goals from the overall ones. There must be a responsible person (Manager of the Network) for all (or several) networking teams, and the team responsibility needs to be clear. The teams are interconnected though autonomous, and they all have their own added value to achieving the relationship management goals. Decisions need to be made about what needs to be done (tasks and responsibilities) within the team as well as for every individual team member in order to be able to achieve those goals. If the teams set their own targets, the side effect will be that employees take more ownership; they will make the commitment to the targets themselves.[28]

This should not lead to fixed job descriptions; it seems more important to have the roles and expectations clear. In that case, taking the core values of the organization as leading the way, it should become clearer for employees what needs to be done to fulfill that role.

> Deloitte joined their observations from their clients and their experiences in reorganization into a paper "Unlocking flexible organizations". In other research they conclude that a so-called "agile" or "nimble" organization is the organization of the future. Main elements are flexibility, team-based and a networked organization that is capable to compete effectively and adapt quickly to an uncertain future.[29-31]

Laloux[32] found in his research that parallel (called by others "heterarchical") teams appear most frequently, leaving the traditional hierarchal pyramid behind. It will lead to a Teal organization in which the parallel teams are used when a high amount of autonomy is possible and there is not too much need for coordination between teams. In practice, it is almost always necessary to have some overall coordinating and/or supporting roles; this leads to more efficiency. This will lead to a different kind of organizational structure, as given in the examples in the figures below.

> The next figure describes the example of Spotify. They have embraced a newer way of organizing. Spotify is built up in "squads" which serve as development teams. Each team is made up of six to twelve developers. Each squad is self-directing, multi-disciplinary, and possesses all the talents and tools to design, develop, test, and launch their part of a product. They decide on their way of working, have a long-term vision, and have a certain number of responsibilities. They can become the experts in their part of the service/product they deliver. The tribes shown in Figure 10.6.3 are the incubators for the squads, and they have freedom and autonomy. The tribe has one lead who will facilitate the best possible working environment for the squads. Part of one tribe is made up of 40 –150 people, however the smaller (closer to 40) the better since the more people work within a tribe, the more rules and bureaucracy will be found necessary.

> It is not only newer organizations that use this new way of organizing. Former traditional organizations like the Dutch bank ING are now front-runners in following Spotify's lead (62); over recent years they are transforming themselves into multi-disciplinary teams.

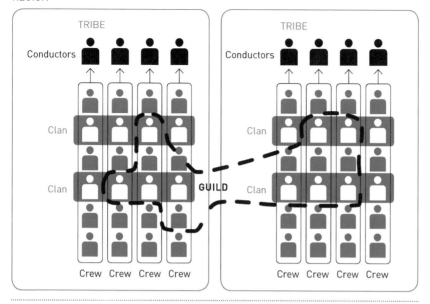

Figure 10.6.3 Example tribe organization chart of Spotify[33]

197

Matching employees to networking tasks

When the best way to organize relationship management has been agreed on, and the best way to structure the activities – when the roles and responsibilities and the profile of the networkers – has been defined, it is time to decide which employee fits the profile of the networker best. As we mentioned earlier and slightly adapted, the method of Kwakman & Burgers[34] is useful here. Here is an example:

Matching networking teams and networkers to stakeholders	
Who are the external stakeholders? – – – –	What networkers are in contact now? – – – –
What is the necessary role to build the relationship? – Creator of commitment – Confidant – Developer – Innovator	Does the role fit the competencies of the current networkers?

What topics are crucial for the most important stakeholders? – – –	Which networker fits best? Which networking team fits best?
What roles are necessary to address these? – Creator of commitment – Confidant – Developer – Innovator	

Figure 10.6.4 Matching networking teams and networkers to stakeholders

Roles and tasks; KPIs

To help define roles and tasks, the Relationship Management Strategy can be translated into KPIs as described in Chapter 9 – first on a business level and then into departmental (team) and individual KPIs and targets. By doing this, the goals can be linked to various Human Resources instruments that are already in place, like the Balanced Scorecard and performance appraisal systems. The more those are linked, the more consistent the coordination will be.

In Chapter 9 examples were given of relationship KPIs on a team level. They could then be translated to an individual level, for example:

Team: Number of meetings $\longrightarrow$ **Individual:** Total number of meetings (people spoken to) at an event, per individual

Total number of meetings (people spoken to)

Team: Social media mentions $\longrightarrow$ **Individual:** Total number of posts on social media of the networking event, per individual

Total number of mentions of the networking event on social media

Team: Thank you emails $\longrightarrow$ **Individual:** Total number of thank you emails after an event, per individual

Total number of thank you emails

When the KPIs for a networking team or networker are defined, it is important to make them as specific as possible; the networking team or individual networker should be able to influence the result of the described target.

Notes

1. Reinventing Organizations, a Guide to Creating Organisations. Inspired by the Next Stage of Human Consciousness, Frederic Laloux, 2014, Nelson Parker

2. General Stanley McChrystal, Team of Teams, Penguin Publishing Group, 2015

3. Handbook of Organisational economics, Milgram Roberts, 2012

4. Paper: Complementarity in Organisations, Erik Brynjolfsson* and Paul Milgrom*, August, 2008; Revised, December, 2010 and January, 2012.; Draft chapter for Handbook of Organisational Economics

5. http://continuingprofessionaldevelopment.org/stakeholder-mapping-key-to-successful-project-management/

6. The Discipline of Market leaders, Addison-Wesley, 1995, Reacy and Wiersema

7. Reinventing organisations, a guide to creating organisations. Inspired by the Next Stage of Human Consciousness, Frederic Laloux, 2014, Nelson Parker

8. ACMP congress 2017, Luc Gallopin

9. https://www.forbes.com/sites/shephyken/2015/12/05/drucker-said-culture-eats-strategy-for-breakfast-and-enterprise-rent-a-car-proves-it/#10c73e082749

10. Stakeholder Relationship Management, Lynda Bourne, 2009

11. https://www.solutionsiq.com/resource/blog-post/what-is-an-empathy-map/

12. 'Solutionsiq.com' https://www.solutionsiq.com/resource/blog-post/what-is-an-empathy-map/

13. Managing Human Resources, Luis R. Gomez-Mejia, David B. Balkin, Robert L. Cardy, 2013 Pearson Education Inc., 7th edition)

14. Unlocking the flexible organization, Organizational design for an uncertain future; copyright 2016 Deloitte Development LLC

15. Social Intelligence, Daniel Goleman, 2007, Arrow Books

16. http://www.idrinstitute.org/page.asp?menu1=15

17. https://www.hofstede-insights.com

18. Creating Capabilities, The Human Development Approach, Martha C. Nussbaum, 2011, The Belknap Press of Harvard University Press

19. Social Intelligence, Daniel Goleman, 2007, Arrow Books

20. McKinsey Quarterly, November 2012

21. https://www.bl.uk/people/albert-mehrabian

22. Beinvloed anderen: begin bij jezelf, Bert van Dijk, Thema, uitgever van Schouten & Nelissen, 2015 Source Chinese sign: http://latcomm.com/2013/03/chinese-character-for-listen-embedded-meanings/

23. Communicatieleer, Frank R. Oomkes, 2013, Boom Lemma

24. https://www.nngroup.com/articles/commitment-levels/Hierarchy of trust: the 5 experiential levels of commitment by Katie Sherwin, March 6, 2016

25. Yes to the Mess: Surprising Leadership Lessons from Jazz, Frank J Barrett, HBR Press, 2012

26. Professionals & relatiemanagement, Frans Kwakman & Jos Burgers, 2005, Sdu

27. Professionals & relatiemanagement, Frans Kwakman & Jos Burgers, 2005, Sdu

28. https://corporate-rebels.com/target-setting

29. Unlocking the flexible organization, Organizational design for an uncertain future; Copyright © 2016 Deloitte Development LLC.

30. Rewriting the rules for the digital age, 2017 Deloitte Global Human Capital Trends

31. Aligning the Organization for Its Digital Future; Findings from the 2016 digital business global executive study and research project, by Gerald C. Kane, Doug Palmer, Anh Nguyen Phillips, David Kiron, and Natasha Buckley

32. Reinventing organisations, a guide to creating organisations. Inspired by the Next Stage of Human Consciousness, Frederic Laloux, 2014, Nelson Parker

33. http://blog.kevingoldsmith.com/2014/03/14 thoughts-on-emulating-spotifys-matrix-organization-in-other-companies/

34. Professionals & relatiemanagement, Frans Kwakman & Jos Burgers, 2005, Sdu

II.   Implementing a Relationship Management Strategy; Implementing Change

Why address the topic of change in a book about Strategic Relationship Management? Organizations invest huge amounts in tools, training, and thousands of books (over 83,000 in Amazon), but studies show a 60–70 percent failure rate for organizational change projects, a rate that has stayed constant from the 1970s to the present (Harvard Business Review).[1]

It is our belief that within ten years most large organizations will have structured their relationship management. By then, it will be part of the day-to-day management, but until then, organizations first need to implement this new strategy.

The implementation of a well-thought-out Relationship Management Strategy is one of the most challenging phases. Strategy, structure, and culture support each other in our daily working life. It will not be enough to just change the strategy (or parts of it) and not support those changes in the structure (the working processes, combined with the necessary skills and systems) and/or the culture (our style and shared values).

Many people across the organization will have to be involved in the process of making changes, but not everyone will be keen on professionalizing the relationship management and having a clear strategy. It might mean that they will have to share their information about their relationships. Also people are not used to putting data and conversations in a database, and it might take some effort to persuade them to start doing so. Another issue is the organization's own networking events; it is not uncommon for employees to prefer to talk to each other than to clients. This also might require some effort to change.

The failure rate can be explained if we understand that it is not only our external stakeholders who want to be part of an authentic relationship; our colleagues do too. Kenneth J. Gergen wrote in *Relational Being*[1] that we are relational beings and that "through relational coordination, organizations come to life." However, most organizations are not applying that principle when implementing new strategies. When something like a Relationship Management Strategy is implemented, it is important to engage your colleagues.

So why is change so difficult? After all, there are many theories and methods that provide us with an almost step-by-step planning format. The difficulty could be that consistency in pulling it through until the end is very hard to achieve, or because it can be a lengthy process and we are easily distracted by the day-to-day business and find it hard to keep to the plan we once had.

Also, the involvement of others in the change can cause a shift in priorities due to different views that could endanger the original Relationship Management Strategy.

Some organizations will find it more difficult than others to implement Strategic Relationship Management because they might have had a negative experience with previous changes within the organization.

Another important factor is the change in our society to how it is today versus the way and the paradigms around which organizations were designed. Most traditional organizations are built on control and management rather than on self-responsibility and leadership. Most employees are only extrinsically motivated, and most management models were designed from around 1800 onwards. That is why most companies are very reluctant to implement more flexible organizational structures, like a network organization where the potential of our intrinsically motivated employees could be far better used for the greater good of the company.

To make an organization ready for a future where Strategic Relationship Management is implemented to its fullest potential, more traditional organizations must go through a paradigm shift; from organizations where people are forced to work in a certain way, with a hierarchal structure and small span of control, to positive organizing and new leadership making use of clear goals and targets in combination with responsibilities, accountability, and authority.

This is exactly why the topic of change needs to be part of this book. The implementation of a Relationship Management Strategy deserves to be well thought out and should be carefully planned.

11.1   Relationship management; how to implement change

If relationship management is a new strategy for your organization, managing change is needed; a Relationship Management Change Project makes it possible for a dedicated team to implement the change in a defined period of time.

The project should lead to a sustainable change, but a project is temporary. The beginning and the end are defined, and therefore the scope and resources are also defined. It will create a unique (tangible or intangible) result. A project is not a routine operation; it is specifically designed to accomplish a unique, complex, and singular goal.

Project teams often include people who do not usually work together, from different departments or organizations, across multiple geographies, and with different needs. A Relationship Management Change Project starts with a clear vision about the desired relationship management approach and a plan for how to implement the change so that there will be a consistent use of a Relationship Management Strategy at all levels of the organization. The project should also include reports on progress and milestones.

Depending on the size of an organization, it is possible to start small with a pilot and use only one department as an example. The Corporate Rebels published an article on their guest blog written by Frank Thun "Adopting Self-Management; Big Bang or Baby Steps."[2] In it, Thun gives a great overview about the choices when implementing change. One view that is mentioned is "if hierarchal organizations are so resistant to change, you cannot change them by evolution. Nothing short of a revolution will suffice."

Organizations do not change. People do.

When an organization undertakes projects or initiatives to improve performance, seize opportunities, or address key issues, they often require change; changes to processes, job roles, organizational structures and types, and uses of technology. However, it is actually the **employees** of the organization who have to ultimately change how they do their jobs. If these individuals are unsuccessful in their personal transitions, if they do not embrace and learn a new way of working, the initiative will fail. If employees embrace and adopt changes required by the initiative, it will deliver the expected results.

Change starts by asking those within the organization who must make the right change the following questions:
· How to decide **what** needs to be changed when implementing a Relationship Management Strategy?
· How to **manage** the change?
· How to use **motivation, power,** and **influence** to engage everyone involved?

One could start by defining the project of implementing a Relationship Management Strategy; it should lead to continuous adaptation to changing principles. It would be helpful if the organization were able to handle change, meaning that there is a certain amount of flexibility in adapting policies and behavior.

11.2 Analyzing the current and desired situation and managing the change

Change starts with acquiring a good overview on the current situation within the organization. Traditionally, this can be achieved by making an analysis to determine what goes well but also what needs to be improved.

The McKinsey 7-S framework[3] is a good model for making an internal analysis and it can be used to make an overview of the current and the desired state. It is a strategic model that can be used for many purposes such as organizational alignment, performance improvement, understanding the core and most influential factors in an organization's strategy, determining how best to realign an organization to a new strategy, and other organization design.

The model, made famous by McKinsey & Company, makes it is easier to see the gaps and create awareness of what needs to be changed. The model provides a good basis for a thorough discussion around an organization's activities, infrastructure, and interactions. By doing this, it is easier to get an overview of what should change when implementing a Relationship Management Strategy and how you can make a comprehensive implementation.

7-S model and its usage

The 7-S model is about the seven elements of an organization. These elements can be defined by:

1. **Strategy**: How to win? How to align vision, strategy, goals, and recourses?
2. **Structure**: How is the organization organized; roles, responsibilities, accountability, relationships, communication, decision making?
3. **Systems**: What business and technical infrastructure do employees use on a day-to-day basis to accomplish aims and goals; systems used, rules and procedures?
4. **Shared values**: What are the traits, behaviors, and characteristics that the organization believes in; corporate culture, mission/vision, core values?
5. **Style:** What behavioral elements does the organizational leadership use? What is the culture of interaction?
6. **Staff**: What is the employee base; size, resources, level or need of training, and talent management?
7. **Skills**: How is the ability (skills available) to do the organization's work coordinated (the performance of the organization and individual performance management of the organization)?

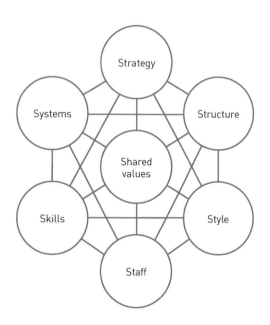

Figure 11.2.1 The McKinsey 7-S framework[3]

Once these questions are answered, the information should be examined. The analysis should look for consistency, alignment, conflicts, gaps, support, strengths and weaknesses. It is important to keep in mind that the S's are linked; if things changed in one S, this might lead to an effect in other S's as well.

The current and the desired situation can be described according to the 7-S's. A comparison of the two will reveal gaps that need to be filled in order for the organization to change. This approach will result in a structured start that will lead to the desired outcome.

By comparing the current and future 7-S's, gaps can be defined which leads to improvement and action plans. For example, in the current structure it is clear that there are many hierarchal layers in the decision making process and the desired situation is self-directed teams with autonomy in decision making. To go from the current to the desired state, new responsibilities for management and teams need to be defined. Several tasks need to be divided up and spread around (among others). Another example; in the analysis of the desired situation of *style*, the conclusion might be that the leadership style and the shared values need to change. Different ways of working together are needed (also affected by the change in structure). The unwritten rules and values are in need of alignment to the new way of working.

An alternative approach is the method developed by Deloitte.[4] This approach starts with developing a vision and forming networked teams. The Deloitte method describes four steps:

1. Protect the core and disrupt at the edges; decide where the organization needs to change and disrupt them with new ways of working.
2. Unleash the networked teams; realign and select existing structures and change into self-managed, networked teams that are focused on a specific outcome.
3. Adopt a collaborative systems mind-set; shift into a transformative power of systems thinking.
4. Create conditions for flexible design; keep the organization connected by creating an ecosystem of open talent with a fail-fast approach and to make use of social technology.

This is more pragmatic and starts from a specific need in the organization, instead of the more traditional way of making a full analysis of strengths and weaknesses and deciding based on that what to change. Depending on the basic questions an organization has regarding implementing Strategic Relationship Management, this could lead to a different approach.

There are many ways of changing organizations and there are many more models and methods, for example, John Kotter's 8 Step Model , Action Research by Kurt Lewin, ADKAR by Jeff Hiatt and the Appreciative Inquiry by David Cooperrider . It is best to pick a method that fits the situation, because the methodology needs to fit the organization's core values and the issues at hand.

How do you know what kind of method you need? There are change consultants that make their own methods out of various existing ones, and most HR departments favor a particular method. A method should provide a structured way of approaching the change and guarantee that all the aspects of change are covered.

Engaging employees

When implementing change, an important step is to engage the employees/ colleagues by touching their Heads, Hearts, and Hands. As we wrote in Chapter 3 about creating a Networking Vision, it is necessary to create understanding (Head), it has to touch the Hearts of the people who are involved, and it needs to be actionable (Hands).

People will not take part in the change if they do not know, understand, or see the reason for the change. Creating a sense of urgency is an extremely important step at the start of an implementation. Creating a so-called burning issue will lead to a burning ambition. When people have that burning ambition, it is easier to make a good start because they feel the necessity for change. Whatever method is chosen, always start with the reasons for change – the "why".

Changes are also more successful if there is a focus on the positive aspects. It is better to focus on the future and not stick to the past, whatever pain there might still be. However, it is also possible to look at pitfalls from a positive perspective by focusing on the values of the organization and searching for aspects that enforce those values. That way pitfalls can become areas of improvement.

Cameron & Quinn[9] have developed a method that has proven effective in changing the organizational culture (so in terms of the 7-S model, the shared values and style among others). Another method is the Appreciative Inquiry.[10] This is another an example of a positive approach that starts from the strengths of an organization.

If employees are conscious about the values of the organization and are able to align them to their own personal values, it will be easier to adapt their behavior accordingly. Combined values are important when creating a burning ambition. Also, an employee will take more responsibility and change/improve his or her behavior when it is clear what the added value of the change is.

Change might lead to letting go of old certainties and this might need support from the organization. Employees will not change their own behavior if the leaders do not walk the talk. The more a new way of working is seen on the work floor, the more chance there is that the employees will move as well.

All the 7-S's are influenced by a new strategy. Leadership styles need to change, but policies and work processes do too; new skills must be developed, and new objectives have to be set. A new way of working as described here (what), will require a new way of cooperating and human interactions (how). The network organization as a community where we tap into our collective potential requires a different way of looking at the organization and one's colleagues. Trust and respect become even more important and the success of one employee is dependent on the success of another employee or even of the team. This will have to lead to new support systems within an organization.

This might also lead to a more philosophical question; where will this lead us? That can be a very unsettling question to ask any employee. Leadership has to show that they will support and show consistent behavior to all employees involved while leading the organization forward.

The tangible (structural and goal setting elements) and the intangible (culture, paradigms and assumptions) need to be connected, and this is why change as part of implementing a Relationship Management Strategy is crucial. The individual and the organizational perspective need to be linked as well as the interior and exterior perspective.

11.3 Motivation

Motivation[11] can be defined as "the internal and external factors that stimulate the desire and energy in people to be continually interested and committed to a job, role, or subject, or to try to attain a goal. Motivation is what drives you to act and it is your inspiration for doing something."

Motivation can be derived from a positive drive, but also from fear.

To implement a Relationship Management Strategy requires motivating people to be part of a change and to embrace the new goals the strategy has set. When employees and colleagues are motivated, it is easier to get them on board and minimize possible resistance. Kim & Mauborgne[12] described it as "Execution is Key! Before people will execute a new strategic plan, their minds and hearts must align with the new strategy."

Motivation can also be used to inspire people to do something in a different way. However, this requires awareness about what behavior exactly needs to be motivated. So, what is motivation, exactly?

People are motivated by different things, and when motivating people, it is important to have various tactics. Motivation results from both conscious and unconscious factors such as:

· The intensity of a desire or need.
· The incentive or reward value of the goal.
· The expectations of the individual and of his or her peers.

These factors are the reasons one has for behaving a certain way. A simple example is a student who spends extra time studying for a test because he or she wants a better grade or because he or she is afraid to fail and disappoint his or her parents.

There are two standard types of motivation:

· **Extrinsic motivation**[13] refers to performing an action or behavior to receive an external reward or outcome. When you are extrinsically motivated to do something, you aren't concerned with whether the action is enjoyable. You are most concerned with the outcomes associated with the action.

The example of the student who is motivated to get a better grade is an example of an extrinsic motivation. Another example is those of us who choose not to wake up early on weekends; we cannot be late for work or school during the week so we are extrinsically motivated to wake up early to receive the outcome of being on time. When you do something to avoid punishment or a negative outcome, you are acting due to extrinsic motivation.

· **Intrinsic motivation**[14] is defined as performing an action or behavior because you enjoy the activity itself. Whereas acting on extrinsic motivation is done for the sake of some external outcome, the inspiration for acting on intrinsic motivation can be found in the action itself.

Many people read books simply because they enjoy reading. Some people collect stamps; most people do it because they like collecting and any potential financial gain is less important as a goal.

In 1959 Frederick Herzberg in his Motivation Hygiene Theory said that external motivators only have a short-term effect. More recently also Daniel Pink came to a similar conclusion – that intrinsic motivators have more effect than extrinsic ones.

When implementing a Relationship Management Strategy, colleagues should also be intrinsically motivated.

Locke's[17] research into motivation showed that clear goals and appropriate feedback also motivate people. In his 1968 article "Toward a Theory of Task Motivation and Incentives" he showed that that working toward a goal is a major source of motivation that in turn improves performance. Locke's research showed that the more difficult and specific a goal is, the harder people tend to work to achieve it.

A more recent example; Elon Musk's Space X program is a great example of how people are motivated to work on a difficult task. The recent successful launch of the space-craft to Mars and the Sun must have created enormous motivation for the people who worked on the project starting in 2002.[18]

11.4   Formal and informal communication; power and influence[19]

Especially when implementing something new, communication is important. In a previous chapter, we discussed the competency of communication and the importance and difference between verbal and nonverbal communication.

This section is on how to communicate with internal stakeholders, those involved in the change and in the Relationship Management Strategy in general. It is important to be aware of the attitude of people, their power and influence and mainly those who might sabotage the whole process. This chapter focuses on internal stakeholders though the information here can be used when dealing with external stakeholders too.

Let us first explain the different kinds of communication lines in organizations:

The **formal** communication lines within the organization are clear and based on the structure and the division of roles and responsibilities. Communication takes place through the formal channels of the organization structure along the lines of authority established by the management. Such communications are generally in writing (policy, manuals, procedures, rule books, memoranda, official meetings, reports, and so forth).

Formal communication is transparent and maintains the formal relationship of authority. But it is also often time consuming, cumbersome, and can lead to distortion.

Informal communication means all forms of communication that arise outside of formal communication. They are built around the social relationships of employees and do not flow along formal lines. Informal communication arises for example, when people want to get their way anyhow or when they want to speed up a decision making process.

Informal communication can make it difficult to fix responsibility about accuracy of information. Such communication is usually oral and may even be conveyed by a glance, gesture, smile, or a silence.

Informal communication lines are very important when influencing the behavior of people and will have to be considered when trying to make a change.

> Power is the capacity or ability to direct or influence the behavior of others or the course of events, according to Oxford dictionaries.

The concept of power and influence is important when discussing internal stakeholders. This aspect can help to prioritize stakeholders.

Power[20]

To lead or influence people effectively, a sufficient power base is needed. There are eleven sources of power: five personal sources, five organizational sources, and one metasource. Below is a brief explanation of each of these power sources.

1. *Personal Sources of Power*

Knowledge, skills, talents, and abilities, as well as learning, wisdom, and accomplishments are important sources of power. Also, the way a person is able to **express** him or herself can be a source. If you are, for example very assertive, attractive, engaging, or charismatic (**attraction**), this can give you power in a relationship. If you know a person well, already did business with the person and the experience was good, it can help you in future dealings (**history**). If you are seen as a person of integrity, honest, brave, or fair, this could give you a certain amount of power. Think back to the different roles of a networker–if you are in the role of a confidant, it helps if you are seen as a person of integrity and a reliable character.

2. *Organizational Sources of Power*

A **role** can have a lot of legitimate power and authority because it is linked to a position. It can be a significant source of power but can also lead to abuses of power if not used wisely. There is more power if the role is combined with the personal sources of power.

The owner of a company or the person in control of important **resources** (such as money or natural resources) will have power to decide, but it is not always perceived as the strongest base for power. In organizations, becoming the budget holder, the one who decides how the money is divided, might lead to a lot of power. Access to and control of **information** is also seen as a power source, if used wisely, while making use of personal sources can be powerful tool. From a relationship management point of view, having a good **network** and knowing the right people can be powerful too. Who you know, your **reputation**, and the quality of your connections can give you a lot of power.

3. *Will Power (a metasource)*

Will power is based on the desire to be more powerful than others. Without having the courage to act, will power cannot lead to results, so it is an essential part.

Influence[20]

Influence is the application of power to accomplish a specific purpose. Research (by Walt Hopkins[20] among others) shows that people typically try to lead and/or influence others using ten positive influence techniques and four negative or "dark side" influence techniques.

Influence can be as complex as forming an alliance of nations or as simple as a child smiling and extending his hand in an offer of friendship. Every time we try to affect how other people think, behave, or decide, we are trying to influence them. A smile and a handshake are attempts to socialize, to form a connection and break down barriers. As people get to know us and like us, they are more likely to say yes to our requests.

1. Positive approaches

By using **logic** to explain what you believe or who you want to try to influence and convince others. It is seen as the number one influence tool throughout the world, used in nearly every culture. However, it does not work with everyone and in some circumstances will not work at all. For example, when emotions take over a rational approach, it might have the opposite effect. Another way is to use your (formal) **authority**. There are bosses who tell their employees, "Because I am your boss, you have to do this...." In the Netherlands, this does not work very well; it influences an employee in a more or less negative way. In other cultures, this way of using authority can work because of a different approach to authority.

On average, using authority is seen as the least effective influence technique in the world, but it will work with some people most of the time and most people some of the time (an example could be the Armed Forces).

A third way could be **exchanging**; if you receive a gift (material or immaterial), you might feel obligated to give something in return – at least it creates awareness of some kind of reciprocity. When it is done in an implicit way, it can be seen as a very effective influencing technique. When you need to ask for something in return, it becomes less effective, sometimes even a bit childish.

The more confident you are in **stating** what you believe in, the more you can influence others, although it can backfire. People can get tired of what they perceive as pushy and perhaps dominating.

2. Social approaches to influencing

Getting to know the other person and being open and friendly is used very often to influence people (**socializing**). You gain more by being friendly than by being nasty to a person. In cross-cultural settings you do need to keep in mind what is done and not done. You also can make use of the fact that you are already in a (long-term) friendship with someone; it is easier to influence the people you have already done business with successfully than new acquaintances (**appealing to the relationship**).

Engaging or stimulating people by asking questions (**consulting**), involving them in the problem or solution, is also often used for influencing others. If you know that the other person is quite convinced about his or her opinion in a certain situation, they are most likely willing to go along with you. This works two ways in influencing the process. The last social approach is to **build alliances**; a group is likely to be more convincing in certain situations.

3. Emotional approaches to influencing

Making an emotional **appeal** or an appeal to the heart is a good way to build a certain commitment. And, if you show people how it is done and they see you as a kind of **role model**, they might emulate your behavior. This is sometimes an unconscious way of influencing.

4. The "dark side" influencing tactics or negative approaches

You do not need to do things openly to effectively influence the process. If you **avoid** taking part in something or are able to **manipulate** a person by having hidden agendas, this could also lead to high influence. This is used in organizations a lot and causes delay or denial of implementation. **Intimidating** or **threatening** are imposing or even harmful to others and in the long run are not effective because people feel it and will most likely try to avoid you in future.

11.5   Conclusion

In the near future, creating authentic relationships will become even more important for organizations. It is a way to distinguish themselves from their competitors. However, even without implementing a Relationship Management Strategy, employees still want to be part of an authentic relationship with their colleagues. To be able to build authentic relationships, internally or externally, creates engagement and loyalty. This requires new competencies and skills from everyone who is involved.

If leaders do decide to implement a Relationship Management Strategy, it is important to translate this to the employees who directly and indirectly are impacted by this decision. You do not want be part of the 60-70 percent failure rate when implementing new strategies.

There is a broad variety of change management methods; align this with the wants and needs of the organization and its employees.
· The "why" of the implementation should be very clear for everybody–it will lead to more engagement.

- The "what" should be defined in terms of roles, tasks, responsibilities, and the way reporting lines are designed. This will create more structure.
- It is important to decide "how" to organize this, the planning and timing of the implementation, but also "how" employees are expected to work together in their networking teams as well as with their external relationships.

It is important to use all the skills available when it comes to influencing the right employees in the right way and at the right time. This can lead to clearer expectations and increased effectiveness.

Notes

1. Relational Being, Beyond Self and Community, Kenneth J. Gergen, Oxford University Press, Inc, 2009
2. https://corporate-rebels.com/guest-blog-adoption-self-management/
3. https://www.mckinsey.com/business-functions/strategy-and-corporate-finance/our-insights/enduring-ideas-the-7-s-framework
4. Unlocking the flexible organization, Organizational design for an uncertain future; Copyright © 2016 Deloitte Development LLC.
5. Leading Change, Auteur: John Kotter, Co-author: Oliver Wyman, Harvard Business School Publishing, 1996
6. Action research, Kurt Lewin; http://cei.ust.hk/files/public/ar_intro_background_of_action_research.pdf, Organization Development and Change 10th Edition, Cummings & Worley
7. ADKAR: https://www.prosci.com/adkar/adkar-model
8. Cooperrider AI: source: Appreciative Inquiry Handbook, David L. Cooperrider, Diana Whitney, Jaqueline M. Stavros, 2nd edition Co-published by Crown Custom Publishing, Inc. and Berrett-Koehler Publishers, Inc.
9. Diagnosing and changing organisational culture; based on competing values framework, Kim S. Cameron and Robert E. Quinn, 2011
10. Appreciative Inquiry Handbook, David L. Cooperrider, Diana Whitney, Jaqueline M. Stavros, 2nd edition Co-published by Crown Custom Publishing, Inc. and Berrett-Koehler Publishers, Inc.
11. Tipping Point leadership, Kim & Maubourgne, 2003 http://study.com/academy/lesson/intrinsic-motivation-in-psychology-definition-examples-factors.html http://www.businessdictionary.com/definition/motivation.htm
12. Tipping Point Leadership, Kim & Maubourgne, 2003
13. https://study.com/academy/lesson/extrinsic-motivation-in-the-workplace-factors-types-examples.html
14. http://study.com/academy/lesson/intrinsic-motivation-in-psychology-definition-examples-factors.html
15. Frederick Herzberg, Motivation Hygiene theory: Writers on Organizations, Derek S. Pugh, David J. Hickson, 6th Edition, Sage Publishing
16. Drive, the surprising truth about what motivates us, Riverhead hardcover, Daniel Pink, 2009
17. www.mindtools.com/pages/article/newHTE_87.htm
18. http://www.spacex.com/elon-musk
19. https://www.mindtools.com/pages/article/newHTE_87.htm39
20. http://www.theelementsofpower.com

How a refugee organization professionalized its relationship management

by Boukje de Haan, Head of Communication and Fundraising, Foundation for Refugee Students UAF

The oldest refugee organization in the Netherlands
The UAF was founded in 1948 in response to the brutal suppression of the student uprising in Prague. A group of fifty Czech students fled to the Netherlands. The Dutch universities decided to set up an organization to help those students continue their education in the Netherlands. The organization was originally called the *University Asylum Fund*, the UAF. Today it is known as the Foundation for Refugee Students UAF.

Each year, the Foundation for Refugee Students UAF supports 3,300 refugees in the Netherlands to prepare for and undertake their education and find suitable employment in the Netherlands.

The UAF is an independent foundation that is able to carry out its work thanks to grants from the Dutch Ministry of Education, Culture, and Science, an annual contribution from the Nationale Postcode Loterij (Dutch Lottery), and the donations and support of the public.

The Foundation for Refugee Students UAF maintains relationships with all parties that can play a role in the development of the talent of the refugee. UAF knows what a refugee needs in order to get viable employment on the Dutch labor market, what facilities are available for refugees, and what steps a refugee has to take in order to achieve economic self-sufficiency. Various organizations play a crucial role along the road to economic self-sufficiency, such as educational institutions, language institutes, local councils, employers, and other refugee organizations. UAF has a detailed knowledge of the fundraising market and knows where to get financial support. UAF is the spider at the center of the web, developing and strengthening relationships and creating links between all the different parties. A plan-based approach to relationship management is crucial in order to support refugees to achieve their full potential.

Why did you initiate a relationship management professionalization program?
Society is changing all the time; the Netherlands is increasingly becoming a networking and participation society, and a growing number of functions and authorities are being decentralized. More and more refugees are turning to the UAF,

and we have therefore set ourselves an ambitious goal; to support as many refugees in our target group as possible to achieve economic self-sufficiency. Until recently, the UAF mainly focused on optimizing the support given to refugees while they were studying in order to maximize their chances of success. Over the coming years we will be intensifying our contact with employers and looking for alternative routes to support refugees find paid employment even faster. The facilitating role of UAF will be scaled down, and UAF will develop into a Network Organization. This means we need to have a clear strategic vision for our relationship management. The role of the student counselor and job consultant will also change; the counselor will become more of a connector (networker) among the organizations that are involved in the integration of refugees. UAF will be transforming its way of working into a regional approach centered on the creation of connections and partnerships. The UAF staff will be working partly in the regions in order to set up networks that refugees can turn to in their regions.

How did the Institute of Strategic Relationship Management (ISRM) and their vision help you?

Most of our employees are not familiar with Strategic Relationship Management, so we asked ISRM to organize an in-company training course for a core team of relationship managers. Step by step, in a number of sessions, all the different aspects of Strategic Relationship Management were covered, and then we translated the theory into practice. We developed our own vision of relationship management, formulated our ambitions and goals, appointed an order winner for each value center, and carried out an internal and external stakeholder analysis. That way, our staff was introduced to Strategic Relationship Management in an organic way, which convinced everyone of the importance of a systematic and proactive approach. In addition to the core team, we involved some internal experts in specific subjects, such as the HR consultant and the Functional Application Manager. By the end of the training course, we had developed a clear and comprehensive overview of the contact people, the relationship goals, and the contact intensity for the relationships in each external relationship segment.

What steps have already been taken?

Because the training sessions included homework assignments, we already had all the documents we needed for Strategic Relationship Management by the end of the course. The first version of the vision and strategy was discussed by the management team and will be ratified soon. Communication of the vision and strategy to the staff started with a presentation to the regional coordinators, and a schedule of needs and requirements for the CRM system has been drawn up.

What difficulties did you encounter, and what are the challenges?

Relationship management does not happen all by itself, and the relationship managers who took the course will play an important role in the implementation and embedding of the strategy. Most of the staff is not used to working on relationship management in a systematic way; they are mainly focused on providing guidance to refugees, and they do not feel like they have the time to proactively initiate and develop relationships. Creating an awareness of the importance of relationship management takes time and effort. Time is a major challenge anyway, not only for the networkers, but also for the Managers of the Network. Another challenge is the creation of the necessary support structure (systems, human resources, coordination) needed to collect, manage, and analyze the relationship data. Dealing with overlapping contacts and segments is also a big challenge; for example, some educational institutions have contact with more than one relationship manager within the UAF. These relationships can cover multiple segments and exist at different levels within these segments. It is essential to know who is responsible for what relationship and where the different relationship managers and their strategies overlap.

What new understanding and insights did you gain?

Thanks to the training course, we are now aware of the necessity of having both a strategic, structured, and methodical approach and regular monitoring in order to be successful. It was also a surprise to find out how much of the staff plays a role in relationship management, and that therefore we have to make sure, for example, that the receptionist is aware of its importance too.

What have the benefits been so far?

The networkers who attended the training course now see relationship management in a completely different way, and we all realize how much time and effort you need to put into it. A mixed, multidisciplinary group took the course together so the connection between the various disciplines was established right away and that highlighted the interrelationships between the disciplines. Thanks to the training course, staff in different disciplines now has tactical meetings to discuss the best way to manage relationships.

Successful Encounters

Officers of the Oude Schutterij in Alkmaar, Claes Pietersz. van der Heck, 1613, panel, 99,2 × 108, 6 cm, collection Stedelijk Museum Alkmaar

LinkedIn or Facebook?

by Paul Mosterd, Deputy Director Hermitage Amsterdam

Were militia portraits in the seventeenth century always intended to benefit one's career and network? Did you invariably have be depicted as confident and proud, do you think? Then you should pay a visit to the Stedelijk Museum in Alkmaar. A militia portrait hangs there which does exactly the opposite of what all those other portraits do; it does not try to impress us at all. It is a curious work. Claes van der Heck painted it in 1613, and he portrays the officers of the Oude Schutterij in Alkmaar, one of the most influential cities in the Netherlands, in a landscape. It seems as if they are having a picnic in the forest! It almost looks like a company outing, complete with awkward, forced poses.

Why is no one wearing a uniform? The men do wear those famous white collars, but the squatting and kneeling on the dirty tree stumps certainly makes the image comical, especially because of the immaculate white collars. The combination is distracting so we are unimpressed by these opulent officers. The viewer's eye is directed to the dunes in the background and to a couple that is gazing toward us. If you look at the picture for a while, you almost start to think the painting was a failure. That, however, is unlikely – Van der Heck was a professional with an excellent clientele. Maybe something else was going on, maybe the commission was unusual – no more power plays or dress to impress. More than anything else, the painting seems to present a group of friends. It is certainly not about ambition, status, or being seen. Perhaps it was not intended to impress the spectator. Not LinkedIn, more a convivial Facebook.

12. Supporting the Networkers; Creating the Networking Tool Kit

This chapter is about supporting colleagues – the networkers – in their networking activities by developing a so-called networking tool kit. Networkers should be informed, involved, and supported in various ways so that they can be successful in their networking activities. This chapter sums up how to provide the right support.

Almost everyone in organizations is in need of a meaningful network and thus almost everyone has to network from time to time. Some employees spend very little time on networking, whereas for others it is a day-to-day activity: account managers, diplomats, fundraisers, or external relations officers.

The networkers should be supported by the Managers of the Network – the readers of this book – to be successful. The Managers of the Network are responsible for the management of the entire network of an organization and thus for supporting the networkers.

12.1 Networking tool kit

The Managers of the Network support the networkers to perform successfully by providing a networking tool kit:

1. Every networker should be **informed** about (and preferably also be **involved** in the development of):
   - The Networking Vision and Relationship Management Strategy.
   - The tasks/responsibilities/competencies/goals of a networker; What is expected of the networker? How to perform these tasks?
2. The networker should be able to **share information** obtained from external stakeholders during the networking activities:
   - By using a CRM system.
   - Via networking team meetings.
3. Be **supported** in developing the necessary **networking skills**.
4. Be supported with and informed about **networking opportunities**.

1. To inform (and involve) the networker

The networkers should preferably be involved in the development of the Networking Vision (Chapter 1 and 3) and Relationship Management Strategy (Chapter 4), but at the very least they should be properly informed; How is the Relationship Management Strategy aligned with the overall strategy? What are our relational goals? How are the relational goals translated into individual goals? How is our network contributing to the success of the organization?

It is vital that all of those involved in the relationship management have a fundamental understanding of the choices that were made in the development of the Networking Vision and Relationship Management Strategy. Yearly or twice-yearly Networking Vision and Relationship Management Strategy sessions could be a way to do this. A written version of the Vision and Strategy should also be available outside these sessions.

It is also good to explain how the responsibility for the relationship management (Chapter 10) is embedded in the organization; Who is responsible for what? And what is the role of the networkers in all of this, what is expected of them? The role of the networker is to build relationships based upon the formulated Networking Vision and Relationship Management Strategy. However, the role of the networker can differ from organization to organization. The definition of clear goals, tasks, responsibilities, and competencies is advised.

2. Share information

Networkers should be able to share useful information within the organization; What has been discussed with external stakeholders? What information has been obtained? What is important to share with colleagues?

To be able to do so, an effective CRM system is essential (Chapter 9). The networkers should be motivated to use the CRM system and fill in the necessary information. Use of a CRM is often not a digital but a motivational challenge.

It is also good to regularly bring together those who operate in the same network via networking team meetings (Chapter 10). These meetings bring networkers together who share the same topic, region, or have other things in common. These meetings are meant to exchange information, specifically the subtler information that is hard to share in a CRM system, and to strengthen each other's networks. The Manager(s) of the Network leads the networking team meetings.

3. Developing networking skills; training and coaching

Not everyone is a born networker; some people lack the necessary experience, knowledge, or skills. During monitoring/evaluation it will become clear whether a networker is effective. If not, the networker should be supported with the appropriate training or coaching.

To determine the effectiveness of a networker, it is important to have a clear definition of the competencies of a professional networker, as described in Chapter 10. This is not only useful for monitoring/evaluation purposes but also for the development of an effective training program and for the recruitment/selection of the best networkers for particular networking events or meetings.

> Change comes when people want it, not before.

Networking skills can be trained but it requires repetition over a long period of time. Not every networker can be trained to the same level and to the same extent. Also, the time frame can be different per individual–for some people it will take longer than for others, and some might have to go through deeper development than others. Effective networking skills training requires a personal approach.

If there is little or no budget for training, a selection could help; only the best networkers are asked to attend a meeting or networking event.

Examples of networking skills that people can learn by training are personal presentation, communication and social skills, nonverbal communication, cross-cultural communication, table manners and other etiquette, practical diplomatic skills, ethics, and integrity.

Specific things that can be taught are how to compose a guest list for a networking event; how to invite guests for an event or meeting; how to prepare for an event or meeting; how to determine goals; how to welcome guests; how to make introductions; how to start and end conversations; what to talk about with the guests; how to process the information obtained; how to decide on the follow-up; and how to use the CRM system effectively. These skills could be trained in group sessions, online courses, on the job, by using role-play, in personal coaching sessions, or by observation reports. See also Chapter 10.

4. Networking activities

The networkers should be involved in and informed about the opportunities for strengthening the network:

· What networking activities are organized by our organization? What stakeholders could be invited for those activities? What networking opportunities do these activities offer us? How do we invite guests for a networking event? What is expected of the networkers during those events? See also Chapter 13.
· What external networking activities does our organization participate in? How to also participate?
· What other opportunities are there to strengthen the network; invite connections to sign up for newsletters or yearly reports, for example.

A bank for wealthy clients conducted several surveys about its networking events. The remark most made by clients was "where was my account manager?" Another bank reviewed the guest lists of its past networking events and found that 20 percent of its clients were invited to 80 percent of the networking events. A lot of networkers invited more or less the same guests to the events put on by the bank.

13. Networking Events or Meetings

Once the organization's Networking Vision and Relationship Management Strategy are ready and after designing the organization's relationship management approach, it is time to stage a real encounter. But how do you organize effective relationship meetings based on the information in the previous chapters? How do you translate the organization's vision and strategy into successful personal encounters, in other words–how do you move from the strategic and tactical level to the operational level?

In this chapter, the process of managing networking events is discussed.

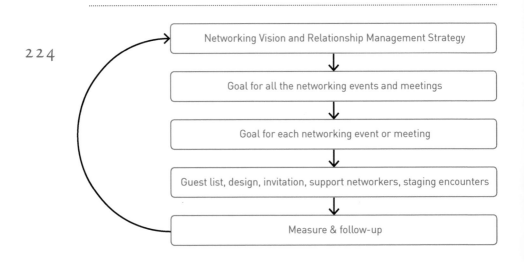

Figure 13.1 Networking events or meetings

13.1   The goal of networking events or meetings

The management of an effective networking event or meeting starts with translating the Networking Vision and Relationship Management Strategy into
· One goal for all the networking events or meetings.
· A specific goal for each networking event or meeting.
Based upon this, you can structure the event or meeting.

The Networking Vision and Relationship Management Strategy is the connective tissue across layers of management and between functions. This vision and strategy provide guidance and link to division, business, and networking activities. The development of a goal for the relationship meeting(s) or event(s) and the networkers should be in line with the development of a Networking Vision and Relationship Management Strategy. For this, the Strategy Cascade can be applied (see paragraph 4.5).

By having a solid understanding of the direction, priorities, and profit model of the overall organization and of the Networking Vision and Relationship Management Strategy, it is easier to identify how an event or meeting and a networker can contribute value to the organization. When it is clear what markets or segments the organization wants to focus on, more meaningful relationship activities can be developed as opposed to a situation in which this is less clear.

13.2   Managing the network event or meeting

This chapter focuses on events or meetings and how to structure them to maximize the Return-on-Relationship. The basis of this vision is a modern application of protocol, as discussed in Chapter 2.

Campaign management
A networking event or meeting is a one-time occurrence. However, when plotted against time there are pre-event, event, and post-event activities. As we see in Figure 13.2.1, the process starts by defining the campaign objectives. Also part of the process are various approval stages (for objectives, for approach, for content, for budget) and a testing phase. When a lot of money will need to be spent, it is useful to conduct testing beforehand. The testing can be simple (for example, test the idea with some relationships) or more sophisticated (an online mini-campaign). The last cluster in the campaign process is the evaluation of the results.
An event is one of the steps in the overall process; #5, campaign delivery.

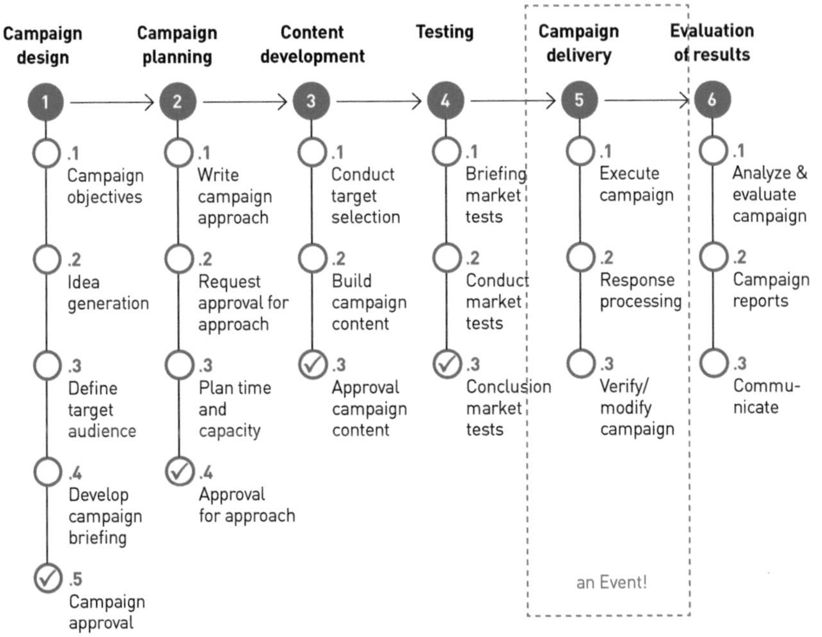

Campaign design	Campaign planning	Content development	Testing	Campaign delivery	Evaluation of results
1	**2**	**3**	**4**	**5**	**6**
.1 Campaign objectives	.1 Write campaign approach	.1 Conduct target selection	.1 Briefing market tests	.1 Execute campaign	.1 Analyze & evaluate campaign
.2 Idea generation	.2 Request approval for approach	.2 Build campaign content	.2 Conduct market tests	.2 Response processing	.2 Campaign reports
.3 Define target audience	.3 Plan time and capacity	✓ .3 Approval campaign content	✓ .3 Conclusion market tests	.3 Verify/ modify campaign	.3 Commu- nicate
.4 Develop campaign briefing	✓ .4 Approval for approach				
✓ .5 Campaign approval				an Event!	

Figure 13.2.1 Campaign management process[1]

An event therefore is part of a bigger process. In the context of relationship management this is called the campaign management process. A campaign process could look like Figure 13.2.1.

If we focus on one single event or meeting, the event can be split into different steps: the selection of attendees, the design of the program, the invitation process, the support for the networkers, the staging of encounters, and the follow-up.

Having the approach written out as a process is helpful to:
· Identify what data is collected during which step.
· Instruct employees on what they should do and when.
· Guarantee consistent quality – no elements are forgotten.
· Identify key requirements that must be fulfilled to run the process smoothly.
The process is a tool to enable the organization to continuously learn, improve, and develop a consistent quality level in managing its strategic relationships.

Networking event or meeting management
Now let's focus on the organization of one event or meeting, as seen in Figure 13.2.2. This process consists of composing a guest list, designing the networking event or meeting, the invitation process, supporting the networkers, staging the encounters and measuring results.

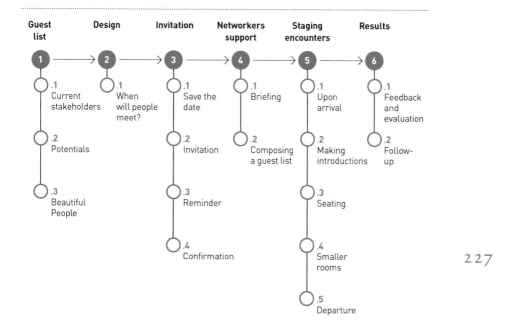

Figure 13.2.2 Networking event or meeting management

1. Composing a guest list

The guest list should support the goals and is the basis for a good networking event or meeting. The desired attendance is largely influenced by the guest list – "who else is invited?" In evaluations, most guests indicate that this is the main reason to attend.

Most organizations consider inviting only their current clients or stakeholders, but from a networking perspective it is advisable to invite more people:
· Current stakeholders.
· Potential stakeholders.
· Beautiful People (people who support the networking function of the event).

> *An example of an event with current and potential stakeholders and Beautiful People*
> A regional bank (in Europe) organized a golf tournament for directors of small and medium-sized businesses. Instead of just inviting current clients, they also invited potential clients and Beautiful People.
>
> Examples of Beautiful People are the city's alderman in charge of economic affairs, the regional chairman of the chamber of commerce, and the chairman of the local school of economics. Beautiful People have a positive effect on the profile of the event and contribute to the networking function; they make it easier to attract other people.

The guest list of this event resulted in the tournament being the number one network for smaller and medium-sized businesses in the region. The attendance increased considerably over the years, and the bank profited from the success of the networking event.

Cross-fertilization and exchange should be the objectives of all relationship events. A guest list should be interesting for the host as well as for the guests. It is also good to find a balance between government officials and business representatives, current clients and potential clients, young and old guests, men and women. A good guest list could also include distinguished personalities from the arts, literature, academia, or media.

A broad mix of guests and stakeholders is very relevant in the cultural and corporate worlds, as is explained by Axel Rüger, director of the Van Gogh Museum in Amsterdam, the Netherlands, in the Dutch magazine Winq (January/February 2015) (translated from Dutch):

"The culture and creative sector should wield more influence. At trade missions of the municipality of Amsterdam, a delegation of the cultural sector is always present, together with the mayor and representatives of the corporate sector. With state visits, that is not often done. If I do attend, I often hear, 'You can talk to the cultural organizations, but nothing more.' I believe we should progress towards a more integrated approach, also in a broader perspective. If you go through the membership lists of the supervisory boards of cultural institutions, you will find all the CEOs of multinationals you can think of. Then have a look at how many leaders from the cultural sector have a commissioner's position at large or mid-sized enterprises. You can almost count them on two fingers. At my museum, we manage a world brand. I do an enormous amount of market research, I have visitors from all over the world, I know quite a bit about the consumer and consumer behavior, and we work closely with the travel industry. We manage an SME with very specific financial goals. We manage a very broad group of stakeholders, much broader than many commercial organizations do. If I mention this to one of those CEOs, there is a minute of silence and then he says, 'You are actually right. Never thought of that.' That is what we should start, much more cross-fertilization, much more exchange."

Another way of constructing the guest list is to think of people who would be happy to receive an invitation and a second group – who we would be happy to have in attendance. The latter group might be harder to get; more effort is needed to persuade them to come.

For recurring events, it might be convenient to use a so-called Iron List, a list of functionaries who should always participate in that particular event. This list keeps you from having to start all over again every time the event is being organized.

2. Designing the networking event or meeting

There are many examples of networking events that do not offer the opportunity for people to actually meet; those with lengthy programs, long dinners, crowded rooms, or loud music. Often most of the budget for networking events is spent on catering, speakers, or entertainment, and events lack the structure needed to support the networking function. The organization of a good networking meeting starts with designing the networking moments; when will people meet?

The program of a networking meeting should leave room for people to meet upon arrival, at the table, during the breaks, after the plenary program, and so forth. Designing an effective program often means reducing the time for plenary sessions.

An example of a traditional program for a networking dinner:

7 p.m.	Arrival of the guests
7:30 p.m.	Start dinner
10:30 p.m.	End dinner

This program leaves very little time for people to meet; many guests arrive five to ten minutes before the start of the dinner and leave immediately afterwards. The majority of the guests have about two conversations; at the table with the people seated to their left and to their right.

A better program could look like this:

From 5:30 p.m.	Arrival of the guests
6:30 p.m.	First course (while standing)
7:15 p.m.	Guests take their seats for the sit-down dinner
8:00 p.m.	*Changement* (change seats)
8:45 p.m.	Continue dinner (at a different table)
9:30 p.m.	End dinner, walking dessert and coffee
11 p.m.	End

This program offers many opportunities to meet; upon arrival, when being served the first course, at the table, during the break (*changement*), and when the last course is served.

3. The invitation process

To go or not to go? That's the question.

Professional invitations support the desire for (high) attendance and play an important role in communicating the networking opportunities. There are, however, many ways in which invitations can be sent, with different degrees of success in attracting the right people.

Invitation route
A classic invitation route as part of a campaign management process consists of the following elements:

  ◯ Save-the-date   ◯ Invitation   ◯ Reminder   ◯ Confirmation

The save-the-date is only used to communicate the date, and the invitation is meant to get a response as to who will attend and who will not. This is often indicated by r.s.v.p. or "répondez s'il vous plaît" which means "please respond." After the rsvp date, a reminder is sent to those who did not respond. Then only those who said they are coming will receive a confirmation with the last details.

To achieve the desired attendance.

Timing
The timing of sending out invitations is important; invitations should be sent out in time to be successful in attracting the right people. This depends to a great extent on the country, the city, the social activity, and the kind of guests involved. In the diplomatic community around the world, invitations for receptions are normally sent out two or three weeks in advance. In the Middle East, however, it can be quite appropriate to send invitations less than a week prior to an event. If the function is larger, three or four weeks may be more suitable. In Western Europe, Australia, and New Zealand, invitations to formal events should ideally be sent four to six weeks prior to the event, otherwise it is likely that only a few people can accept, because of other engagements made earlier. For high-level events this is even more the case.

Digital or printed
Colorful multi-folded cards, traditional engraved invitations for embassy receptions, well-designed electronic seminar invitations, birthday invitations on Facebook – a wide range of invitations is common nowadays. Because so many invitations are sent via email, a printed invitation attracts more attention and is therefore often more successful in realizing the desired attendance. Invitations sent

via SMS, Facebook, Twitter, or any other kind of social media are, especially for formal occasions, often not very successful.

Basic elements

Invitations that lack the most basic information are not very effective in attracting the right people. A professional invitation provides the invitee with the essential details of the event. This is the same for digital invitations, despite their more informal nature.

Professional invitations should include an answer to the following W's:
1. Who is inviting?
2. Why is he or she inviting?
3. What kind of function is it?
4. Who is invited?
5. Where is the event being held?
6. When is the event taking place?
7. What dress code applies?
8. Who to contact with reply?
9. Whatever information is also relevant to know.

Personal

Personal invitations are more successful than standardized invitations. Starting an invitation text with "Dear client" communicates the mass production of the invitation and thus of the event. Most people will think, "How likely is it I will meet someone of interest?"

Personal invitations include the name of the guest. It is even better if the name is handwritten or engraved. What also helps is the indication "strictly personal and non-transferable" or a short handwritten personal note from the host or hostess.

Who is invited?

It is not common to send guests a guest list, but to clarify the networking opportunity it is wise to include some general information about the target group of the event. One could add to the invitation text a sentence describing the type of guest being invited; "This invitation has been sent to communications managers of large corporates and other communication experts." Other ways to support the networking opportunity is to add a committee of recommendation of people of interest to the target group.

Official invitations; forms of address

There are certain universal conventions governing forms of address, but every country has its particular style. Generally, the way of addressing a person is determined by his or her status as well as the relationship between that person and the speaker or writer.

> Many books and manuals have been written on forms of address, but the following book is recommended and constitutes points of reference for the various forms of address for heads of state and government, as well as other religious, legal, diplomatic, royal, and political officials from around the world: Hickey, R., *Honor & Respect: The Official Guide to Names, Titles, and Forms of Address*, The Protocol School of Washington, 2008

4. Supporting the networkers; those interacting with external stakeholders
Even the best-organized networking events are not successful without professional networkers. As discussed in Chapter 10 and 12, if the networkers do not understand the role they must play, nothing will be achieved.

> In the movie *The Devil Wears Prada*, Meryl Streep plays the chief editor Miranda Priestly of the renowned fashion magazine Runway. During the reception given by Runway at Paris Fashion Week, Miranda is assisted by her two PAs. They whisper the name and function of the guests approaching Miranda, enabling her to give everyone a warm and personal welcome.
>   Miranda Priestly must be one of the best networkers in the business and is well aware of the networking game that has to be played to achieve goals. Not knowing someone's name is not an option for someone in her position.

Whether you are hosting numerous dignitaries from around the world at a high-level event or you host an intimate dinner for a couple of close business partners, the networkers will have to pay attention to all their guests. It depends on their charm, social capabilities, and networking skills to make this happen.

In doing so, being authentic is key. The networker must show a genuine interest in others and be a gracious host who makes sure that people feel comfortable in the presence of everyone there. He or she ensures an atmosphere of mutual understanding.

At the same time the networker must achieve a certain networking goal by talking to certain guests for a certain reason. This seems to present a paradox – is this not in contradiction with the desire to be genuine? A lot of networkers find it difficult to comply with both.

What is asked of a networker?
· The networker composes a list of guests suitable for the event (if asked to do so by the Manager of the Network).
· The networker prepares him or herself for each event; who would I like to meet?

What would I like to achieve? When am I successful?
- The networker does research on the guests he or she would like to meet; what useful information can be found in our CRM and online?
- The networker is present before the guests arrive and leaves after they have left.
- The networker greets his or her guests upon arrival and says goodbye at the end.
- The networker initiates conversations.
- The networker introduces guests to guests, colleagues to guests, and so on.
- The networker shows sincere and genuine interest in guests, makes everyone feel at ease, and creates mutual understanding.
- The networker spreads his or her attention to all the guests.
- After the guests have left, the results are entered in a CRM system; who did I talk with? What was discussed? Was the event successful for me?
- A follow-up is determined.

The networker should be supported by the Manager of the Network as discussed in Chapter 10 and 12. This support starts with determining:
- Who will be acting as networker? Who will be the (main) host(s)?
- What support is required?

Briefing
A preferably written briefing should contain the following information for the networkers:
- The networking goal of the event; what should be achieved?
- A program including the necessary background information.
- Information on the goal and role of the networkers; what is expected of them?
- Who will I meet; a guest list including a book of faces and background information (what should be achieved, with whom, what is our mutual relationship/interest?).
- All practical and logistical information (address, dress code, menu, seating).

Composing a guest list
In larger organizations, the networkers are often asked to provide a list of guests for the networking event or meeting. Not every networker knows how to do this, so support or guidelines should be provided:
- How to invite the guests; what is the communication message?
- How to choose the guests; what should be their profile?
- How to make sure they will attend; how to guarantee they will come?

The networker who is also the main host
Acting as the main host requires a different support; the main host will have to welcome everyone upon arrival and most guests expect him or her to know their name. The main host will also have to welcome the guests in his or her speech and

maybe even personally welcome the special guests. The main host is also responsible for the seating arrangements and determines who sits where. Most guests will want to say goodbye to him or her before they leave.

5. Staging the encounter; making sure people will actually meet

How do you guarantee that people will actually meet? The best way is to proactively stage encounters or arrange meetings. The best moments for this are before and after the official parts of a program. Upon arrival, for example, it is common to escort guests to the networkers. Seating guests is also an effective way to ensure certain people will meet.

Here are the chronological elements of a seminar program. Each black element takes only a few minutes per guest but offers an opportunity for the organization to stage encounters.

Arrival Coffee/tea Seating Seminar Movement Reception Farewell

The role of the usher
Ushers are part of the organizing committee and focus on facilitating the encounters and escorting guests to the networkers (or the other way around). Ushers can be very useful in increasing the number of meaningful encounters by supporting the networkers.

Upon arrival
Upon arrival guests could be escorted first to the main host and then to one of the other hosts (networkers). This way it is possible to stage specific encounters and determine in advance which meetings will take place.

This approach requires a certain preparation. It must be determined who should meet whom and this information will have to be included in the guest list and registration. Upon arrival, guests are escorted to the main host and other hosts (networkers) by ushers, who are able to perform this task in a professional and informal manner and ideally are able to inform the guest and host(s) of each other's name and function.

In advance, the hosts (networkers) will have to be told about this procedure or maybe even receive training. And the networkers will have to be strategically placed in the reception area so ushers are able to find them.

This approach increases the meaningful encounters considerably. Where people are normally able to meet about four to five people they already know, this approach arranges ten to twelve meetings with people who have never met before. The Protocolbureau in The Hague is one of the experts in arranging meetings this way, and they are called upon for assistance for many networking events.

The ushers of the Protocolbureau are trained in making introductions by remembering the following steps; name guest, name host, name guest. The first step is to find out the name and function of the guest. The second step is to explain to the guest who they are taking him or her to. The third step is to announce the guest (with his or her function title) to the host. This may sound easy, but it requires some practice to make professional introductions. The extensive training program for the ushers consists of several role-plays to practice this.

Making introductions during the event
Making introductions (other than upon arrival) is also a very effective way to increase the number of meaningful encounters; people are introduced to each other by name and function. Ushers can assist in finding the guests and bringing the host (networker) to the guest or the other way around. Introductions start by telling who you want to introduce, after which people are brought together and introductions are made.

Introducing guests to a guest of honor at formal receptions
If special introduction rounds are foreseen during an official reception, the host remains with the guest of honor at the same place in the reception area. An usher takes care of finding the guests and escorting them to the host who will then introduce them to the guest of honor.

These special introductions should be arranged in advance and should look as informal as possible in order to create an atmosphere in which everyone feels comfortable. Quite often the guests who are participating in the introduction rounds will be informed accordingly in advance or upon arrival.

By seating
Seating people is an effective way to support the networking function of an event. By seating people next to each other, a meeting can be guaranteed. This is the case at lunches and dinners, but also at plenary sessions where an encounter can occur when sitting down and shortly before the program starts/ends.

Seating people means making a seating plan, and these plans change until the last moment as the guest lists change until the last moment. Digital seating programs are very useful as it is much easier to process last-minute changes. Seating people also requires seating cards (to hand out to the guest upon arrival indicating where they are seated) and table/chair cards (with the name of the guest). For the ushers, seating plans and guest lists will have to be printed.

In the 16 October 2014 online article "Drama. Ego. Protocol: Washington dinners have it all" in *The Washington Post*, Roxanne Roberts provides the following example of mixing guests at formal dinners:

"*Rima Al-Sabah, wife of the Kuwaiti ambassador in Washington DC, is an expert at the gentle art of managing a room full of big names. She says protocol is of 'paramount importance' because diplomats expect to be treated according to their rank. 'It would be insulting to do otherwise.' Several A-list ambassadors were deployed around the room – Al-Sabah uses them as anchors for different tables – and then she seats people with similar interests so they have plenty to talk about. 'I mix all of the guests, after the basic protocol has been set, because I don't like the idea of a host taking all of the most important VIPs to their table and putting all the other guests together at what might feel like a lesser table,' she says.*"

Smaller rooms
At large events the use of smaller rooms can be helpful to increase the number of meaningful encounters. Upon arrival or during breaks, people are escorted to a certain room based upon mutual interest.

Engagements during farewell and on departure
Farewell and departure are as important as the arrival and welcome due to the fact that the first and last five minutes leave a long-lasting impression. The hosts (networkers) should be positioned in such a way that guests can easily say goodbye on the way out.

6. Measuring results
After the event, it is important to find out the outcome of the event. What are the results? What did we achieve? How did individual networkers perform? To what extent have they shown the desired behavior and used the expected skills?

Those who fail to learn from history are doomed to repeat it.

Asking the guests for feedback
It is common to ask the ushers to escort the guests outside to ask them for feedback. This works best if it does not feel like an official evaluation. Most feedback is given about the event and some feedback is received on more general matters. Also, the first reaction of a guest is usually positive, out of politeness, so it is important to ask a second more in-depth question like, "Is there anything we should improve next time?"

Evaluation with the networkers
The most important evaluation is the one given by the networkers themselves; what was discussed with the people that were brought into contact with them? And did they meet anyone else? This evaluation usually brings a lot of valuable information and leads.

It is best to conduct this evaluation before the networkers go home, so they still remember most of what happened. Sometimes there is resistance from the networkers; they do not like to give details about what was discussed, or they are afraid the evaluation will make painfully clear they lack the necessary networking skills.

Follow-up
Measuring results is one step; determining how the follow-up is managed is another. Who will make sure the results are entered into the CRM system? Who will check that the necessary steps are taken?

In the days after the event, plan time to determine and execute the follow-up. The next steps will have to be made while the event is still fresh in the memory of the guests.

A networking event is nothing more than a snapshot. The effectiveness of it hinges very much on good preparation but also on good follow-up. Many organizations fail to measure results and ask their employees who they met and what was discussed. Experience, however, has proven that most events, when staged and evaluated appropriately, are very effective and bring a lot of useful results.

Notes
1. Source: Deloitte Consulting

The authors, from left to right: Robert Collignon, Prof. René Foqué, Gerty Smit, Monica Bakker, Jean Paul Wijers.

The authors

Jean Paul Wijers

Jean Paul Wijers is the founder and director of the Institute of Strategic Relationship Management (ISRM). In 1996 he graduated from the Hotelschool The Hague, one year after starting his first company, Protocolbureau. Between 2001 and 2009, Jean Paul Wijers worked as head usher for the Master of Ceremonies of H.M. Queen Beatrix, at royal weddings, state funerals, and royal baptisms.

Jean Paul used his unique experience in protocol to develop a method for organizing effective networking meetings with measurable results. In a modern application, protocol is a way to increase the number of meaningful encounters at networking events.

His vision of effective relationship management resulted in the foundation of the ISRM. Jean Paul is also the initiator of the postgraduate program about Strategic Relationship Management and the initiator and editor of this book, *Managing Authentic Relationships; Facing New Challenges in a Changing Context.*

Prof. Dr. René Foqué

René Foqué is emeritus Professor at the Law Faculty of the University of Leuven and at the Erasmus Law School in Rotterdam. He still teaches at the European Interuniversity Centre in Venice. He is the academic coordinator of the Comenius Leadership Course in Bologna. He served previously as chairman of the jury of the International Spinoza Prize. He is a correspondent fellow of the Dutch Royal Academy of Sciences. He studied law and philosophy at the University of Leuven and French language and literature at the Université de Lille.

Monica Bakker

Monica Bakker is a sinologist and lived for several years in Beijing. At the Dutch institute Comenius Courses which is related to University of Groningen, she is a program director of new programs on executive leadership development. Besides that, Monica is a Socratic Dialogue facilitator and lecturer on Innovation Leadership and Chinese Innovation Mindset at Inholland University of Applied Science.

At the ISRM, Monica is a trainer and consultant on relational leadership and vision development; to what end and on the basis of what attitude do organizations create their Networking Vision and bring it to life?

Robert Collignon

Robert Collignon has more than twenty years of experience in marketing, sales, and customer service. He is a director of (customer) strategy at Monitor Deloitte. In addition to his work at Deloitte, he lectures at the ISRM and the Hotelschool The Hague.

His client list includes Swiss Life, Aegon, Procter & Gamble, Pfizer, TUI, Sol Melia, KLM, AB Inbev, ABN AMRO and RTL.

A Dutch national, Robert has a Master's degree in Business Law and in Business Administration and he is a Registered Marketeer (RM). Robert has contributed to numerous marketing and business publications.

Robert Collignon is chairman of the United World Colleges (UWC) Netherlands. UWC is a non-profit organization that makes education a force to unite people, nations, and cultures for peace and a sustainable future.

Gerty Smit

Gerty Smit is an expert in change management and human resources management. As an independent Birkman consultant, she is an experienced coach in career development, team development, and personal development. Since 2001 she is also a lecturer at Hotelschool The Hague and is responsible for developing and teaching the courses Strategic Relationship Management and Change Management at Bachelor level. Before 2001 Gerty was a (senior) HR advisor/manager at the Dutch telecom company KPN.

She has a Master's degree in Public Law and Management (Rijksuniversiteit Groningen) and a postgraduate education in Psychology (Centrum voor Beleid en Management/Rijksuniversiteit Utrecht).

The Institute of Strategic Relationship Management

The Institute of Strategic Relationship Management (ISRM) is the founder of modern relationship management. The unique approach of ISRM is based on more than twenty years of practical experience. ISRM is a network of relationship management experts.

The consultancy and training of ISRM help organizations in the transition to a modern and effective network organization that employs a purposeful and structured relationship management policy. Professional relationship management ensures that a network contributes to the achievement of an organization's targets, providing access to the right networks and creating mutual relations with the right people.

In addition, ISRM organizes the postgraduate training program Strategic Relationship Management for professionals who are responsible for the management and development of network management within organizations.

More information:
www.relationshipmanagement.eu
info@relationshipmanagement.eu

Institute of
Strategic Relationship
Management

Enroll in the postgraduate program Strategic Relationship Management of the Institute of Strategic Relationship Management

The Strategic Relationship Management program (postgraduate) teaches participants how to professionalize the relationship management of an organization. The aim is to enable the participants to make it possible for the network of an organization to both structurally and measurably contribute to achieving the organization's targets. The basis of this is the structuring of the entire relationship management – one policy from strategy to implementation.

Structuring relationship management.

The relationship management program begins with refining the vision of the participants concerning the importance of having a network and establishing an effective Relationship Management Strategy that is aligned with the strategy of the organization. Participants of the postgraduate training program also learn how to calculate Return-on-Relationship, how best to identify the external and internal stakeholders, how to deal with the complexity of the management of relations, and how to set up internal responsibility and implementation for relationship management. The training program also focuses on the transition of organizations to a network organization and concludes with the development of network competencies and the organization of measurable, effective networking meetings.

Who should participate?
Participants in the Strategic Relationship Management program deal with complex relationship management issues on both a strategic, tactical and operational level. They come from different fields including government institutions, non-profit organizations, and commercial environments:
· Marketing and communication managers, account managers, event managers, sales support staff, investor relations staff, PAs (business and industry).
· Cabinet staff, policy assistants, communication staff (government).
· Fundraisers, business developers, communication staff (cultural sector).

More information:
www.relationshipmanagement.eu/srm
info@relationshipmanagement.eu

Glossary[1]

- **Contacts:** Individuals with whom the organization is or has been in contact.
- **Customer Relationship Management (CRM):** Software that facilitates data storage, reporting and analytics for high volume relationships.
- **Customers:** Individuals purchasing services or goods from the organization.
- **Internal stakeholders:** All employees who are involved in the (implementation of a) Relationship Management Strategy.
- **Manager of the Network:** Those responsible for the facilitation and management of the entire network of an organization (not to confuse with the networker).
- **Network density:** The amount of interrelatedness of the network.
- **Network organization:** Organizational structures in the form of a network of shared tangible and intangible resources that are formed to achieve specific or general objectives. These organizations are more horizontally structured based on the relevance of the roles played by the parties in the structure.
- **Networker:** Networkers are those internal stakeholders who are in need of a meaningful network. For the success of their job, knowing the right people is essential. Building and/or maintaining a meaningful network is part of their work, preferably supported by a professional relationship management.
- **Networking events or meetings:** An event meant for networking.
- **Networking team:** A cooperation of internal stakeholders operating in the same network.
- **Networking Vision:** The vision of the organization on why having a meaningful and reciprocal network is important.
- **Networking:** The activity specifically meant to build or strengthen/maintain a network of relationships.
- **Reciprocity:** The exchange of something between people or groups of people for mutual benefit.

- **Relationship Management Strategy**: The definition of the ambition of the organization with regards to relationship management and the way it intends to achieve this ambition.
- **Relationship management**: The approach that intends to create positive and constructive relationships with those selected stakeholders who can support the organization achieving its strategic ambition.
- **Relationships**: The way in which two or more people (or things) are connected and the way in which two or more people or groups feel about and behave towards each other.
- **Return-on-Relationship (RoR)**: The financial return generated by the relationship minus the financial investments in the relationship.
- **Segments**: Stakeholders with similar characteristics clustered together, like echelons.
- **Stakeholder**: The individual with whom the organization has a connection (relationship).
- **Symbolic relations**: Relationships governed by shared values.
- **Systemic relations**: Relationships governed by market thinking, in which results and pragmatic transactions are leading.
- **Value network**: A network of organizations and/or individuals interacting with each other to benefit the entire group.

Note
1.   Source: Oxford dictionary

Index

250

251

Thank you

On behalf of all the writers of this book, our sincere gratitude goes out to:

Margie Alders, Fabienne Baart, Alco Bakker, General Dick Berlijn, Ange de Beer, Rob Brons, Jan Willem van Brouwershaven, Prof. Douwe Breimer, Adriana Collignon-de Medeiros, Janny Diepenhorst, Tanja Dik, Janine Dijkmeijer, Phine van Doorne, Thea Enting, Franck Erkens, Quinten Gazendam, Gert van der Houwen, Ngoc Xuan Huynh, Dorianne van Heeswijk, Joep C. De Jong, Ajay Kapur, Jan Keijzer, Jeroen Koks, Victor de Leeuw, Marielle Konings, Madelon van Leeuwen, Ilya van Marle, Alexandra Messervy, Will van Middelkoop, Gilbert Monod de Froideville, Wendela Manting, Eric Niehe, Rutger van Nouhuijs, Sylvia den Ouden†, Aad Otto, Martin van Pernis, Dr Zeynep Sayim, Céderick Schoneveld, Frans van Steenis, Hans Storm, Susanne Stolte, Eline van Stralen, Tijmen Struijk, Sylvia van der Tuin, Kevin Verbaas, Mark Verheul, Mabel Verwer, Loes Vink, Elly van der Vliet, Katrien de Vreese, Wilma Wijers-Smeets, Joop Wijn, Olof van Winden, Tess Wouda Kuipers, Haagse Hogeschool, Hotelschool The Hague, the Supervisory and Advisory Board of Protocolbureau, Hermitage Amsterdam, Rijksmuseum Amsterdam, Norbert Middelkoop and others of the Amsterdam Museum and Stedelijk Museum Alkmaar.

Without your inspiration, advice and help, this book would never have been possible.

Colophon

Text
Jean Paul Wijers
Monica Bakker
Robert Collignon
Gerty Smit
Prof. Dr. René Foqué
Paul Mosterd
Paul Spies
Tom Verbelen

Design
DeLeeuwOntwerper(s), The Hague

Cover
Banquet of Guardsmen from the District IV under Captain Jacob Backer and Lieutenant Jacob Rogh, Nicolaes Pickenoy, 1632 (detail), canvas, 198 × 531 cm, collection Amsterdam Museum / DeLeeuwOntwerper(s), The Hague

Photo's
· Group portraits: Amsterdam Museum and Stedelijk Museum Alkmaar (cover, page 20-22, 82-84 and 216-218).
· *The Night Watch*: Rijksmuseum Amsterdam (page 69)
· Unsplash (page 93, 118)
· I-stock (page 93)
· Wilma Smeets (page 240)
· Jeroen Koks (page 245)

Group portraits from the Amsterdam Museum and the Rijksmuseum collections are now on display together in the Hermitage Amsterdam.

ISBN   978 94 6298 861 3
NUR   801